Steady Steady

THE LIFE AND MUSIC OF SEAMAN DAN

Henry 'Seaman' Dan and Karl Neuenfeldt

Aboriginal Studies Press

Aboriginal Studies Press
First published in 2013 by Aboriginal Studies Press

© Henry 'Seaman' Dan and Karl Neuenfeldt 2013

All rights reserved. No part of this book may be reproduced or transmitted in any form or by any means, electronic or mechanical, including photocopying, recording or by any information storage and retrieval system, without prior permission in writing from the publisher. The Australian *Copyright Act 1968* (the Act) allows a maximum of one chapter or 10 per cent of this book, whichever is the greater, to be photocopied by any educational institution for its education purposes provided that the educational institution (or body that administers it) has given a remuneration notice to Copyright Agency Limited (CAL) under the Act.

Aboriginal Studies Press
is the publishing arm of the
Australian Institute of Aboriginal
and Torres Strait Islander Studies.
GPO Box 553, Canberra, ACT 2601
Phone: (61 2) 6246 1183
Fax: (61 2) 6261 4288
Email: asp@aiatsis.gov.au
Web: www.aiatsis.gov.au/asp/about.html

National Library of Australia Cataloguing-In-Publication data:

Author: Dan, Henry "Seaman" 1929–, author.

Title: Steady steady : the life and music of Seaman Dan/Henry 'Seaman' Dan, Karl Neuenfeldt.

ISBN: 9781922059208 (pbk.)
ISBN: 9781922059437 (ebook PDF)

Notes: Includes bibliographical references and index.

Subjects: Dan, Henry "Seaman" 1929 — Songs and music. Singers — Torres Strait —Biography. Musicians — Torres Strait — Biography. Torres Strait — Social life and customs.

Other Authors/Contributors: Neuenfeldt, Karl, author.

Dewey Number: 305.89915

Printed in Australia by the Opus Print Group

Cover and text design by: Sprout Design

Cover (front): main photo by Karl Neuenfeldt; lower panel (left) The Pearl Fleet [at Thursday Island] c. late 19th century, Julian Rossi Ashton; (middle) courtesy Tim Peek. Cover (back): (left) courtesy Oliver Strewe; (middle) aerial view of Thursday Island, courtesy Kim Wirth; (right) courtesy Kerry Trapnell.

Every effort has been made to trace the original source of copyright material contained in this book. The publisher would be pleased to hear from copyright holders of any errors or omissions.

Aboriginal and Torres Strait Islander people are advised that this publication contains names and images of people who have passed away.

Cessa and I first heard of Bala* Seaman when we were at the Catholic convent on Thursday Island in the 1930s. All civilians were evacuated off the island in December, 1941. We married and raised our families and it was years later before we met up with Bala Seaman. He was good mates with Eddie Dubbins who worked for the DNA [Department of Native Affairs] and lived with other blokes at the Batch, short for Bachelor Pad.

There were weekend parties at the Batch and Bala Seaman was always there with his guitar, entertaining everyone. Talk about sing all night. Us girls, Cessa, Rita and me were always invited to these parties which was before we started singing as The Mills Sisters at the pubs on TI.

We first heard TI Blues in the 1970s and loved it. It became part of The Mills Sisters' repertoire in the 1980s when we were doing the folk festival circuit. Then in the mid-1990s, as we were retiring, we said to Bala Seaman, Get out there and start recording your music! And he did.

We love the way he mixes the blues and Torres Strait music, especially that he also sings in traditional languages.

Everyone loves Bala Seaman and his music. He's a great ambassador for the Torres Strait because he brings together Indigenous and non-Indigenous people through his unique style of music.

Cessa Nakata and Ina Titasey, the Torres Strait Mills Sisters

In earlier times the Darwin people of mixed-race Aboriginal descent were encouraged to identify with the 'other' side of their inheritance — Malay, Filipino, Chinese, whatever. As a result, culturally, they were somewhat lost. But they cherished their contacts with people from Torres Strait.

So when Seaman Dan came to Darwin in the early 1950s he was made very welcome. For one thing he was a beaut, good-looking bloke, musical, played nice guitar, knew all the 'pearling' songs and the marvellous traditional songs of Torres Strait.

His second big attribute was that he took a job at Koolpinyah Butchers and they also made ice. Very few people had refrigerators in those days and 'The Ice Man' was probably the most popular man in town. The many parties at 118 Parap Camp and the Police Paddock were enhanced by the arrival of Seaman: The Ice Man Cometh.

There was a group of us: Seaman, Rusty Perez, Steve Abala, Gabe Hazelbane, Peter Cardona and me. We would sing all night. And lower the odd beer!

Seaman represented 'the genuine article' to us in respect of the pearling industry. He was a 'blue water' man. He had practical experience as a diver and his arrival would usually prompt the cry: 'Stand back you shallow water mob: make way for a deep sea diver.'

His musical career, his entire life since, has been nothing short of remarkable. Australia is indeed a lucky country.

Ted Egan, OAM

* In the Torres Strait Bala means 'brother'; not as in biological brother but rather as a term of respect.

FOREWORD

My oldest memories of Seaman Dan hark back to the early 1950s — I was five or six years old. At the time, I was playing in the front yard of our house in John Street, TI when I heard a stranger speaking to me. 'Hiya, Guy! Your Mum and Dad home?' he asked in his quiet silken-toned drawl. He had a brown paper bag with a few large bottles of beer in one arm and was balancing a guitar on the gatepost with the other. How did I know it was beer? Come on … this *was* TI, aka 'Thirsty Island' back then! The guitar I recognised from pictures on the covers of vinyl records I'd seen at Uncle Porgie's place next door.

The ensuing party that day was one of many such spontaneous events at our place as well as other friends' and relatives' houses — gatherings that were pretty common in our little cultural melting pot of a community whenever certain luggers were in port. They would doubtlessly have happened before this particular time, and I clearly recall them as being joyous, happy and exciting times for the grownups and kids alike. Sometimes these visitors were straight off the boat and smelled strongly of the ocean and the gifts of salted pearl shell meat they brought ashore — a delicacy when cooking 'Long Soup'. At other times, they were all spruced up and ready to relax with some serious all-night partying. I only ever remember Mr Dan as always looking very cool and dapper.

Over the ensuing couple of decades, the four remaining pubs on TI slowly became more of a focal point for entertainment from the old house parties. By then, younger people were plugging electric guitars into their amps and had taken over the pub lounges and beer gardens at what were known locally as 'cabarets'. However, fans of good old-timey tropical tunes were still able to join mainstay acoustic minstrels such as Uncle Seaman, the Mills Sisters and a handful of other talented musicians such as the late George Dewis and the late Izzie Shibasaki for a big singalong in the public bar. These events were hugely popular, and on Friday nights the number of sweaty bodies packed into the old Grand Hotel made it almost impossible to get into the place after 7.30 p.m.

The live music scene on TI tended to lose its way somewhat throughout most of the 1980s and early 1990s, and consisted mostly of disco beats pumped out by anonymous DJs working canned dance beats through a reel-to-reel tape machine. However, the famous Mills Sisters had recorded their CD during this period and were becoming very popular with audiences on the mainland and overseas. The fact that one of the songs on their CD was written by Uncle Seaman helped remind people of his place in the Torres Strait music scene. However, we need to 'fast forward' to the late 1990s, just as things really started to come together for him.

It was at this time that he met Karl Neuenfeldt, who was visiting TI to interview people as part of a research project on which he was working. This meeting at the Torres Strait Media Association's radio broadcasting studio was to be the beginning of a strong musical and personal friendship/partnership that has proved mutually beneficial and that has endured to this day.

I'm not quite sure how my own involvement came about, but somehow I've had the honour of having been a tiny part of Uncle Seaman's wonderful journey ever since Karl's visit. This special privilege has allowed me to be in the studio with him as part of the *Mata Loose* backing group (under the skilful engineering, co-production and guidance of Nigel Pegrum), to feel his personal glee over the phone when he received the first of three national music awards — 'Hey guy, I did it! … won this trophy … woohooo!' I also did a stint as his tour manager on a highly eventful road trip visiting several communities across Cape York Peninsula from TI to Cairns. You wouldn't believe how many hula dancers there are in these remote places — testament to the goodwill from visiting boat crews back in the old pearling days, no doubt! I even learned his main weapon for maintaining that super-smooth voice, but you'll have to ask him for that secret recipe yourself.

One of the things that has fascinated me as I have followed Uncle Seaman's career over the years has been the wide range of people that enjoy his music. The fact that he is loved and appreciated in the Torres Strait and by people of his own vintage elsewhere is understandable, but his following among younger audiences (especially women!) is quite special. A friend from Canberra once told me that his children (all under seven years of age) insisted on having Seaman Dan CDs played at the start of every single long-distance car trip they ever did.

My personal observation is that his fans simply enjoy the way he tells such great stories through music, with so much grace, enthusiasm and fun. The smile is also totally sincere both on and off stage, and his genuine joy in what he does is absolutely contagious.

There are so many facets to this great man's life, and I trust you'll enjoy reading about these as much as I have. I'm sure there are many of you — especially his family and close friends — who could easily fill many more chapters with your own stories and experiences.

In the 60 years that I've been fortunate to know Uncle Seaman, I can wholeheartedly say that I feel blessed to have experienced the good fortune to have grown up as a TI boy in these beautiful Torres Strait homelands, with such wonderful role models as Henry Seaman Dan … a humble human being with a zestful appreciation of life and love of people second to none. He is a true world ambassador to his people through his dignified charm and music, and I am sure you'll all join me in saying '*au esoau/koeyma eso/*many thanks' to Uncle Seaman for making our lives richer and for just being who he is.

'You can take the man out of the sea but you can't take the sea out of this man … well, certainly not out of his songs!'

Vic McGrath

CONTENTS

Foreword by Vic McGrath — v
Preface — viii
Acknowledgments — x
Maps of the Torres Strait and Top End of Australia — xi

Part I: The Life of Henry 'Seaman' Dan — 1
1. An Island Home in the Torres Strait — 2
2. Cape York Time — 18
3. Cairns During the Second World War — 28
4. Learning to Live a Diver's Life — 34
5. Adventures Across Northern Australia — 39
6. Working Adventures on Sea and Land — 51

Part II: The Music and Recordings of Henry 'Seaman' Dan — 65
7. The Opportunity of a Lifetime — 66
8. *Follow the Sun* — 68
9. *Steady, Steady* — 85
10. *Perfect Pearl* — 101
11. *Island Way* — 118
12. *Sailing Home* — 133
13. *Sunnyside* and *Still on Deck: Personal Favourites* — 149
Epilogue — 153

References and Further Reading — 154
Select Discography — 160
Select Filmography — 162
Awards — 163
Index — 164

PREFACE

I was walking with Henry 'Seaman' Dan at the Cairns Indigenous Arts Fair in August 2010. We were making slow progress, partly because Uncle Seaman was using a walking frame and was careful to watch where he was going.

It was also very crowded, and every few metres or so someone would stop to say hello — either introducing themselves as a relative (usually explaining how they were related) or complimenting him on his music and telling him what it meant to them. Many people were genuinely keen to meet Uncle Seaman, and he was equally pleased to meet them — which is typical of his politeness and friendliness towards everyone, regardless of their age, culture or station in life.

In his quiet way, he was understandably honoured that in a large gathering of people from across northern Queensland and Australia, so many people recognised him — and, probably more importantly, that they recognised his music as something that brought them joy. For Uncle Seaman, this transcended the remarkable journey of how he came to be a professional performer in his early seventies and was still winning major music awards in his eighties.

Although 'semi-retired' for health reasons, the previous night he had been a guest artist at a concert by emerging and established Indigenous musicians and singers. Crooning as smoothly as ever, Seaman was happy to be singing publicly again, and proud to show people that he was still one of the best at making music 'ailan style'.

Seaman has always encouraged younger musicians — Indigenous and non-Indigenous, female and male — to 'give it a go'. As far as he is concerned, coming from a humble background and living in a remote part of Australia shouldn't hold anyone back — in fact, it can be helpful if performers with talent and persistence are true to what is unique to them: their music and their culture. Uncle Seaman achieved success late in life, and he advises younger musicians to take heart: 'If this old fella can make it, you can too. Just take things "steady, steady",' he says.

This book is a biographical account of how he 'made it': the music, the friends, and earning a living on the sea and land across tropical Australia. It is about how he has brought happiness to others with his music and stories, and how as a Torres Strait Islander he made history by using his musical gifts to make other Australians more aware of his culture — while they smiled and quite often hummed along to his songs.

My role in Seaman Dan's story for over a decade has been as a co-producer (with Nigel Pegrum), co-songwriter and musician in his band, and de facto manager. In some ways, Seaman Dan and I are a bit of a mismatch: he's an elderly Torres Strait Islander and ex-pearl diver and I'm an immigrant academic from Canada. Sort of 'the bluesman and the boffin' from one perspective, but from another we are not mismatched at all. We both love music — especially music from the Torres Strait

Seaman Dan and Karl Neuenfeldt.

region. That is what has underpinned our friendship, which has grown increasingly close over our years together in the studio, performing and touring, and in our music-making.

And that is what this book is about: Seaman Dan making music '*ailan* style'. His story is told mostly in his own words, gathered from taped interviews about his music and recollections of a long life lived — as he often says — 'steady, steady', but also with quite a few adventures along the way.

Karl Neuenfeldt
Central Queensland University, Bundaberg Queensland

ACKNOWLEDGMENTS

The authors would like to thank the many people who contributed to researching, preparing and publishing this book. In particular, our thanks go to Rhonda Black, Rachel Ippoliti, Lisa Fuller and Kim Johnston at Aboriginal Studies Press for their professionalism and suggestions; Sue Jarvis for her exacting and sympathetic editing; and all the individuals, families, photographers, public archives and museums that facilitated finding and permitting the use of photographs.

Henry 'Seaman' Dan very much thanks his family, friends and fans for inspiring and encouraging him to write and sing his songs and record them. As well, he thanks his fellow Torres Strait musicians for all the music and good times over the years, especially Cessa Nakata, Ina Titasey, Jerry Lewin, Russell Barkus and all the members of the Ramblers band. He also salutes the memory of the late Rita Mills, the late Hismile 'Izzie' Shibasaki and the late George Dewis. Thanks also to the following hoteliers for giving him the chance to keep performing: Bob and Jeanette Wescome at the Wongai Hotel (Horn Island); and Chris, Leigh and Jarod Lemke, Tony Mack and Bec Harrex at the Torres Hotel (Thursday Island). At 83 years of age, Seaman is very happy to still be 'singing for his supper'!

Karl Neuenfeldt thanks for their research assistance and willingness to provide help — usually at very short notice — Vic McGrath, Bua Mabo, Mary Bowie, Cessa Nakata, Dana Ober, Pauline Mills, Ina Titasey, Ida Tillett, Silen David, Anna Shnukal, Steve Mullins, Jeremy Beckett, Lyn Costigan, Jeff Corfield, Joy Cardona, Jean and Peter Mathams, Vanessa and Liberty Seekee, and Philip Hayward, who originally suggested he explore the music of the Torres Strait region. Central Queensland University provided leave to facilitate the research and writing.

Henry and Karl most especially thank co-producer and audio engineer Nigel Pegrum and all the collaborators whose contributions have been so important in funding, recording, designing, distributing and promoting the music. They include: the Australia Council for the Arts, Graeme Regan, Lynlea McIntyre, Carmel Nunan, Tony Hillier, David Hudson, Terri Janke, David Bridie, Graham McDonald, MGM Distribution, Hot Records, all the session musicians, singers, songwriters and arrangers, and members of the Soother Band. We also thank the following media and broadcasters for helping circulate the music: ABC and SBS Radio and Television, Radio 4 MW-Thursday Island, Aven Noah, Jenny Enosa, Sylvia Tabuai, Stephan Armbruster, Nancia Guivarra, Rhianna Patrick, Fiona Cochrane, and Rhoda Roberts and *Deadly Vibes*.

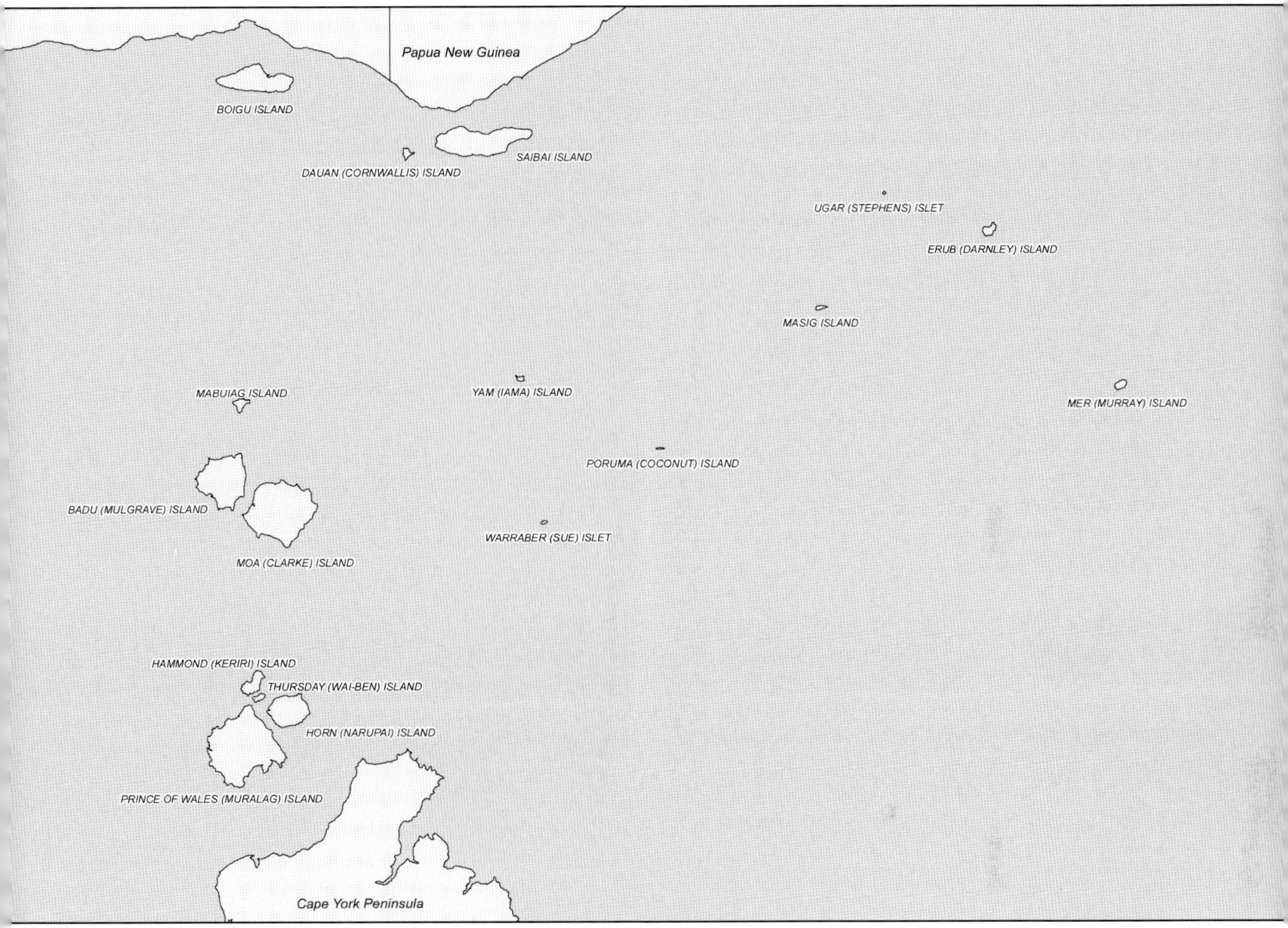

xi

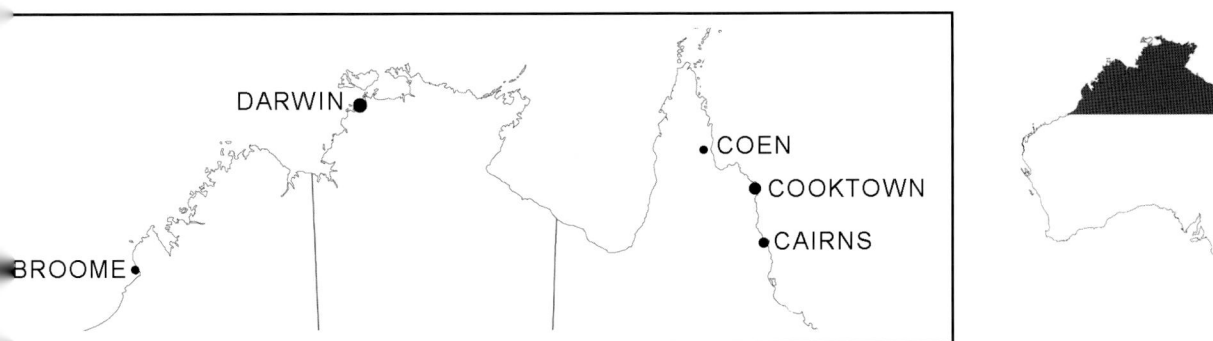

Map of the Torres Strait inhabited islands, courtesy of the Torres Strait Regional Authority.

General location of places mentioned in the text, base map © Geoscience Australia.

PART I

THE LIFE OF HENRY 'SEAMAN' DAN

CHAPTER 1

An Island Home in the Torres Strait

*Take me across the sea / Over the deep blue sea /
Darling won't you take me / Back to my home TI.*

'Old TI' [1] ⛵

The Torres Strait Islander flag was recognised under federal legislation in 1995. Designed by Bernard Namok.

Torres Strait, Torres Strait Islanders and their music

Before recounting the story of the life and music of Seaman Dan, it is useful to appreciate three key influences: the Torres Strait region where he was born, grew up and still lives; his Torres Strait Islander culture; and the region's music. His careers as a community and later professional musician have been celebrations of the uniqueness of the Torres Strait and its culture.

The Torres Strait region lies between Australia and New Guinea, and contains myriad islands, reefs and channels. It is named after the Spanish explorer Luis Váez de Torres, who passed through the region in 1606. Torres Strait was annexed by the colony of Queensland in 1879, and after Federation in 1901, it became part of Australia. However, full rights were denied to its Indigenous citizens until race-based restrictions gradually lessened by the 1970s.

The region is a major marine passageway between the Pacific and Indian Oceans, and also connects the diverse cultures and nation-states along its borders. Before European colonisation, extensive trade networks criss-crossed the region, linking its Torres Strait Islander, Aboriginal and Melanesian populations. With European colonisation, the region was incorporated into global mercantile and transport networks. However, some regional traditional trade networks still survive. The

---

1 ⛵ Songs marked with a boat are on the compilation CD included with this book, *Still on Deck: Personal Favourites*.

region contains Australia's only nearby national borders, with Papua New Guinea (PNG) and Indonesia. Consequently, it remains of political, economic and cultural importance, although it is geographically distant from Australia's centres of power.

Ever since the colonial era, the region has been very multicultural. Migrants came from all over the world to extract its maritime resources, working alongside Torres Strait Islanders and Aborigines. From the mid-1860s, bêche-de-mer (trepang) was harvested, and soon pearl and trochus shells were gathered. Relatively rare pearls were also collected, and the region became known as one of the world's premier sources of high-quality pearl shells and pearls. Although the maritime industries experienced periods of boom and bust, they continued until the 1970s. The region still extracts some marine resources, such as fish, crayfish and cultured pearls.

Torres Strait Islanders

Torres Strait Islanders are Australia's minority within a total Indigenous minority of approximately 550,000 people, which constitutes 2.5 per cent of the general population. In the Australian Bureau of Statistics' 2011 Census, approximately 52,000 Australians identified as Torres Strait Islanders, including those who also identified as Aborigines. It was only after the Second World War that unfettered migration to the mainland was permitted. Torres Strait Islanders now live across Australia, with approximately 33,000 settled in Queensland. In the Torres Strait region itself, approximately 6000 Islanders live in 17 island communities and in two settlements on Cape York Peninsula.

The current culture of Torres Strait Islanders — known as *ailan kastom* — can be characterised as a complex mixture of Indigenous and non-Indigenous elements and influences. Importantly, given that it is a small and dispersed population, it has been adaptable and persistent over time, place and situation. As anthropologist Jeremy Beckett (1987) observes, '[It] is a lived and living culture, strong enough to survive not only a succession of changes in its original environment, but also transplanting;

Lieutenant James Cook claimed British sovereignty over the eastern part of Australia in 1770. When he sailed through the Torres Strait region, he named Thursday Island and some other islands. A replica of Cook's *Endeavour* visited Torres Strait in 2011. Courtesy Liberty Seekee.

a culture capable of taking new meanings and functions.' One cultural area where this ability to adapt and persist is quite apparent is in its diverse musi

Torres Strait Islander music

Traditional — or what is sometimes termed ancestral — music was an important part of pre-colonial Torres Strait Islander culture. When the Haddon Anthropological Expedition to Torres Strait recorded music (and filmed dance) in 1898, memories of earlier music were still relatively recent, although some practices and repertoire had either been suppressed by missionaries or supplanted by migrants' music. As well, epidemic diseases had reduced the region's population. Among those affected would have been musicians and singers. Nonetheless, the recordings from 1898 document musical styles capable of providing crucial musical underpinnings to socio-cultural life.

When colonial era migrants came to the Torres Strait region from Melanesia, Polynesia, South-East and North Asia, the Americas, Europe and mainland Australia, they also brought their music with them. These styles mixed with the traditional/ancestral music of the region's Indigenous inhabitants to create what has been termed modern/contemporary music. For example, in the Eastern Islands, music and dance styles such as the South Sea Islander-influenced Taibobo, Segur Kaba Wed (play dance and songs) and Kole Kabem Wed (songs for European-style dances) arose. Comparable adaptations took place elsewhere, and in both the Western and Eastern Islands skills in composing and writing songs (and choreographing dances) were highly regarded, with particular extended families even establishing musical reputations that in some cases have lasted for generations.

Traditional/ancestral and modern/contemporary music styles encompassed not only the secular but also the sacred. Introduced Christian hymns initially replaced the sacred musical aspect of pre-colonial socio-cultural life, and notably also included both men and women as active participants. Later, as well as hymns, locally composed sacred songs known as *kores* (choruses) became important in worship, and also as an outlet for creativity. Consequently, there is a rich repertoire of Torres Strait Islander sacred music in both of the traditional languages, Meriam Mir and Kala Lagaw Ya, as well as in English.

The processes of musical adoption, adaptation and innovation varied locally, but over the post-colonial generations a multicultural, eclectic regional musical style has evolved. This is what Seaman Dan heard from childhood, and later performed and recorded.

Thursday Island

The largest settlement in the Torres Strait, Thursday Island (also known as TI), is a unique Australian community. It was established in 1877 and currently has 2,600 residents. It became the centre of the region for several reasons: its strategic importance as an excellent harbour near to a major shipping lane; its mercantile role in the provisioning and processing of maritime industries such as bêche-de-mer, pearl and trochus shelling; and its government services, such as customs and courts.

To some early observers, TI was a notorious place. AB 'Banjo' Paterson referred to it as 'Thirsty Island' because of its rowdy pubs and hotels. Somerset Maugham set his short stories 'French Joe' and 'German Harry' in its multilingual, multicultural community. As a new settlement, it was a tiny town (3.5 square kilometres in size) on the frontier of Far North Queensland, but also a place where Indigenous and non-Indigenous cultures met and where people had to learn to accommodate and adapt to one another. Not only did they create a unique society; they also created a unique musical culture that resonates today in the songs of Seaman Dan, as well as other Torres Strait Islander musicians and singers.

Left top: SS *Changte* of the Australian Oriental Line at Thursday Island post-1925. Courtesy Torres Strait Historical Society.

Left centre: Torres Strait pearl shellers, undated. Courtesy National Library of Australia.

Left bottom: Torres Strait maritime workers at Thursday Island (Wyben), undated. Courtesy Torres Strait Historical Society.

Right: SS *Airlie* and SS *Chingtu* advertisement, *The Pilot*, 16 May 1903.

Thursday Island sketch, c.1880s.

Thursday Island town site and harbour, c.1924. Courtesy State Library Queensland, image no. 204885.

Birth and ancestors

TI also has a regional hospital, and Henry Gibson Dan was born there on 24 August 1929. His birth mother was Kitty Savage (1903–81), later Kitty Ware, from Erub (Darnley Island), and his birth certificate lists him as Henry Savage. Historically, adoption was quite common in the Torres Strait region, with children frequently being raised by extended family or friends. Catherine Jaira (née Amboyn) (c.1898–1968) and Henry Maynard Dan (c.1895–1970) (also known as Henry Daniel Maynard) adopted young Henry at an early age, and he took the family name of Dan. For most of his life, he has been known by the nickname 'Seaman'.

Like many people in the Torres Strait region, Seaman has a multicultural ancestry, with African-American, Polynesian and Melanesian ancestors. Two male ancestors of note are his great-grandfather, Douglas Pitt Senior from Jamaica, and his grandfather, Sam Savage (Tehega Afugia Toa) from Niue. Douglas Pitt Senior, a sailor, came to the Torres Strait region in 1871 on boats carrying missionaries from the London Missionary Society. Also travelling with Pitt was his wife, Sopa Kalemo, Seaman's great-grandmother. She was from Lifou in the Loyalty Islands group in present-day New Caledonia. Their eldest daughter was Maryann, Seaman's grandmother.

Catherine Jaira Dan (née Amboyn), undated.

Douglas (Sr) and Sopa Pitt, undated.

Kitty Savage, Darnley Island c.1920. Courtesy Ada Tillett and the Australian Institute of Aboriginal and Torres Strait Islander Studies, Phillip Macfarlane collection, image no. N003968_05.

Sam Savage came to Torres Strait from Niue. Seaman recalls hearing a family story speculating on how Tehega Afugia Toa may have acquired the name 'Sam Savage':

> He came by a vessel from Niue and he met my grandmother Maryann Pitt [at Erub/Darnley Island]. Then they fell in love and he wanted to marry her so he sailed to Thursday Island … to become an Australian citizen … He went up to the administration office … the fellow said, 'what's your name?' He said, 'My language name is Tehega Toa'. The fellow asked him, 'How do you spell it?' and Sam said 'Well, I don't know.' 'What island do you come from?' 'Savage Island, Niue.' The fellow said, 'We'll call you Sam Savage.' So he was registered as Sam Savage.

According to Seaman, they settled for a time at Mauar (Rennel Island), west of Masig (Yorke Island) in the Central Islands cluster. In Seaman's words, Sam and Maryann Savage 'grew their family up from there'. He also recalls that whenever the Savage family came to visit TI, they stayed with his adoptive family, the Dans:

> I used to run to the corner shop for [grandfather Sam Savage] and get him his tobacco and cigarette papers and he'd give me three pence to buy a packet of peanuts. I can still remember him. He was a very big man.

Seaman's direct ancestors were resourceful people who established what are today very large extended families: the Pitts and the Savages. Many of them migrated from the Torres Strait region, some before and many after the Second World War. They left for work, employment and educational opportunities, and their descendants can now be found across Australia. However, like many other Torres Strait Islanders, some remain connected to their home islands, especially through music, dance, art and cultural practices — and some through the music and songs of Seaman Dan.

Early years on TI

Kitty Ware (née Savage), undated. Courtesy Ada Tillett.

At the time Seaman was growing up on TI in the early 1930s, the maritime industries had declined from their heyday around the turn of the 20th century. But they were still active, and for men a life at sea was one of the few available employment options.

Some of Seaman's earliest memories of his adoptive parents are that his adoptive father, Henry — also known as 'Darkie' Dan — was often away working as captain of a bêche-de-mer vessel, gathering and processing trepang for Morey and Company:

We saw very little of him when the weather was good to go out to work. The season for that type of work up in the Torres Strait region is sign-on 15 March and that season is cyclone-free weather right through to 15 January the following year. That's when they sign off.

Henry Maynard Dan c.1960s

His adoptive mother, Catherine — also known as 'Granny' Dan — worked as a cook at TI's old Royal Hotel. Seaman remembers her with great fondness as a hard worker and a kind-hearted woman with strong values:

> [She] was my inspiration. If I did something wrong she'd screw my ear. It hurt, but screwed some sense into me. She always tried to put me on the right track — respect others and they will respect you. It comes back to you.

With regard to his own education at Our Lady of the Sacred Heart School on TI, Seaman recalls that the nuns were 'very strict but they taught you manners, they taught you properly. [Their priorities were] religion, then manners and education. They all came into one.' He also remembers that:

> [My parents] had me baptised in the Catholic Church and I started school when I was five years old … At certain times of the year we had a school picnic and the priests and nuns — well, the priests mainly — they chartered a vessel from the Department of Native Affairs to take all the convent school children from Thursday Island to Hammond Island on the school picnic. And we'd have racing and baseball on Hammond Island and for little fellows growing up it was a good, happy time.

One of TI's iconic hotels, the old Grand, c.1960. Courtesy Ian Pearson.

He even recalls his first 'paying' job, earning him a bit of money to go to movies at the cinema — known locally as the 'picture shows':

> I was about six or seven years old when Mrs Watson [from the old Royal Hotel] said to my mum, 'If you want Henry to rake the leaves in front of the hotel, we'll pay him two shillings every Saturday.' Mum told me this and said, 'You know you could earn your picture money — two shillings.' For children, it was ninepence to go into the movie, ninepence for a bottle of lemonade — a big 26-ounce bottle — and sixpence for a packet of peanuts. Well, that was all right with me. Two shillings! Raking the yard for two shillings, that was great!

For a youngster, the movies were great fun, and also offered a chance to imagine the bigger world outside of isolated TI:

> There was an open-air [cinema] and we had Hopalong Cassidy and Westerns lots of children used to like. Us boys especially would sit in the front and you'd have to look up to the screen. There'd be Cowboys and Indians. They'd inspire us too when we're out playing, to play Cowboys and Indians.

What Seaman would not necessarily have known at such a young age was that the cinema on TI was racially segregated, and that was why he was seated where he was. People classified as 'European' sat upstairs in the covered dress circle section on leather seats; those who were what was then termed 'mixed race' sat below them on the ground floor in the partially covered stalls section on canvas seats; Torres Strait Islander and Aboriginal people were seated in the uncovered area of the stalls section on hard benches.

Left: Thursday Island cinema showing lower stalls (non-European) and upper circle (European) sections c. mid-1930s. Courtesy of Jean Mathams (née Sullivan).

Right: Thursday Island cinema showing screen and lower stalls (non-European) section c. mid-1930s. Courtesy of Jean Mathams (née Sullivan).

Race-based laws and regulations were a fact of life in the region when Seaman was growing up. They were originally introduced by the Queensland government to deal with what it considered to be a 'native problem', and initially were aimed primarily at Aboriginal people, but eventually included Torres Strait Islanders. According to Margaret Reid of Queensland's Department of Aboriginal and Torres Strait Islander and Multicultural Affairs (2012), the legislations and regulations, and their applications, were complex:

> The legislation was applied differently depending on where [Torres Strait] Islanders were living at the time, and how they were defined for the purposes of the particular Act that applied at the time [because] the definitions about who was subject to the Act changed with the legislation.

In general terms, the laws and regulations meant most Indigenous people in the region — particularly those living outside of TI in the outer islands — were restricted with regard to personal matters such as where they could live and travel, what they could do with their wages and even whom they could marry. Visits to TI by people 'under the Act' were regulated — but, interestingly, visitors were allowed to participate as dance groups in civic events such as the 50-year anniversary of TI's establishment in 1877, which took place in 1927.

Maritime work away from home islands in particular did allow men some degree of independence, and also the opportunity to travel, but Indigenous women were usually restricted to their homes or home islands. However, TI was sometimes an exception because it was very multicultural and, after decades of intermarriage between migrants and Indigenous peoples, trying to define who was or was not Indigenous became increasingly problematic. As well, TI had pubs and hotels serving alcohol — something that was restricted for Indigenous peoples. However, as Seaman recounts:

> My uncles, they come in from hard working out on the sea, [gathering] trochus shell, bêche-de-mer, pearl shell — they don't worry about alcohol. They just worry about food for the family.

Seaman's personal situation was different. He remembers that Henry Maynard Dan could drink in the Royal Hotel, where Seaman's mother was the cook, so his father was not under the Act.

Seaman was later to write and record a song, 'The Ukulele Waltz', ⛵ about the effect such laws and regulations could have on the social and musical lives of people who otherwise mixed together, regardless of Queensland's laws. However, as a child growing up on TI, he recalls: 'Everybody just played with everybody. We were all one — Chinese, Japanese, whites. We were all good friends, all good mates. Yes, there was no friction.'

Thursday Island social scene, 1907. Courtesy Torres Strait Historical Society.

Community music and entertainment on TI

Seaman has many fond memories of growing up in a multiracial extended family and a multicultural community, where music was an important part of social life and the different Indigenous and migrant groups mixed their music and their cultural traditions. An account from 1896 by Thomas Eyken, a visiting Church of England parson, provides a good example of the variety of music circulating in the community from its early days, and also a glimpse of social life for TI's European elite:

> On Christmas Eve, after dinner at the Residency, numbers of Manilamen labourers came to give their Christmas performances. Chinese lanterns swung from the flagstaff on the lawn, beneath which, with the aid of the moon, they played and sang … The band consisted of a concertina, a penny whistle, and a lovely Japanese drum played with vigour, and without cessation. The repertoire consisted of the 'Marseillaise', 'The Spanish Anthem', 'Grandfather Clock' and 'Rule Britannia' … On New Year's Eve the same thing was repeated, with the addition of an illumination of the shelling fleet and the yacht; and the full moon shone down upon the beautiful scene with intense luster. At twelve o'clock twenty-one guns were fired from the [steam] yacht [170 tons]. They were answered by every sort of gun from the lawn; while islands across the glittering channel resounded with reports of rifles and revolvers.

On the outer islands, too, music and dance were important aspects of entertainment. In 1927, the Reverend WH MacFarlane reported on a church event at Erub (Darnley Island) combining Indigenous and non-Indigenous elements:

> There was a procession of people, with drums, etc., as on festival, round the precincts. Looked very festive; bright colours of dresses, flowers,

etc. ... Singing sounded very fine, and whole proceedings were worthily carried out ... In the afternoon [of the following day], play was resumed on mission ground. Darnley contingent led off as a military regiment, in uniform copied from Zouaves as seen in *National Geographic* magazine. A 'band' accompanied the turnout: it was exceedingly well done. Other good dances were figures from the old Malu dances (put on by Murray [Islanders]), and a splendid 'play' — 'The Landing of Captain Cook at the Endeavor [River]'. The whole thing was very striking.

Although TI had a cinema and also occasional entertainment troupes visiting off the many in-transit passenger liners, when Seaman was a young boy, homemade entertainment was very important because people had to amuse each other, often at 'house parties':

> Every so often, certain locals would get together and they'd have what we called a 'house party'. Each family would take it in turn to have a house party at their place. This is always what they'd call a 'surprise party'. The owner or tenant at that particular house, they don't know there's going to be a party at their place. It's a surprise party so they could be sitting down at suppertime. We'd all go in a group. Then when we're about, oh say a 100 yards (90 metres) away from the house, THEN THE MUSIC WOULD STRIKE! My mother would start the button accordion. Dad would rattle the bones and [everyone would be] yelling with the guitars and the ukuleles. And everyone'd start to sing till we got to the house. And the people in the house, they'd hear this music and the singing and say, 'Oh, there's a surprise party coming to our place.' So they'd clear the table, clear the dance floor and there you go, a house party would start. And this happens to all the friends in that

Dulla Solomon (née Jia) c. mid-1930s Thursday Island. Courtesy of Gladys Bingarape, Seriba Shibasaki and Tatipata families.

Thursday Island entertainment group c.1920s. Back row [l-r]: unknown, Henry Maynard Dan (holding bones percussion), Billy Dubbins, Wally Woods Snr, unknown, Eddie Seranealis, Hubby Seranealis. Front row: unknown. Courtesy Wally Woods Jnr.

particular group. It's open house, so you've got to be prepared all the time but you don't know when that house party's going to come to *your* house. We children used to go along just to play. That's all we could do, just watch the grown-ups enjoy themselves. It was good fun for us children. We'd get to meet our school friends. We'd enjoy ourselves. We'd just play outside and the grown-ups would sing and dance in the house. It was good fun in those early days. It was, say, mid-1930s, early 1930s. Yes, they were good days — happy days.

At such a young age, Seaman was mainly a spectator: 'I couldn't play the guitar or the ukulele but I just watched the elders play the instruments and I used to sing.'

There were also other kinds of musical entertainment on TI, although not radio at home in those days:

[We had] no wireless but Mum and Dad had a wind-up gramophone and she had a lot of Tex Morton records. You know, my favourite song was Tex Morton's 'I'll be Hanged if They're Gonna Hang Me'. And she had one record [I also remember]. She [had been] asked to accompany and be carer for this crippled girl to go to Cairns … While in Cairns she bought one [by] Bobby Breen. Oh, he had a beautiful voice … His song was 'Rainbow on the River'.

TI had a dedicated entertainment venue, the Victoria Memorial Institute Hall, built in 1903. A playbill for a concert by a local entertainment group, the Merry Magpies, in September 1934 (opposite) gives a good idea of the kinds of eclectic music and dance Seaman encountered as a child.

Thursday Island musicians, c.1920s. [l–r]: Baddah Bin Gapore, Ketchell Anno, Manji Ah Boo, Johannes Tatipata (standing), Jaffa Ah Mat, Solomon Toulasik, Jeffrey Doolah. Courtesy of Gladys Bingarape (née Tatipata).

TOWN HALL THURSDAY ISLAND
MONDAY, 3rd SEPTEMBER, 1934

GRAND CONCERT BY THE MERRY MAGPIES

PROGRAMME

Overture K. Anno & Company
1 Opening Chorus 'Happy Days' The Company
2 Song and Chorus 'Roll on Mississippi' J. Thompson & Co.
3 Duologue 'I'm Married' J. Sariman & Co.
4 Song 'Among the Sugarcane' D. Drummond
5 Recitation 'Magpies Nest' S. Subideen
6 Dance 'Samoan Dance' J. Sariman & Co.
7 Duologue 'Grandma Advice' B. Ahfat & Co.
8 Dance 'Malay Dance' The Company
9 Song 'Doctors Fight' B. Anno & Co.
10 Song 'Silver in my Mother's Hair' D. Jia
11 Ribbon Dance The Company

INTERVAL

1 Song 'Why Shouldn't I' J. Dubbins, J. Thompson & Company
2 Song 'Medicine Jack' P. Lewis
3 Paddle Dance J. Sariman & Co.
4 Fan Dance A. Bargo & J. Davies
5 Song 'Senor Alfonso' R. Bin Gapore
6 Song 'South Sea Rose' D. Jia & Company
7 Recitation 'Woods' A. Bargo
8 Song 'Whispering Hope' The Company
9 'Lady of Spain' R. Hondo
10 Song '[My Old] Kentucky Home' Sambo & Alabama

Thursday Island Hula Dance Group, c. late 1930s. Standing [l–r]: Jenap Bin Dol (née Jia), Jumila Dubbins (née Ah Mat), Dahlia Bin Hoosen (née Malay). Kneeling [l–r]: Kathleen Taylor (née Jia), Dahlia Seden (née Drummond). Sitting: Edna Mohamad (née Anno), Patty Hodges (née Dewis), Dulla Solomon (née Jia), Doseena Bin Garape (née Jia), Jane Thompson (née Adams) Bottom [l–r]: Jessie Moyden, Gladys Hondo (née Anno). Courtesy McGrath family.

The concert is musically interesting because it highlights the wide range of music and dance circulating on TI: everything from Samoan and Malay dances to the 1931 British song 'Lady of Spain' and American songs from the black-face minstrel tradition of the late 19th and early 20th centuries, such as '[My Old] Kentucky Home', performed by Sambo and Alabama. The family names of the performers also highlight TI's multicultural mix. Religious music also had an influence, as Seaman recalls: 'You got taught to sing at school, at school concerts, and the nuns would teach us how to sing and how to sing certain songs.'

While at the convent school on TI in the 1930s, Seaman also met two young Torres Strait Islander singers who, later in life, would be important in his own musical career. Twins Ina and Cessa Mills were from Naghir (Mount Ernest Island) and, along with their younger sister Rita, would eventually form the Mills Sisters singing group, tour nationally and internationally, and record the first song Seaman wrote, 'TI Blues' ⛴ :

> They come from an island called Naghir which is 30–35 miles [46–48 kilometres] northeast of Thursday Island but being that far away and going to school, they go to the convent [and board there] and the nuns look after these outer island children. They were very good singers and they were brought into the choir then.

From those early days, they established a lifetime connection, which would include collaborating with Seaman on recordings more than 60 years later. Seaman says:

> They used to sing at the [Grand] Hotel and when I'm up there in port [on TI] they'd invite me to sing with them. It was inspiring for me, very inspirational.

When Seaman was a young boy, music was something everyone enjoyed, and he professes that he had no special aptitude. However, he did notice the importance of music in the community: 'People were always happy, there was always music going on.'

Seaman lived on TI until 1938, when he and his mother relocated to Cape York Peninsula on the Australian mainland, setting the stage for adventures and events that would change his life — and his music — forever.

Thursday Island 'Hula, Hula Dancing Party', postcard, c. mid-1930s. Top row [l–r]: Solomon Toulasik, Dulla Solomon (née Jia), unknown, Jenap Bin Dol (née Jia), Roy Williams. Middle row: unknown, Kathleen Jia. Bottom row: Tidja Adams, Seri Jia, unknown. Reclining: Sam Savage.

CHAPTER 2
Cape York Time

Come on little pony eat up your crackers and corn / When mustering time is all through / There'll be no more work for me and you / Come on little pony you just keep jogging along.

'Little Pony'

Relocation to Cape York

In 1938, Seaman's mother had an opportunity to take a job on the Australian mainland — at Coen on Queensland's Cape York Peninsula — and convinced him that it would be a good move:

> Mum Dan was a cook at the old Royal Hotel on Thursday Island and word had spread even to Coen. The [Exchange Hotel] owners, Mr and Mrs [Herbert and Amelia] Thompson wrote to Mum and offered her a job as a cook … When Mum asked me about what I think about going to Coen from TI, leaving all my school mates behind, making new school friends in Coen. Oh I'd take a long time to think this over and make my mind up. Then Mum made my mind up for me. She said, 'You know, Mr and Mrs Thompson, they own a cattle station and there's plenty of horses there.' [And me being a Hopalong Cassidy movie fan] I said, 'Mum, let's go. Let's go to Coen.' So Mum gave notice and she accepted that position … and we flew to Coen mid-1938.

Young Henry and his mother left TI on a Gypsy Moth plane piloted by aviation pioneer Tom MacDonald, departing from the tiny airstrip that now is the site of Tamwoy Town and the secondary school. It was the first time he had flown, and it was a long and bumpy ride. He remembers it to this day: 'Well, I got air sick all the way down to Coen.'

Tom McDonald (left) and Ted Mansfield (right) with Gypsy Moth 'Miss Cairns' De Havilland at Coen, 1928. Courtesy State Library of Queensland, image no. 69595.

When they got to Coen, Seaman's mother wanted him to continue his education. However, Seaman says:

> It was prior to the start of the Second World War, [and] the school teacher, he resigned and flew to Cairns to join the Armed Forces … The school was there — a nice big school it was too — but no school teacher.

The only alternative was to take correspondence lessons, supervised by a married daughter of the Thompsons, Ann Prideaux. The lessons arrived via overland mail, and Seaman remembers the mailman:

Jim McDowall carried mail by packhorse on Cape York Peninsula during the period 1934–51. In the dry season, the trip was about 13 days but in the wet season, it could take six or more weeks. Courtesy National Archives of Australia, 1934, image no. J2879:QTH247B.

The mail used to go from Cairns to Cooktown [and then] to Laura by rail motor and then by the mailman on horseback [to Coen]. It used to take him weeks [for] a round trip … flood, rain or shine. He might be two [or three] days late during the Wet [season], but he would always get through. Mr Jim McDowall, that was his name.

Unfortunately, Mrs Prideaux also eventually had to leave Coen, so Seaman's formal education ended when he was just 11 years of age. But that did not mean he was free to fritter away the time: his mother made sure he was busy, as there were many odd jobs around the hotel that he could do at his age:

> It was my job to make sure the chooks get fed … I [would] feed them every morning and go and check for eggs, take the eggs up into the kitchen. Then walk about 2 miles up to the goat yard and let the goats

out. There was about 25–30 head of goats that I had to look after too. It was good because it kept me occupied because there were [not many] playmates there. There was one Aboriginal boy, Aboriginal family, Mr and Mrs Port. The eldest boy [Alfie] he was about my age too so we got on well together … When I had time off, I'd ask [Mum] if I could go and play at Alfie's house. She'd let me go.

But it was not all hard work. Seaman recalls with fondness that:

When Mum knocks off work it would be hot in the room, so we'd go outside in the yard, then on the lawn. Take soft drink out, maybe a lemonade, and she'd put the [wind-up] gramophone on then. We had seventy-eight [78 rpm] records of Tex Morton, Jimmie Rodgers, hillbilly [music].

One other job he could do was help out when freshly butchered meat was brought into the hotel:

The system was [Mr and Mrs Thompson] had this cattle station at Silver Plains, 30 miles north-east of Coen, on the coast there, near Princess Charlotte Bay [and] every two weeks they'd do a kill no matter where they are mustering. They'd do a kill early in the evening and they'd put the meat on two packhorses in the pack bags and one of the Aboriginal stockmen would ride and take the horses with the meat for the hotel. He'd leave about seven o'clock that evening and he'd get there about three o'clock [the morning of] the next day … He'd arrive at the hotel and Mr Thompson would be waiting for him in front of the butcher shop. So the stockman would give Mr Thompson a hand to offload the pack bags, take the meat out and put it in the butcher shop. He'd help Mr Thompson to cut it up into steaks and corned beef and that, and Mr Thompson would dry-salt the meat himself. After, the stockman would go back the next morning. It was my job to look after the horses — ride bareback on one and drive them down to the creek, which was about half a mile away, give them water and drive them back and put them back in the yard again. So that was a big thing for me and young Alfie Port; he taught me how to ride a horse in Coen. They're quiet horses, so I could handle that. It was good fun for me. I'd imagine that I'm Hopalong Cassidy taking the horses [down to the river for water].

Doing odd jobs kept Seaman busy around Coen, and even gave him opportunities to play out his fantasies of being a cowboy like Hopalong Cassidy. However, he soon had the opportunity to embark on a much more exciting and real adventure: mustering on a cattle drive, where he even got his own horse — to be immortalised many decades later in his song 'Little Pony'.

Young Henry Dan (left), aged 11, and head stockman Romeo Thompson (right) droving at Silver Plains Station Cape York c.1939–40. Courtesy Henry Dan Private Collection.

In 1941, Seaman's mother told him he could go to Silver Plains Station if Mr Thompson had work for him. Seaman remembers that, 'She got me a sombrero, leggings [chaps] … if you bump up against a tree your leather leggings would protect your legs. Spurs, stockman boots, [with] the elastic sides.' With the outbreak of the Second World War, some of the cattleman on Cape York, such as Mr Thompson, gathered herds to move them south to railheads for shipment to larger centres where beef was in demand, especially for military personnel. Seaman recollects:

> We're into the [Second World War] now. So [Mr Thompson] donated 200 head but we had to go and muster 200 head of scrub cattle and they were wild cattle. So we'd go out with 15–20 head of 'coaches', which is quiet cattle. You have to know how to handle these scrub cattle. They'd come down from the scrub early in the evening. They'd get out on the plains so you've got to catch them [there]. So we'd wait; the manager would make us wait until four o'clock the next morning. Then we'd

ride in and circle behind the scrubbers — scrub cattle — get between them and the scrub at the foot of the hill. And when the manager knew everyone was in position, he'd whistle and crack his whip and it was all 'yakka' and 'crackka' and a race with the scrubbers because the 'coaches' are already in with the scrub cattle. So they're out in the open and we'd run 'em til they start to slow down and [then] let them walk and stop, get their breath back, then walk them slowly to a temporary holding yard that we'd built the day before. It was there waiting for these scrubbers. We'd put them in with the quiet cattle, left them there for one day and we still had 20 miles [32 kilometres] to [get them] back to our [cattle dip where you get all the ticks off] … Then the following day, we'd brand them and the young 'mickies' — the young bulls — they'd get de-nutted to make them a bullock.

Once the cattle were all gathered up and the scrub cattle calmed down, the real adventure could begin. Nevertheless, Henry wanted to let his mother know he was all right:

> I was still 11 years old but I was halfway — well, say a third of the way — to being an experienced stockman, but there's a long, long way to go yet. I wrote a letter to Mum telling her that I [would] go along to take these cattle to Mungana [near Chillagoe]. It's a long walk overland … I didn't realise how far away it was but it took us six weeks, travelling from waterhole to waterhole every day. But it was good experience for an 11-year-old. It teaches you discipline and patience.

A big challenge was learning to ride mustering horses, not the tamer horses around Coen:

> I could ride reasonably well — well, I thought I could until I got down to the station and tried to ride these frisky horses. Different story altogether! This particular time we were out and we were doing this racing, getting the cattle out and I fell off three times. So the third time I fell off they were taking the cattle back to the main homestead. It was only about 2 miles [3.2 kilometres] away then. So after I fell down a third time I said, 'Oh blow it, I'll walk back to the camp!' So I walked the 2 miles back to camp! And after that I said, 'Well, you've got to learn to ride properly!' And you soon learned.

As a youngster, Seaman's role while mustering was to help out wherever he could:

> I was the youngest in the team then. So I'd help the cook wash the pots. When you're out in the bush like that you'd just use a tin plate and you look after your own plate. You've got your own cutlery, your own pannikin and your own tin plate. They're yours, so it's up to you to look after them.

Part of the discipline was learning that the work went on all day, every day from dawn until dusk. It was also always unpredictable because the drovers and the cattle travelled across bush country without tracks, but the drovers were expert bushmen.

> You'd get up at dark. The manager used to wake us up at four o'clock [in the morning]. The boy would light the fire. Then we'd have damper cooked the night before, just have a slice of damper and a cup of tea. Just on daybreak you start walking your cattle then and they'd walk 8–10 miles [13–16 kilometres] to the next waterhole. That's how you'd pace it out so the cattle don't get too tired or lose their condition, because they're going to markets now.

There was little time to rest during the day, because such a large herd required constant monitoring:

> Well, you're in the saddle most of the day. The only time you stop is when you want to give the cattle a break. That's lunch and then you take it in turns to do what we call tailing the cattle. You just ride around them and make sure they don't stray, so they know that there's someone there all the time.

Towards late afternoon, it was time to prepare for that day's camp and an evening meal — which, not surprisingly, often consisted of beef. Seaman recollects that the meals were 'beef and more beef, and it's corned beef. Only time you have fresh beef is when you run out of corned beef. Then you do a kill.' Vegetables were rare, but tea and damper were always available, and often there was a bit of golden syrup.

Sometimes Seaman had to work at night as well, although he was not too successful the first time:

> Each person had his own night watch. You circle the cattle and make sure that they're resting in the night. So they don't stray. When it was my turn to do night watch, three of the cattle, they strayed away from me! The manager went round did a head count. It took us [a total of] six weeks [for the muster] but we were four weeks on the trail [by then] and you get to know each beast. You're with them all the time every day and there was three missing. He said, 'Oh Henry, you lost three beasts, they're gone.' When they go like that, they go straight back home again. It's their sense of direction. He sent one of the Aboriginal stockmen to go and track [them] down and bring them back. We kept on going, and early that evening the Aboriginal stockman arrived with the three beasts that were making their way home. He brought them back again. They are good stockmen, good bushmen!

Seaman remembers the boss's reaction: 'Oh well, you must have dozed off, so I'll put you on the early shift so you're not sleepy.' That's exactly what he did.

Droving required many skills, and Seaman learnt some of them from Romeo Thompson, the Aboriginal head stockman of Silver Plains:

> He's experienced and he could handle cattle. He was one of the stockmen who breaks in these young horses when they come of age … who rides it, [and] breaks in the [unbroken horses]. He taught me how to ride 'buck jumpers'.

It was crucial that the drovers work together as a team, each with their particular role to play. It was also important that expert stockmen such as Romeo Thompson taught the younger drovers what to do and how to navigate the bush.

While on the muster, Seaman also encountered a variety of wildlife, such as snakes, feral pigs and especially wild horses:

> You've got to watch out for these brumbies, these stallions, and if one of the stock horses are on heat, the brumby would hang around and try to drag her away. And the mare being on heat, she'd go too. So you've got to tie her up — all the mares, tie them up, hobble them.

After six weeks, the drovers finally arrived at their destination. When the train arrived and the cattle were loaded on to the cattle cars, the manager, three Aboriginal stockmen and young Henry hopped on to the last carriage:

> We left all our droving gear, droving plant behind at Mangana, and the horses, and just took our swag and clothes and hopped on the van and we went into Mareeba [and the cattle eventually to a meatworks near Cairns].

After returning to Mangana, it took another two weeks for the drovers to return home to Silver Plains. By then, Seaman was getting homesick and missing his mother:

> I stayed there another week and [we] made another kill to go back up to the hotel again. Then the manager asked me if I'd like to go home and see Mum, and I said, 'Please, yeah.' 'Alright,' he said, 'you can go and if you don't want to come back, you don't have to.' And I said, 'I might not come back then', because I'd had enough of that. He said, 'Oh, you'll be right, you'll be right.'

His mother noticed that he had grown up a bit, and he was glad to be home:

> It was strange, the first time I'd been that long away from Mum, you know, and I was happy to see her again. I'm 12 years old and I'm back home! That was great.

As to whether or not it was a job or fun, he recalls:

> I was on five shillings a week and that was plenty for a young fellow when you're having fun riding horses every day. My wages went back to Mum. It was money for soft drink!

The bush skills Seaman learned droving cattle were later put to good use when he worked as a mineral prospector in remote areas of Queensland, and also in the highlands of Papua New Guinea.

Learning guitar and music

Around the time Seaman was embarking on his adventures as a young drover, he met Valentine Bynoe McGinness, better known as Val McGinness. Val was an Aboriginal mechanic and musician from the Northern Territory who was then working around Coen. Seaman credits Val with being the person who first inspired him to play guitar and sing, and he recalls vividly his early encounters with a guitar: 'Val had a battered old guitar and he showed me a few chords, how to play the guitar then. Being there [in Coen] he helped me with my music also.' Val also socialised with Seaman and his mother, and other people at the hotel:

> [Val] had a room in the hotel. After the kitchen work was done, we'd go sit out on the lawn, and he would bring his guitar along. Mum would have a wind-up gramophone, we'd be all singing. [As well], he'd take Mum Dan and I out on Sunday when we'd have our day off, take us fishing on the Coen River. He'd take a panning dish and he'd show me how to pan for gold, alluvial gold.

This early introduction to gold panning was also to be a help in the future: '[It] helped me as regard my training when I went to work for a mining company later on in life. I sort of knew a little bit about it then.'

Val McGinness went on to be an important community musician in Darwin, where his descendants — such as Kath, Ali and June Mills — continue to perform unique Indigenous music as the Darwin-based Mills Sisters and as solo artists. Val also wrote a popular version of 'Waltzing Matilda', 'Waltjim Bat Matilda', in the Gurindji-Kungarakan language, which was recorded and popularised by Ali Mills in 2010. Seaman would later write and record his personal celebration of community music and musicians in Darwin, 'Waiting for the Ice Man'.

Reflecting on his time on Cape York, Seaman remembers having a very close relationship with his mother; however, because of isolation and the advent of the Second World War, he also had little opportunity to receive more formal education. However, he observes:

> I don't regret [the lack of formal education] at all. Due to my outside experience I've gained more than I would have if I'd kept going to school. There'd be just that one road but [because of] me going out to work there's different work that I could take on and do it properly.

In any case, children of his generation growing up during the Great Depression were expected to go out to work early, and Seaman was no exception.

Life in the dry, dusty inland cattle country of Cape York was a world away from TI's humid, tropical seaside. However, later in life the adventures and the skills Seaman learned on Cape York proved useful — and would also provide the inspiration for songs chronicling that period of his life. So would the next period of his life: moving to the north Queensland regional centre of Cairns for the duration of the Second World War — definitely the 'big smoke' in comparison to tiny TI and even tinier Coen.

Val McGuinness performing in Darwin, c.1970s. Courtesy of Mills family of Darwin and Jeff Corfield.

CHAPTER 3

Cairns During the Second World War

Let's have a house party hula / I wanna hula-hula with you.

'House Party Hula'

The Second World War and evacuation from TI

The Second World War led to the relocation and dispersal of many residents of TI, including all non-combatants. TI also had a sizeable Japanese male population because of the key role played by Japanese men in Australia's maritime industries. Once war was declared, they were rounded up and interned on the mainland. TI became a military centre, as did Horn Island with its important airport, which was first bombed by the Japanese in March 1942. Many Torres Strait Islander men enlisted in the Torres Strait Light Infantry, and served in active combat and crucial support roles, while many non-combatant Islanders living throughout the Torres Strait were confined to their home islands.

On Tuesday, 27 January 1942, the following notice appeared on page one of the *Torres Strait Pilot*:

> NOTICE TO THURSDAY ISLAND PUBLIC. Decision has been given that the women and children of Thursday Island be compulsorily evacuated. All women and children, white and coloured, will therefore be prepared to leave Thursday Island by ship at 6 p.m. on 28th January. Suitcases and personal effects only may be taken. Further notice will be given if additional belongings are later allowed. Port of disembarkation will be notified later.
>
> – RJR HURST, Lt-Col. Staff Corps, Fortress Commander, Thursday Island

Some people departed on large passenger boats such as the *Ormiston* and *Wandana*, and evacuees recall singing Jaffa Ah Mat's popular song 'Old TI' 🔊 as they left. However, others left on whatever boats were available, including the *Goodwill*, a small freight boat. Some of the *Goodwill*'s evacuees composed a song of farewell and remembrance to a melody reminiscent of 'When Irish Eyes are Smiling'. In a community recording done for the National Museum of Australia in 2003 for the *Paipa/Windward Exhibition* CD, on which Seaman was one of the singers, the words to 'As the *Goodwill* Sailed Away' were recalled as:

> *We left our dear old TI with tear drops in our eyes / We can only hope to be back there in dear old TI / We left our dear old TI with tear drops in our eyes / We could see the folks still waving as the* Goodwill *sailed away / We missed our palms and fishes which surround our island home / And never more we'll dream of leaving dear old TI.*

Evacuees recalled singing 'As the *Goodwill* Sailed Away' and 'Old TI' 🔊 later when they returned to TI in the late 1940s. The Second World War marked a major change in life for many residents of the Torres Strait: many of the old ways of life and the old attitudes could not be sustained when evacuees returned to rebuild and re-establish a new society.

Social and cultural life in Cairns

Seaman and his mother were already on the mainland at Coen, so they were not TI evacuees; nonetheless, the Second World War also changed their lives irrevocably. In 1943, Seaman had the chance to relocate to Cairns. Grannie Dan's son and Seaman's step-brother, Jack Smoke, had joined the Australian army, so Grannie Dan asked him, 'Would you like to go to Cairns, stay at your brother's place?' Seaman was ready for a change after his years in the tiny community of Coen, but he knew that he would have to find work in order to contribute to the household. He recalls his first job in Cairns:

> We were staying in Bunda Street not far from the gasworks and the National Hotel [was] on the corner of Bunda and Spence Street. It's now called the Cape York Hotel … So I got a job there as a yardman. I used to scrub the floor in the hotel. There was no long-handled deck broom. I used to [sweep it clean first and] get down on my knees, kneel on a sack bag, and scrub that bar floor! I was 13 and you wanted to do something so it didn't worry me. My wage then was 15 shillings a week. I thought, 'Gee whiz, that's much more than five shillings a week when I was in Coen!'

Social life for Seaman centred on the now-defunct nearby area known as Malay Town. It was a multicultural community along Alligator Creek, where Torres Strait Islanders, Malays, Chinese, Indians and other non-European people lived.

Malay Town and Alligator Creek, 1920. Courtesy Cairns Historical Society, image no. P02207.

What Seaman remembers most vividly is the homegrown entertainment that made the community a lively place. It was especially important because, as on TI, Queensland's race-based laws and regulations restricted who could go where. Seaman recollects that the music was an important part of maintaining a sense of community for all the evacuees. The music he heard there was also his first exposure to African-American culture:

> I had a lot of young mates there, some down from TI, and I used to muck around with Kasim Raymond's uncle, 'Slicky' [Lawrence] Raymond. We were about the same age, we went to the same convent school on TI … And there was a young uncle of mine, Fred Sailor, his mother [Louisa] was one of the [Pitt] sisters, sisters of my grandmother Maryann Pitt. And they used to live in Malay Town and Fred used to play the guitar. He played jazz guitar, followed the American style. The American Negroes [soldiers] had a camp out at Redlynch. When they'd get their liberty they'd come into Cairns. They used to jive. An old fellow, Harry Hodges, used to play the button accordion. And another uncle, Fred Sailor's older brother, Ben Jacob, he'd play the mandolin. He was very good. They had good parties there. The [African-]Americans they'd sing their blues and the jazz songs and they'd do jitterbug. And I kept on watching them and I used to think to myself, 'Gee, I'd like to play like those fellows' … and that's how I got into jazz and blues. Just watching the American Negroes play, listening to them sing, you soon pick it up.

As part of the homegrown entertainment, the young women would do hula dancing, while the older people would clear a space to dance and socialise. As well as music and dancing, other Islander cultural practices such as feasting were important:

> When there's a special feasting, in their backyard they'd do the underground cooking, *kapmauri*. They still had that tradition. Even though we were in a big city, in Cairns, we still held our tradition.

Seaman developed a positive attitude to trying to make the best of the difficulties people faced:

> You're in a different place, different cultures, but you still uphold your culture. You have to make a new life, you gotta start somewhere. It's no good sort of moping and being sad all the time. You try to be happy. Even though that was the war years you meet other people, meet a lot of nice people and you [adjust] … life must go on. So you just carry on.

Hula dancers, Cairns, c.1946. [l–r]: Clare Mcgrath (née Dubbins), Sarina Ah Mat (née Adams), Betty Bin Juda (née Ah Mat), Lala Nicols (née Walters), Mary Bowie (née Galora).

Savage family entertainment group, Cairns, c.1930s. Back row [l–r]: Willy Savage, Pensio Cedar, Kenny Thaiday, Freddie Ware, George Jose(?). Middle row (l–r): Cecilia Jacobs, Winnie Collis, Kaffa Savage, Ellen Savage, Lilly Savage, Olive Cedar. Front row (l–r): Dorrie Hippie(?), Sam Savage (Seaman's maternal grandfather), Becky Jose. Courtesy Henry Dan Personal Collection.

Decades later, Seaman wrote the song 'House Party Hula' as a tribute to the homegrown entertainment in Malay Town and the cultural practices that helped create and sustain a sense of community for him and others during the Second World War years they spent in Cairns.

Making a contribution to the war effort

As Seaman adjusted to life in Cairns, he felt he needed to be making some kind of contribution to the war effort, as its consequences were felt across all communities and by all generations:

Friends in Cairns c.1945 Top row [l-r]: Henry Dan, Raymond Perry, Len Pitt, Francis Sebasio Middle row: Siti Bingarape, Kenny Sebasio, Loyola Canuto, Elsie Williams, Joe Ah Mat, Pauline Savage, unknown child Bottom row [l-r]: Cecilia Canuto, Selena Lewin, Gloria Botha, Mary Guivarra, Sarina Adams, Lucy Gaiba Pitt Front row: unknown children. Courtesy Pauline Mills (née Savage).

> I was 14 and this mate, Jerry Lewin, his brother, Sammy Lewin, and another mate, Budden Ah Mat, joined the American small ships, went over to New Guinea. And these other [TI] boys they joined the Merchant Marines and they'd come ashore, come up to party when they were in Cairns. They were neat, well-dressed. [And I thought] I would really like to join the Merchant Marines, too. There was a Manpower office in Cairns. He'd make sure that everyone was working. It was still war years, it was 1944 ... so I went up to the Manpower office, rode my pushbike. He said, 'Yes?' I said, 'Please sir, I want to join the Merchant Marine.' 'How old are you?' 'Fourteen, I'll be 15 next month.' 'Ah, come back in another two years' time and I'll think about it.'

Although Seaman was far too young for the Merchant Navy, there were other jobs he could do.

> The Manpower officer said: 'I can get you work if you want to do work for the war effort.' So he gave me this address, Hancock and Gore Ply Mill, which wasn't far from my place in Cairns, I lived in the Bungalow area too. So I rode my pushbike down to this ply mill and went to the office. [The officer said] 'What's your name? How old are you?' 'Henry Gibson Dan, 14 years old.' 'Alright, you looking for work?' 'Please sir, yes.' 'Okay, come in on Monday. We start at seven o'clock. This is wartime, we're doing our war effort.' So we used to work from seven o'clock [in the morning] til six in the evening. And there was no smoko breaks, half an hour break for lunch ... You really worked but there was a lot of teenagers working there too and oh we all had fun together. Then just before peace was declared, that's when we could have smoko and the work hours was cut back.

Tropical Troubadours, c. early 1940s. Back row [l–r]: Heather Pitt, Amy Walters, Arthur Pitt, Francis Guivarra, Bill Paterson, Thomas Guivarra, Fred Walters Jnr, Lucy Gaiba Pitt, Maisie Pitt. Middle row [l–r]: Ketchell Anno, Nocky Delacruz, Dorrie Delacruz, Dulcie Pitt, Agnes Pitt, George Noble, Fred Walters Snr. Front row: Hazel Meredith, Sophie Pitt, Ivy Guivarra, Joan Guivarra. Courtesy Cairns Museum, image no. P10824.

Hula Group, Cairns, c.1945, Standing [l-r]: Lucy Gaiba Maza (née Pitt), Pauline Mills (née Savage), May Oui (née Addo), Elsie Smith (née Williams), Daphne Noble, Mary Bowie (née Galora) Kneeling: Betty Bin Juda (née Ah Mat), Gloria Guivarra (née Botha), Sarina Ah Mat (née Adams), Flo Ludwig, Clare Filewood (née Chin Soon), Lala Nicols (née Walters) Front: Florence Kennedy (née Savage). Courtesy Pauline Mills.

Notwithstanding his and other Islanders' contributions to the war effort, the racial aspects of Queensland's laws and regulations were still enforced — for example, in the pubs:

> In Cairns, the big city, if the barman or the manager don't know you, well, he won't take you in, he won't serve you. But if a friend takes you in and identifies you, it's all right. You can go back to the hotel and have a drink then, as long as you behave yourself.

As demeaning as it could sometimes be, Seaman says at the time the general attitude was: 'If you get knocked back from a hotel you don't worry about that. You just walk out. You don't create any disturbance at all.' Seaman recalls such restrictions with a level of understandable resentment. However, he also appreciates that after the Second World War, things did change — albeit slowly.

The years that Seaman spent in Cairns during the Second World War gave him many new experiences and work skills. Crucially, he also began to develop his love of music. He was still absorbing musical styles, but the blues, hula, jazz and traditional music he heard gave him a solid background in the music his community enjoyed. The end of the war also meant he could join other Torres Strait Islander men returning to work in the rejuvenated maritime industries. There was once again consumer demand for pearl and trochus shells for buttons and decorations and pearls for jewellry. Seaman was about to embark on his working life as a man of the sea.

CHAPTER 4

Learning to Live a Diver's Life

*Divers down getting shells / Tender watches the ocean swells /
Out on the reef ... / Seven men out on the sea /
Work as one quietly / Watching the weather.*

'Watching the Weather' ⛵

After the Second World War ended, TI people living on the mainland had to decide whether to return to the Torres Strait or remain where they were. For some, there were more opportunities on the mainland and for others there was little to which they wanted to return. Their families had dispersed, and houses and businesses had degenerated during the years TI was occupied by the military. The social mix had changed too, with many Europeans choosing to remain on the mainland and very few Japanese allowed to return. Pre-Second World War TI was but a memory, and Seaman recalls:

> When I went back to TI again [in 1947] after leaving in 1938 … nothing was like it was when I was a young boy of eight years old there. A lot of things that I knew existed [then], they were no longer there.

Seaman Dan's mother decided to stay on the mainland, eventually settling in Cairns. However, he took up the opportunity to start his sea-going career with his uncle, Thomas Savage:

> After the war finished, I come out of the ply mill then. I was 16 years old when I first went out to sea, swimming for trochus shells. In 1947, [my uncle] was going to work from Cairns up to the Torres Straits. So I joined his ship as a crew member.

It was also around this time that Henry Dan acquired his lifelong nickname, 'Seaman' Dan — nicknames were common among Torres Strait Islanders, as were other maritime-related terms that became family names, such as Mast, Jib and Sailor. In a maritime environment, many men were technically 'seaman' but for some unknown reason the nickname 'Seaman' stuck with Henry to the extent that many people today do not know his real name.

His uncle soon retired, so Seaman joined the *Idalia* as an engineer and then moved to the *Yola*, where he got his first chance to put on a diver's helmet:

> The skipper, head diver George Elarde, gave me the opportunity to put the helmet on, to work as a learner diver. I was 18 years old then. I'd seen the bottom of the sea through a facemask when you're swimming for trochus shell on the Great Barrier Reef, all different sights. But when you put the helmet on to go and look for pearl shell, it's a different feeling altogether.

One major difference, according to Seaman, was that 'you're not holding your breath like when you're shallow-water diving for trochus shells [without a helmet or compressed air, but only a face mask]. So you've got more than two minutes to admire the scenery underneath.' However, gathering pearl shells required concentration:

Top: Pearl shell diver's helmet, date unknown. Brass, glass and copper, loaned by Peter Ahloy, photo by George Serras, National Museum of Australia.

Left: Torres Strait (A52/Enby) and Broome (Richard Mail) lugger models. Norman Savage, Photo by George Serras, National Museum of Australia.

> You've got to think all the time you're looking for pearl shell, to get that diving experience. So when I'm on the bottom I only take about three or four seconds just to admire what I can and then start looking for pearl shells. You've gotta think that way all the time. You're down there to eat, sleep, dream, pearl shell. So you pick up pearl shell. That's the way … you could become a good diver, a working diver. You learn the trade as you go, to be a good diver, to be a responsible person, that way people can trust you.

Depending on the size of the lugger (boat), a crew would commonly be between seven and 12 men, comprising a skipper, lead divers, tenders, learner divers/deckies, an engineer and a cook.

Despite its often-romanticised depiction in movies and literature, work on a pearling lugger was hard and at times relentless. The water was only clear enough for picking up shells at neap tides, when the currents were calmer and did not stir up the bottom. As Seaman recounts: 'When it's spring tide, the current runs too strong, too fast, stirs all the bottom up, you can't see then. It's impossible to work.' However, there would usually only be three to four clear days in the neap tide in the first quarter of the moon, and six to seven in the last quarter. Consequently, when conditions were suitable, the working days were very long:

> The stern tender [who looks after the boat for the skipper] wakes up at four [o'clock in the morning]. He rouses the crew. The divers they can sleep in. At five o'clock the stern tender approaches the skipper. By that time the skipper's awake. So the skipper in turn wakes the other divers then.

In the tropics, the length of daylight is fairly constant all year. Given the limited times each month to gather shells, daytime meant it was work time:

> At five o'clock the stern tender gets the engineer to start the motor and it's still dark. You need to run up to the buoy, you always anchor where the buoy is so we'd get an early start. You're there right on the working bottom, the working area. It's just a matter of winding the anchor up, getting the boat in position, the drift position. Then the diver, he stands on the ladder. He's got his lead weights on and he stands on the ladder and waits. As soon as [the water was clear enough to see], you fall off the ladder then. That way you're using all the clear water, all the visibility that you can. It's a long day's work.

Around midday there would be a short break, but it was hard to predict exactly when it would be:

> There's no [set] time. When you are running up for another drift [a passage over a shell-bearing area] the tender tells the engineer to run

up slowly, so that gives everyone the chance to have a cup of tea and something to eat. By the time you finish [eating] you're up at your starting point again. That's how you gotta work it out.

The work continued apace while there was daylight, as the crew kept their focus on gathering and cleaning shells:

You start work as soon as you can see. You stop work when you cannot see. That's when you run up to anchor and then the last bags of shells that's been sent up [are cleaned]. The deckies, they scrape the shells on the outside, take all the dirt off — mud, seaweed that's growing on there, bits of coral, bits of shell stuck to that shell. Then they open it up. When that's being done, [we're] running up to anchor. By the time the anchor goes down, all the shell that'd been picked up on that last drift, on the last dive, is already cleaned and stacked into what we call a measuring box. It was an old beer crate, when it's full that's 200-weight of pearl shells there. So you just count the boxes then. It gives you a fair idea [of tonnage] and you're not much out when you weigh it on the scale itself in town, when you go back into port.

Opened pearl shell showing meat. Courtesy Betty Foster and family.

Food was very basic, but it was also very important because diving was exhausting work — especially doing repeated dives in a day. In the early morning:

Tea, coffee, and a slice of damper if you wanna eat, or you would normally just wait until lunchtime. Might have one slice of damper at lunchtime … [but] at lunchtime you've still got to go down and work, pick up pearl shells. It's very uncomfortable when you are trying to do this on a full stomach. I've tried that once as a young diver — I soon learned my lesson. When you're working, especially on the bottom under the sea, you don't feel like eating.

At night, there was time for a full meal and perhaps to reminisce a bit or just relax:

The cook dishes your meal out for you, which is normally rice and curried tinned meat, or hamper corned beef, which is all right too. When you're out at sea you're not allowed to fish. There's to be no blood on deck. [That's because] it brings the sharks around quick, very quick. You're only out [on the open ocean] for [a few days at the first and third quarters] then you're back in shelter again. You stay out from TI for, say, two to three weeks because you don't want to run in [to TI] every spring tide. That's about usually 60, 70 miles [120 to 140 kilometres] away. And that uses up a lot of fuel. So you just anchor not far from the working ground, but you're in a sheltered area, where you can go ashore, relax there, nice beach there. And the crew, well, they do all the fishing. The boat's got a set net or a drag net. Set that to get fish.

Unknown musician on Torres Strait lugger, undated. Frank Hurley, National Library image no. 23200265.

Another part of the diet was salted and dried pearl shell meat strung on a piece of casing wire and hung up on the rigging so it would cure and keep. It could be added to a curry on board or taken home to distribute to families and friends.

Seaman emphasises that accommodation on board was very basic: 'Nothing frivolous. It's a working vessel and that's what it is. You are working men and that's how you are, that's what you are.' On a lugger that he skippered, there were:

> bunks in the fo'c'sle [forecastle], that's in the fore'ard [bow area]. There's usually four bunks there. The engineer has his own bunk in the engine room. And in the stern cabin that's where all the divers sleep. Mine used to be overhead up the top. From port to starboard [there was] my bunk and then that made room for the other divers to sleep in their own bunks. Two, four, six, seven of us could sleep there in the cabin. Some lucky boats [had mattresses and pillows], we just had blankets and that's your mattress, you double your blanket up. But you're young and you're working, you don't worry about [discomfort].

Working on a pearl or trochus lugger required cooperation and trust, and there was a clear line of authority and a strict division of labour. Seaman explains the line of authority:

> Your first sense of loyalty is to your skipper, then your shipmates. So whatever he says you've got to go by his word, even though you don't agree with it, but it's not up to you to disagree. If he makes a mistake, it's his mistake. But if it's to endanger someone's life, well then we'd talk to the stern tender then the stern tender would talk to the skipper. You don't overrule his word. So that's how you work on the ship. You hold your crew with you all the time. You all work together.

Cooperation was all-important, and to encourage a harmonious crew some were made up of relatives or men from the same islands. If it was a mixed crew — such as one with both Western and Eastern Islanders and mainlanders — then men were chosen who were considered accommodating and level-headed. A small boat was certainly no place for big disputes. The work was dangerous and the livelihoods of everyone on board depended on cooperation.

The maritime and diving skills Seaman learned as a young man in Queensland would serve him well when he later had the chance to work in the Northern Territory and Western Australia — other places where the maritime industries were booming after the interruption of the Second World War. In Darwin and Broome, he would have more adventures and also make his first forays into actually performing music himself, and not just listening to it.

CHAPTER 5

ADVENTURES ACROSS NORTHERN AUSTRALIA

Saturday night at the Sunshine Club [Darwin] / Jumping around with the one you love / Doing the twist / Singing the blues / Do any dance that you wanna do / 'Cuz when you heat up you gotta cool down / That's when the ice man comes around.

'Waiting for the Ice Man' ⛵

In the late 1940s and early 1950s, Torres Strait Islander men began working in maritime industries across tropical Australia. Working out from TI, with crews recruited there, as well as from the outer islands and Cape York communities, they sailed luggers and gathered pearl and trochus shells from Broome on the west coast to Mackay in the east. As experienced and hard workers, the Islanders' skills were in demand, and it was part of a pattern of work-based migration that also took Torres Strait Islanders to the canefields of north Queensland and railway lines in remote regions of Queensland and Western Australia. Those emigrants who left the Torres Strait after the Second World War for employment and educational opportunities helped establish the Torres Strait Islander communities now scattered across Australia. However, some men also left for adventures, to see something of the world after decades of restricted movement under Queensland's race-based laws and regulations, and the Second World War. Seaman was one of those single, young TI men who were keen to travel, learn new skills and meet new people.

Seaman had learnt basic maritime skills in Queensland before learning to dive, and he loved life at sea. It opened up opportunities for travel, and he first sailed to the Northern Territory on board the *Fram*, skippered by his cousin, Pedro Guivarra. The *Fram* had been converted from a trochus to a pearling lugger in Cairns, and needed new equipment:

> [So in] early 1952 we sailed up to Thursday Island to hire some pearling gear like divers' helmets and air hoses. And … get a Southern Cross diesel motor to pump compressed air into the two 150 pound air tanks on board the boat for the divers down below picking up pearl shells.

Seaman recalls that the crew mostly consisted of 'TI boys':

> There was Budden Ah Mat, Pedro Wallace [Wallis], Robert Wallace [Wallis], Reggie Lee and Henry Solomon, he was our stern tender … Joe Garcia, he was our cook. I was the engineer on board. We finished end of 1952 [and] we had Christmas in Darwin. The skipper planned to leave the lugger at the end of the season and the owner Dick Tate wanted to take the lugger back to Cairns. But some of the crew wanted to stay on in Darwin so when they were discharged they found work ashore.

Seaman worked for a bit at the Municipal Council's Botanical Gardens, but then he received a better offer:

> I was offered a job in a butcher's shop at the Koolpinyah Cool Stores Ice Making and Butcher Shop. They had a cattle station about 15 miles [24 kilometres] from Darwin at Adelaide River. They'd do the kill there late in the evening and the meat truck would go out there five days a week to get the fresh kill and bring it into the butcher's shop.

It was at Koolpinyah Cool Stores that Seaman first learnt to drive and also learned the new skill of making ice:

> We had three ice tanks [about 2 metres high]. We were making these 45-pound [20.4 kilogram] moulds [blocks] of ice, big slabs … every morning [you'd have to do] what we'd call 'pull the ice'. There's a special hook that you have. There's two holes on either side of the mould on top. Just put the hook on either side and pull it out … [Then] you stack [the moulds] neatly, lean them up against the tank itself and then you'd turn them over and you'd hose 'em to get the ice to fall out. The ice would land on the concrete floor [and then] go into the cold room. They're there [for] whoever wants to buy ice.

Seaman also delivered ice to homes and businesses — something that was common before the advent of widespread refrigeration. Delivering ice also meant he got to drive around in a nice cool truck in Darwin's oppressive heat and humidity:

> I used to do a delivery in the morning and in the afternoon after lunch. I'd take 16 moulds in the morning and I'd have a big ice chopper. Some people they just want half a block of ice, chop it in half. Some — hotels especially — they'd take a full [block of ice]. So I'd carry that

in for them. Then in the afternoon there'd be about 10 blocks, go to restaurants then. And before I do the delivery, the empty moulds that I tipped upside down up against the tank, I'd put them all in and then fill them up with water so they can be frozen overnight for the next day's delivery. [Ice making] goes on in rotation.

Aside from being a cool workplace, it was a good job for other reasons:

> Upstairs above the butcher shop there's accommodation for the workers. So we get free accommodation and meat — the best cuts of meat, like fillet steak, T-bone, rump steak, porterhouse. The staff would pay a shilling a pound, which is real good. Because you work at the butcher shop, you know what sorts of cuts are really good.

While his day job kept him busy, Seaman was also involved in the active social and athletic life centred on an area of Darwin known as Parap Camp. It was ex-army housing left over from the Second World War (118 Parap Camp, now Stuart Park). The war had also scattered the civilian Darwin community, and when they returned, the 'mixed-race' and non-European population was centred on Parap. It was basic housing and times were tough, but strong communal bonds were established and a rich social and cultural life emerged, including active music and dance groups. Athletic groups were also important, and Seaman played Rugby Union and Australian Rules Football with multicultural teams, which included many TI and Aboriginal players, and also the future singer-songwriter and Administrator of the Northern Territory, Ted Egan. Seaman would later record Egan's 'Sayonara Nakamura', 🎵 an iconic song about the dangers of pearling.

At Parap Camp around this time, Seaman had his first opportunity to perform with other musicians. Recalling those first performances there, he recalls:

118 Parap camp housing, Darwin, c. mid- to late 1950s. Courtesy NT Library, Roderick Collection, image no. PH0110/0426.

Darwin musicians c. mid-1950s, [l–r]: Peter Cardona, Ken Hazelbane, Seaman Dan, Rusty Perez. Courtesy Jeff Corfield.

> There were a lot of nice Darwin people there. We used to go to dances and I used to sit in with the Darwin boys [Peter Cardona, Rusty Perez, Russell Cruz, Clive Dowling, Delfin Cubillo, Dave and Ken Hazelbane]. We formed a musical group, like a band sort of thing, and we were often invited to play at dances. We were young and happy. It was the first time I started singing for my supper.

He also reflects that, even now in his mid-eighties when performing on TI and Horn Island, 'Nothing's changed! I still sing for my supper — and I like it!'

There were particular styles of music that were very popular with the Parap audiences:

> It was after [the Second World War], so it used to be [slow fox trot or 'slow drag'] where you could hold your partner close. Another favourite would be the progressive barn dance. You form a circle and you dance on and change partners as you go along and you go [steadily] around that circle.

Darwin musicians c. mid-1950s, [l–r]: Seaman Dan, Peter Cardona, Rusty Perez, Clive Dowling. Courtesy Joy Cardona and Cardona family.

The progressive barn dance was also an effective way for young men and women to meet, and some relationships and even marriages resulted from these social events.

Moving from performing casually for friends at small community dances into a more professional context in public was the next step in Seaman's musical education:

> I went to a party one night in Darwin, and I'm playing away and singing away and this mate of mine [Div Collinson] he plays in a four-piece combo in the Hotel Darwin. So [Div] said, 'You know, you don't sound

Darwin musicians c. mid-1950s at Parap Camp, [l–r]: Clive Dowling, Ray Perez, Ken Hazelbane, Delfin Cubillo, Seaman Dan. Courtesy Joy Cardona and Cardona family.

too bad. How would you like to come up to the Hotel Darwin on a Saturday evening and when we have our 30-minute break, sit in for half an hour?' He said, 'I don't think we could pay you but, you know, you can sing for your supper.' I said, 'You're on, mate!'

What Seaman needed then were more songs to sing. At the time, he had a girlfriend, Mary Powers from Cairns, and she had a 45-rpm record of Nat King Cole singing 'Embraceable You' and 'Makin' Whoopee'. ⛵ So he learnt them, and they were the first songs he sang professionally in public. Almost 60 years later, in 2012, he would record them for *Sunnyside*, an album of his favourite Nat King Cole songs. Aside from singing at hotels, he also performed at Darwin's multicultural Sunshine Club, a venue for community dances and social functions set up because the Northern Territory's race-based laws and regulations prevented Aboriginal, Torres Strait Islander and 'mixed-race' people from entering local venues. The range of music and dancing styles at the Sunshine Club was eclectic, and hearing and performing many different styles of music provided Seaman with a very useful musical training ground.

As much as he loved singing, Seaman still had to earn a living with a day job, and singing inadvertently led him back to sea. He explains:

Once the audience [in Darwin] knew I was from TI they always asked me to sing 'Old TI', ⛵ which is a very nice song, [but] it makes me homesick every time I sing it.

Seaman's home back on TI was never forgotten while he was working away, and he knew he would return eventually.

Top: Seaman Dan with diving equipment in Darwin, c. mid-1950s. Courtesy Henry Dan Private Collection.

Bottom: Seaman Dan (right) being helped on to the deck of the CSIRO research vessel *Paxie* off Western Australia or the Northern Territory, c. late 1950s. Courtesy Vern Wells Collection and Peter Illidge.

After several years working ashore in Darwin, Seaman desperately wanted to return to the sea, and also to North Queensland. This was partly because he wanted to see his mother in Cairns, but he also felt he 'had been away too long [from TI]'. So in 1956 he signed on to the *Paxie*, a vessel gathering data for the pearling industry:

> Commonwealth Fisheries chartered this vessel to do surveys on pearling beds. They were looking for new pearling beds to help our pearling industry out from Darwin, out from Thursday Island, out from Broome. Because there were too many pearling vessels out working, they were depleting the shell-bearing areas. So we had to have more areas. They were in Darwin at this particular time and I knew the research officer, Cliff Middleton. He was a good friend of mine from Thursday Island. Every time that vessel leaves port there's always a research officer from the Commonwealth Scientific and Industrial Research Organisation [CSIRO] on board.

Seaman told Cliff he was homesick — even though 'I had a good job there at the butcher shop. I was on seventeen pounds a week plus free accommodation and when I worked Saturday and Sunday I get another three pounds each couple of hours that I worked, but I wanted to get back home to TI'. However, the *Paxie* was headed out first to do some surveys:

> Cliff Middleton said, 'We're leaving tomorrow to work out from Darwin; we've just come back from Broome. And we'll be out at sea for ten days and when we come back I'll introduce you to the skipper. If you want to come back to TI with us you can come and be a deckie or a diver like you used to be, to go back home.' I said, 'All right.' So [later], when I spoke to the skipper, he said, 'All right, I'll sign you up as a diver, so instead of just working your way back to TI you'll be getting diver's wages.' At that particular time, it was £49, 19 shillings a fortnight. So I signed up as a pearl diver then, went back to pearling again.

When Seaman had learned to dive in Queensland, he was either free diving for trochus shells or using only the helmet and corselet to dive for pearl shells — he had never used a full diving suit. However, the *Paxie* used half-suits.

> I had to learn to use the half-suit, which was much better than just the helmet and corselet. There's hardly any weight at all for the tender, the man that looks after your lifeline on deck. Because with the helmet and corselet, to bring you back up on deck he's got to 'skull drag' you up but with the half suit you can inflate yourself and come up slowly, come up gently. And [a tender] can see the loose lifeline in front of [him] and he just takes in the slack as you're coming up to the surface, which is much easier.

Paxie at sea off Western Australia or Northern Territory, c. late 1950s. Courtesy Vern Wells Collection and Peter Illidge.

The full suit was sometimes used by Western Australian divers, but according to Seaman:

> It's too cumbersome, you can't zig-zag, there's no freedom of movement, not like the half suits. You can cross, zig-zag, from side to side — you cover a lot of area. But with the full suit you get dragged behind the drift of the boat, you just go in that one direction.

However, as he soon discovered, a full suit had its benefits:

> In 1957, we went down [diving] in July, wintertime. And we were wondering, Gee, these Broome divers here they're using the full suit. They're too cumbersome. They're too slow. We soon found out why they were using the full suit. They were warm inside! We were all wet and cold [just wearing diving flannels]! So when we used to come up on deck and take the suit off we would dive straight down into the galley. And the cook, George Dewis, he'd always have the kettle on and he would make a cup of tea or coffee for us until it was our time to go back up on deck again to go [back] down.

Avoiding decompression sickness — or 'the bends' — was a major concern for divers. There were other underwater dangers from sharks, gropers and strong tides, but the bends was a constant threat, especially for men who dived several times a day. Seaman explains how divers 'staged' safely after diving to depth for any length of time:

> You've got to come up in stages. So your first staging level from [say] 28 fathoms is 15 fathoms and you hang there for five minutes. [Then]

> 10 minutes at 10 fathoms, 15 minutes at 5 fathoms and the most critical is two and a half fathoms before you come up on deck, 20 minutes at two and a half fathoms. That's to make sure all of the bubbles [of nitrogen and inert gases] are out of your blood stream so you don't get the bends. We were using our Australian Navy staging tables and that proved real good, very successful.

Nonetheless, even with precautions, divers did get the bends — as would happen later to Seaman when diving in the Torres Strait at the dangerous Darnley Deeps.

Seaman did the season with the *Paxie* but, before he was discharged, the skipper asked him:

> You're a very good diver — would you like to come back and work on the *Paxie* with me next year? We're going to do another survey, possibly the year after that too. And if you know some good workers like you, TI boys, I'd like to sign them on too.' And this is how I signed on Kasim Raymond, George Dewis and Raymond Adams. Kasim was our stern tender, George was our cook and Raymond was our forward tender. So I went back to sea again in 1957.

Over several seasons, the *Paxie* surveyed pearl beds across a vast area of the Australian tropics, introducing Seaman to a wide range of marine environments:

> We worked out from TI into the Gulf of Carpentaria all along that west coast of Cape York Peninsula [down to Mornington Island, then right up to Elcho Island, then Croker Island] and dived all throughout that area. Went into the Arafura Sea, dived there, then we went into Darwin. We spent six weeks there just surveying out from Darwin into the Timor Sea. All throughout Flat Top Shoal, Parry Shoal and we went over to the [Tiwi Islands].

He also got to work in the Indian Ocean off Western Australia, where the diving was different due to the large tidal movements of up to 10 metres and the cyclonic conditions:

> We went over to Broome from Darwin. We called in at Kuri Bay — the pearl farm, Paspaley's pearl farm. It's big business today [but then] there were only two pearl rafts and two Japanese caretaker scientists; now there's a lot of people. We worked out from Broome part-way into the Indian Ocean and we went 60 miles [95 kilometres] south of Broome. But we were always out at sea and never a long time along the coast. Only when we were outside of Broome we'd go in for fuel and stores and water. You're out working all the time. Even on the way to Darwin the ship was controlled by [the CSIRO in] Canberra. The radio message

Shells collected on *Paxie* off Western Australia or the Northern Territory, c. late 1950s, [l–r]: Seaman Dan, Kasim Raymond, Ken Rehder. Courtesy Vern Wells Collection and Peter Illidge.

[would] come through straight to the ship telling the skipper to have a look at certain areas, just check that area out.

The *Paxie*'s surveys were designed to identify possible new pearl beds, so part of the work was gathering scientific data — something Seaman found interesting:

> I was head diver on board then, so it was always me to go down first to have a look. Sometimes you only just have time for the one dip. But you have a special pocket sewn into your diver's trousers to get a handful of the sand, put that in your pocket. That's the first thing you do when you hit bottom. Most times when you're travelling like this the water's really dirty. It's pitch black. So you just hit bottom, grab that handful of sand, [then after staging] you come straight back up again. You go on to another point that we've been told to have a look at. The research officer on board describes the handful [of sand], what you picked up. It's mainly sand and shell, broken coral and through that they get an idea what the bottom is like even though you can't see it to describe it. It was interesting work because it was something different: not working to pick up a lot of shells for your wages, or crew's wages. You're there doing something scientific [for the industry].

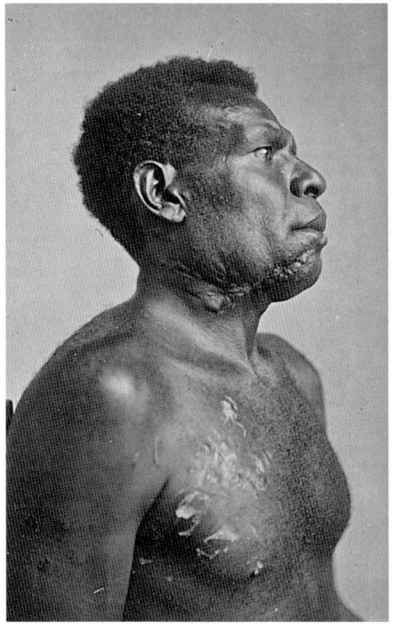 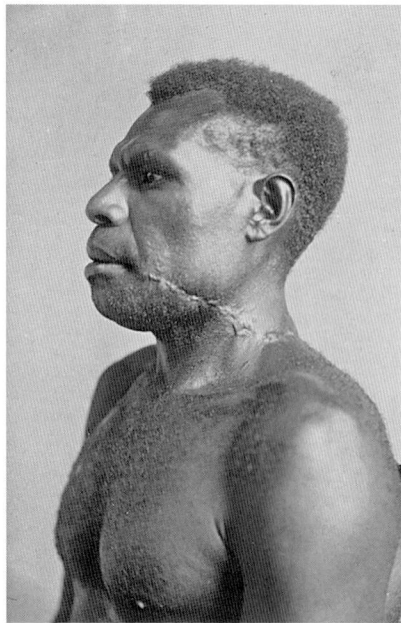 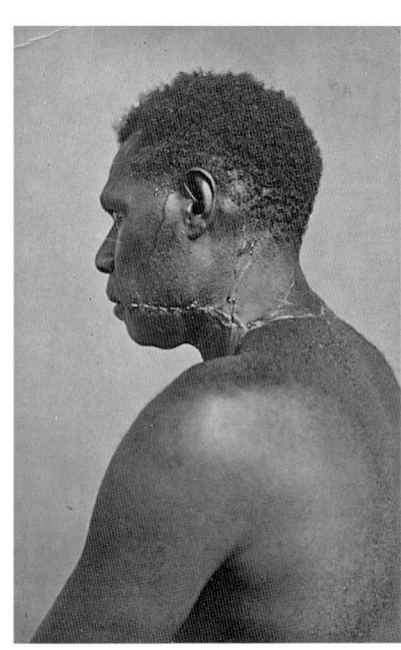

Diver Iona Asai showing wounds from a shark attack. His whole head was in the shark's mouth and he jabbed its eyes with his hands to free himself. Used courtesy of the Asai and Manas families. Photo courtesy Wally Woods Jnr.

While diving in the Timor Sea, Seaman also had close encounters with sharks — which, by and large, were more inquisitive than aggressive. Several instances stood out:

> We had done our one-hour [bottom survey]. I was in the stern helmet and William Busch was in the forward helmet. We had done our staging and had come up to the 5 fathoms staging level and then this school of bronze whalers started to circle around us. We were about 50–70 feet [15–25 metres] apart, visibility was clear [so] we could see each other. He could see all these sharks circling around me and I am saying to the sharks: 'Get over to that other diver! Get over to that other diver!' So they left me and they circled around him … He looked and said: 'Get back to that other diver! Get back to that other diver!' Oh, these bronze whalers! There were about seven or eight in the school. They were about 10–12 feet [3–3.6 metres] long and built for speed! It's scary, but you can't do anything; you just have to hang there and stage to get all of the bubbles out of your bloodstream. The experienced divers used to tell us young divers: 'Whenever you see a shark, you signal for more air and the extra air bubbles keep them away from you.' At this particular time I'm praying that the old fellas were right! It must have been they were right because I am still here!

Learning from experience, Seaman knew when sharks might be present and how to deal with them:

There was another incident. I am on the way down and I am in amongst a school of golden trevally. Once you see a school like that there is a shark around somewhere. So I just inflated myself and I stayed with the school of golden trevally. Then I looked down and here is this huge tiger shark — you could see all of the strips on his back from the dorsal fin down his sides. He was 15 or 16 feet [4.5–5 metres] I reckon — he was huge — so I just stayed there and just hovered there, inflated the suit and just stayed there in among the fishes. When he got out of sight I let the air out, went down the bottom and started picking up pearl shells again and I said to myself, 'Well, you go your way, I will stay here and pick up pearl shells!'

The divers did talk about sharks when they were sighted and also took precautions:

> Once you see sharks like that you let the other boys know that there's a shark in the area. So they don't throw any scraps over the side while you are working because that attracts sharks straight away. We don't do any fishing at all when we are out in a working area; we just open a tin of bully beef, cook bully beef. If you are there for [up] to eight days, well you anchor out at the working ground because land is about 20, 30 miles [32–48 kilometres] away so [you eat] bully beef. And you hold that tin, you don't throw that tin over the side until you get back into port again. Then you take it ashore, put it in a garbage bin on shore. You have got to be careful what you do on board.

Tiger sharks and unidentified child at Thursday Island wharf, undated. Courtesy Wally Woods Jnr.

Once, in the Gulf of Carpentaria near Weipa, Seaman encountered a different kind of potential danger: a saw-shark, which is actually a kind of ray:

> There are a lot of saw-sharks there. We were working about 8 or 9 fathoms, working this sandy area. Both of us saw each other at the same time, this huge saw-shark and me. It was a sandy bottom, no growth, no rocks and he was probably curious. He came straight at me and I am trying to duck in the helmet, [but] there's nowhere to hide! The saw itself I reckon it would have been 6 feet [2 metres] long. That was huge. He pulled up about 6 feet away from me and he turned around and just slowly swam away. I thought to myself, 'Jeepers, with that huge saw he could have ripped me to pieces.' That's how big it was. I was really scared.

Another time, in the Timor Sea, Seaman had a close encounter with a very dangerous fish, a large groper. He was tracking down some pearl shells collected, measured and tagged by the CSIRO to gauge their growth:

> Canberra radioed the skipper on the [*Paxie*] that a pearling vessel had been seen at Flat Top Shoal. [They said] 'Check the shells on your way

Large grouper at Thursday Island wharf, c.1920s, undated. Courtesy Wally Woods Jnr.

back to Darwin from Broome.' Me being the head diver on board, it was up to me to go down and check if the shells were still there. So I went down and I walked all over that shoal and [there had been divers from Broome there] because there were only two shells left there out of the 1000 that we planted. So I picked up the two shells. So with these two shells in the bag, I am walking along and I turn around and I see this huge groper. He is about 10, 15 feet [16–24 metres] away from me and I thought, 'Well, I can't out-swim him', so I unhooked the bag and I went for him with the two shells in the bag and he swam away from me. [I did] this four times and I said, 'Oh no, this groper wants me for dinner!' So the last time I went for him, as soon as he swam away from me I stirred all the mud up. With the half-suit you can inflate yourself and come straight up, so that is what I did. I lost both of us in all of that dirty water I stirred up. [The tender] stopped me at the first staging level and I left the groper down there. He's probably still looking for me!

Seaman says he could sense something was stalking him, although he didn't know what:

> I had that feeling as if something is watching me and I turned around and here is this huge groper and I thought jeepers! He had a huge head on him, holy moley!! He could have swallowed me in one gulp, helmet and all!

Regardless of the sometimes dangerous maritime work Seaman was doing, music was always important to him. It was something to look forward to — especially when the crews came into port. It provided an instant social life for men far away from homes and families:

> They got to know us in Broome and Darwin. [They'd say] 'The TI boys are in, let's make a party.' George Dewis would imitate Satchmo [Louis Armstrong] and I'd sing. Oh, we had a lot of fun!

However, there was no music-making while at sea:

> It's only when you're in port, then you have time. When you're out working on the pearling vessel, especially at peak tide when the currents are not very strong, then you work. Then when you get into port when it's spring tide [and difficult to dive], then you can have time off. Then it's time to play.

The pattern of working hard and then playing music for relaxation and socialising continued when Seaman made his way back to TI for the next stage of his life: marriage, family and some more adventures on land and sea, ranging from deep-water diving for pearl shells in the Darnley Deeps to gold prospecting in the highlands of Papua New Guinea and driving a TI taxi.

CHAPTER 6
Working Adventures on Sea and Land

Diving down to forty fathoms at the Darnley Deeps / Searching for the precious pearl shells / The pearls to keep.

'Forty Fathoms' ⛵

TI taxi driver going round and round / A giant traffic circle in a tiny town / Knows everybody's business / What's going on / TI taxi driver going round and round

'TI Taxi Driver' ⛵

The years Seaman spent away from TI in the 1950s, working in the Northern Territory and Western Australia, developed his work skills and also widened his view of the world — or at least of Australia. Life in the various parts of the tropics was broadly similar, but each place in which he lived and worked had its differences — and also diverse cultures and music. All those influences would eventually come together in his songs and recordings, many decades ahead in the future.

When Seaman returned permanently to the Torres Strait and TI in 1958, he was able to sign on to pearling lugger crews as a much more experienced diver than when he had left. His time on the *Paxie* survey vessel had honed his diving skills, and also his sense of teamwork and responsibility. Maritime work was still viable in the Torres Strait, although it was approaching the end of its post-Second World War boom, with the increasing substitution of plastics for pearl and trochus

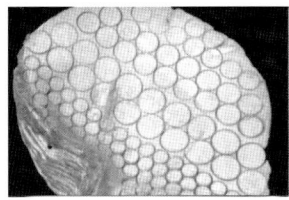

Pearl shell, showing how many buttons could be cut from it.

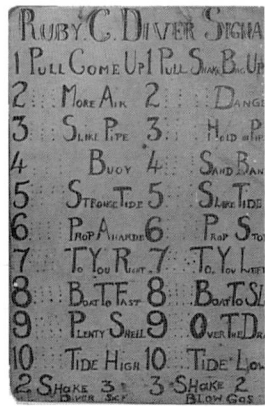

Ruby C's lifeline signals for communication between diver and tender. Courtesy National Museum of Australia.

buttons, and also the non-recovery of shell stock from the over-harvesting of the pre-Second World War era.

Maritime work in Torres Strait, as elsewhere, depended on everyone in the crew working together and paying attention — especially when divers were working underwater. On one occasion, Seaman almost got into serious trouble when his air supply was inadvertently turned off while he was gathering pearl shells:

> We were working the Old Ground, about 15 miles [24 kilometres] west of TI and we had a young engineer. When the stern diver came on deck [after a dive], they took his helmet off and I'm still down below picking up pearl shells. And the engineer, instead of closing the air lock on [the stern diver's helmet], he closed my air lock! And I'm still down below working and I signalled [with] two tugs [on the lifeline] for more air. Two tugs came back and I'm waiting [but] no air comes through. I'm half puffed and I've got all this woollen gear on: shirt, flannel, collar, so I get the helmet off. Just as well it's only 7 fathoms but when you're winded and you've been running backwards and forwards picking up pearl shells, it's hard with all that flannel on trying to swim up to the surface. It was just as well it was flat calm. [But] when I surfaced I was going back down again [immediately].

Luckily the middle tender saw Seaman struggling in the water about 20 metres from the boat:

> He happened to have a single lifeline loose and he signalled towards two other crew members who jumped overboard too to help him. So just as I was going down again, [one] got under me and lifted me up. The other two crew members helped him hold the line-weight too. So, they put that lifeline around me and the crew on deck pulled me aboard then. It was another lucky escape. It was my first step to heaven.

The young engineer got a roasting from the skipper for his almost fatal lack of attention, but Seaman had again escaped a potentially serious accident unscathed.

Back on TI, Seaman first met his wife to be, Clare Dorante from Hammond Island, at a dance. They eventually married in 1958, but later divorced in 1979. They had five children: Connie, Henry Jnr, Simon, Bill and Elvianna. Tragically, Simon was killed in a motorcycle accident when he was just 16. Having a family changed Seaman's working life, especially when it came to considering the dangers of deep-water diving in a place renowned for many pearl shells, but also notorious for many potential hazards: the Darnley Deeps in Eastern Torres Strait. Seaman recalls how he decided to work there, despite his misgivings:

> My two brothers-in-law, Vincent Dorante and [the late] James Dorante, were skippering two Burns Philp pearling luggers. Vincent skippered

the *Floria* and James skippered the *Galton*, and there was the *Grafton* vacant. So [me having been with] Commonwealth Fisheries, they both approached me and asked if I wanted to skipper the *Grafton*, so it'd be like the family working for the one company then. So I said, 'Yeah, all right. I'll come along.' So we went to see Joe Maher, the manager. 'Oh yes,' he said. 'I know your reputation. You worked for Commonwealth Fisheries there for a couple of years.' He said, 'You ever worked the Darnley Deeps?' I said, 'No, my motto is why go to the Darnley Deeps when there's a lot of pearl shells in the shallow areas and it's safer to work the shallow area. Darnley Deeps is a very dangerous place.'

Over the decades of the pearling industry, many divers had lost their lives there —through air hoses and lifelines getting snagged on coral ledges, or early engines being too under-powered to fight the strong currents, or divers getting the bends from deep dives without proper staging.

At the time, Seaman had young divers on the crew of the *Grafton*: Norman and Stephen Daniel, Elda Harry, Murray George and Michael David. They had been working at less than 10 fathoms' depth, and consequently no staging was required. They were keen to work the Darnley Deeps, even though Seaman had said to them: 'Listen fellows, only the game divers and the crazy divers go to the Darnley Deeps. Let's work in the shallow area where it's safe.' However, the reality was that so many

Top: Pearl shells at Darnley Island, c.1948. Courtesy State Library of Queensland, image no. 65437.

Left: Thursday Island pearl shell sorter, c.1930. Frank Hurley, National Library of Australia, image no. 23221101.

pearling vessels were working the shallow areas of the Torres Strait that stocks were being depleted. But the Darnley Deeps still had rich pearl shell beds.

Seaman vividly remembers his first dive in the Darnley Deeps:

> Me being the skipper and the most experienced diver, I said [to the crew], 'I'll go and test this bottom out first.' We had no depth sounder. We were just using the old lead line with bottom markings depicting the fathoms, different-colour[ed] cloths at each different level to give you the depth … I get one of the deckies to throw the lead line down. So he took the measure and yells, 'Twenty-three fathoms, skipper.' [I said], 'Throw the buoy marker.' [Then I said] to the tiller man, 'Change course, run west 20 minutes [then] stop [and throw the] lead line.' [The deckie yells], 'Twenty-four fathoms, skipper.' [We set] another buoy [and I said], 'All right, run back up to that first buoy. I'll take the first dive.'

When divers are working underwater, the stern tender is in control of the boat. The stern tender knew the staging tables, so Seaman said to him: 'Just stick your eye on that clock.' While working for Commonwealth Fisheries, the average time spent on the bottom was one hour, but at the greater depths of the Darnley Deeps, the bottom time was reduced to 15 minutes. Seaman recalls:

> I [went] down and I was astounded. I'd never seen a shell-bearing area like this. It looked like [the tight, overlapping] squares on this [interview room's] floor. That's how the shells were and I knew I had only 15 minutes. I just took two seconds to admire that [view] and just shake my head, and started kneeling down picking up shells. Within those 15 minutes, I sent three full bags up with 75 shells in each bag and I was happy inside. So I signalled to come up. After that first dive, I instructed each diver to be careful, look after yourself. I spoke loud so that the divers could hear me. They're all standing in front of me, so nothing could be mistaken. None of my divers got sick. They were good young divers, keen workers.

However, even with precautions, Seaman did get the bends in 1963. He admits it was 'due to my own stupidity':

> I went down to 30 fathoms and the boat had drifted off the shell-bearing area, just slightly but enough to put me away from the pearl shells. So, I wanted to beat the tide, but you can't beat nature. So, without staging, from that 30 fathoms, I came straight up to the top. Silly thing to do; my own fault. [I was an] experienced diver and I just had one — almost fatal — mistake.

When he got on deck the stern tender looked at him and said, 'You feeling alright?' Seaman said, 'Yes, take this suit off and I'll put it on that young diver.' He sat down and the next thing he knew:

> All of a sudden everything went blurry and [there was] a sharp stab of pain across my back and I collapsed on the deck. So, what [the stern tender] did, he got the crew to carry me over towards the ladder, take the half-suit off the young diver again and put it on me. And I have to go back to the same depth at 30 fathoms where I got sick. Two of my crew jumped over the side to hold me up against the ladder while they put the lead weight and the helmet on. When the air came through, they tapped the helmet. Then they jumped to one side and I fell back into the water. As soon as I got under the surface, everything came back into focus again. No more pain, but I had to go back down to 30 fathoms again and stage for four hours, to make sure there were no bubbles in my bloodstream.

Seaman learned that in deep water diving 'there are no shortcuts'. The incident was a wake-up call for him, and it changed both his working and family life:

> We went back into Darnley Harbour that evening. I wasn't allowed ashore in case I had a relapse and everyone was to stay on deck. So I stayed on board for two days. We didn't go out to work — naturally you couldn't. My crew kept a close watch on me and so when they were satisfied I was all right I could go [ashore]. My wife, Clare, she was ashore. Connie, my eldest daughter, was three years old then and my son, Simon, had just started to walk. So I said, 'This is my last year of diving. I may not get a second chance if I go back down.' And I kept my promise: I never put the helmet back on again after I finished up that year. I was very lucky.

Seaman's maritime adventures in the Torres Strait were later recollected in songs such as 'Forty Fathoms', ⛴ 'Watching the Weather' ⛴ and 'The *Floria* Sails Again' — all musical depictions of his life at sea at a time when the pearl and trochus shell industries were still economically viable in the region.

Leaving a diver's life behind for one working on land did not mean an end to his adventures, however. For men of Seaman's generation in the Torres Strait, there were limited job opportunities — due to the region's isolation, the lack of access to formal education and training, and racial aspects of Queensland's laws. Consequently, many of them turned their hands to whatever jobs were available. Seaman was no exception, and he found some maritime work as a boat skipper but also took up jobs in mineral exploration and even drove a TI taxi. Each job involved its own unique adventures.

Seaman had first met mineral exploration expert Jim Quinn while working on the lugger *Fram*:

> We got caught in a cyclone at the Tiwi Islands. We had to go running to shelter from the working area to get away from these very strong winds. And through that cyclone I met Jim Quinn. He was a field supervisor for Consolidated Mining Industries, this exploration company owned by Clive Foyster, millionaire in Brisbane. He asked me if I'd like to sign up as a prospector and I said, 'Oh well, yeah.' So, I signed up as a prospector then. At the start, they had this exploration barge, the *Seafoy 2*, based in Cairns. It was newly built with two industrial chemists on board.

Seaman started off as a deckie, but later became caretaker for a company speedboat based in the Torres Strait:

> [Consolidated Mining Industries] had an exploration lease on Horn Island [for] the old gold mine. I was based on Horn Island, where I lived, to help the young geologist. So, I'd organise a boat for him to come and go to Horn Island [from TI] and also organise a truck. So money was

Seaman Dan (centre with hat), gold prospecting in the Kainantu area of the Eastern Highlands, Papua New Guinea, 1971. Courtesy Henry Dan Personal Collection.

> sent up … to pay for expenses, accommodation for the geologists plus pocket money for the crew.

The chance for a more exciting adventure with the company came about when Jim Quinn was taking a mineral exploration team up to the Eastern Highlands of Papua New Guinea, and Seaman got the chance to join the expedition as a prospector:

> Jim Quinn and I flew from Cairns to Port Moresby and caught a connecting flight from there [to Goroka]. We were to be based [at Kainantu] to have a look at a gold mine owned by Ken Rehder, who used to be one of the divers onboard the Commonwealth Fisheries survey vessel the *Paxie* … Alan Knight was there to meet us [and] he drove us back to Kainantu, 50 miles [90 kilometres] away.

When the prospectors first visited the local area, the people were very friendly. They were shown around the villages where the people were putting new roofs of thatched plaited palm leaves on their huts. However, there was soon a serious problem with getting to Ken's isolated gold mine:

> The reason [was] that the airfield in Kainantu was overrun by the locals. There were too many crossing the airfield without any authority at all and it was dangerous to land. So [the airport people] put a fence around the airfield for the people's own protection but they sort of read that as an insult, not as a protection. They said, 'All right, you won't let us walk across the airfield. We won't let you drive across the bridge.'

Clearly the locals and the airport officials were having a serious disagreement, and travelling cross-country in the rugged terrain was very difficult for the prospectors as there were only basic tracks and — of more concern — makeshift bridges. So when the prospectors wanted to try to get to Ken's gold mine amidst the social turmoil, they took along two boys from the village where they were staying as interpreters and also the Acting Administrator, all to no avail:

> There were two logs at a bridge crossing. Just two ordinary trees cut down and you had to sort of balance yourself across this 100 foot-drop [30 metres] ravine and it's scary! Alan Knight and I went there first with the other prospector and we just made it across. And coming back to where our vehicle was parked [high above by the bridge], you had to climb up 700 or 800 feet [210–240 metres]. And Alan said, 'I think I'd rather walk down the riverbed road' — even though we have to climb up and down boulders — rather than taking a risk crossing that two-log bridge again, [with] that 100-foot fall into the gap. So we walked down the riverbed then, even though we had to climb the boulders. It was much safer than crossing that two-log bridge again. We made it, anyway — got back safely.

It became clear that the standoff would not be resolved quickly or amicably, as Seaman explains:

> So, we couldn't do anything. It's their country, their land. So, we didn't have a look at the gold mine. But Ken had a huge boulder in his backyard studded with gold from his mine [and] he offered [us] to take whatever chips of gold back to Australia, which we did.

Seaman sums up the adventure:

> You know, they think differently up there [in PNG] … so, we just came back to Australia, but I didn't mind because I didn't want to argue with them. It's their land. They know what they want.

A more rewarding result from Seaman's time in PNG was the opportunity to hear local string-band music. Decades later, he recorded a PNG song, 'Veiga, Veiga', about the sea breezes that blow across the Papuan Gulf, in string-band style. He also later recorded a string-band version of one of his favourite Nat King Cole songs, 'Makin' Whoopee'. ⛵

Another working adventure came about when Seaman took up taxi driving on TI. Although the island is only tiny — roughly 3.5 square kilometres — with 4.7 kilometres of roads, it has quite a few taxis to service its population of approximately 2600 people. It might seem on the surface to be a fairly unadventurous kind of job, but that wasn't how it turned out — especially when Seaman not only had to row to work from nearby Hammond Island, but sometimes also had to swim ashore when he reached TI. He recalls:

> Ah, it was tiring work. I didn't have a dinghy [with a motor] to come back [and forth from Hammond Island where my family was living]. The mother- and father-in-law lent me their dinghy to row to the back of Thursday Island and I'd walk to the taxi rank on the waterfront, which was owned by Sidney Laifoo. He owned two taxis and I used to drive one of them. I used to work all day until I did the night shift too. Then after the picture run [after the cinema closed], Sidney would drive me at night around to the back of TI to the landing where I had [anchored] the dinghy.

What made getting home more difficult was that sometimes:

> When I'd come over in the morning to pick the taxi up, it's low tide and I'd have to anchor the dinghy way out. So when I go back after the picture run around 11.30 p.m., Sidney would put the car lights on to show me where the dinghy is and watch me swim after the dinghy. Yes, swim after the dinghy! As soon as I was on board, I'd wave to him that I'm okay and he'd switch the light off and go back into town and I'd row all the way back to Hammond [Island].

Seaman Dan and Jerry Lewin performing at the Victoria Memorial Hall, Thursday Island, c.1970s.

Part of the challenge was that the tides running between TI and Hammond Island were very strong. Luckily, as an experienced sailor, Seaman had learned how to use tides:

> You've got to work the tides. I'd row up against the tide, all in the shelter of TI and when I'm far up enough then I'd get the current and the wind would take me over … to Hammond Island beach in front of the mission. I'd get home about one o'clock in the morning and make sure everything's right for the next morning's row over to TI. My wife would still be awake and the stove still hot, water hot for my tea, have something to eat then dive into a shower then into bed. Five o'clock the next morning, I'm awake again, same thing again, make sure the dinghy's okay. She'd give me breakfast and make a sandwich for me, then away I'd go again.

As if such a daily grind were not hard enough, sometimes an element of real adventure was added to the working day. Seaman remembers encounters with something that most taxi drivers don't have to face during their shifts — saltwater crocodiles:

> In those days the council workers that do the garbage run, they'd tip the wet garbage at the landing on the beach there where I anchored my dinghy. So this particular night, I knocked off early and Sidney Laifoo dropped me round the back and there was this ex-croc shooter from Mornington Island, Gerry Blitner, and he had a rifle with a telescopic sight. He wanted to shoot this croc there, and I didn't know this was happening at the time and when I saw this croc, oh he was a huge croc! He's on this pile of garbage and he's gorging himself. So Gerry Blitner went right up close, it was about 10 metres. I don't know how he missed that croc but the shot went over the croc's head. It left everything and slipped into the water. It was only knee-deep water. As soon as he got there, there wasn't much movement. He just crawled on the bottom straight out to sea, towards my dinghy, the dinghy I was using. So after that night, I said to the boss, 'Well, I'm knocking off at five o'clock every afternoon. No more picture runs!'

Some of Seaman's experiences as a taxi driver were later recounted in 'TI Taxi Driver', 🔊 a song that is not only an homage to some TI taxi drivers but also some of the passengers encountered while, according to the song's lyrics, he was 'going round and round' on a 'giant traffic circle in a tiny town'. Interestingly, there was an unwritten 'code of silence': taxi drivers often observed a lot going on in people's private lives, but said nothing about it.

Seaman and his family moved to Cairns for various periods of time, where he worked on construction sites as a labourer, but the majority of the time they were in Torres Strait. He did get the chance to do some maritime work — not as a diver, but most often as a skipper. Along with collecting 'chicken-shell' (small pearl shells) for a Torres Strait pearl-farming operation, one time he was employed to transport a fishing boat from TI to Tweed Heads in New South Wales. He engaged two of his brothers-in-law, Bert and Owen Dorante, as crew. He remembers that what should have been an uneventful voyage ended up as another hazardous adventure:

> We steamed from TI to Cairns, fuelled up from there. Samuel and Allens, a big company, were the agents for this company that bought this vessel. I had had some trouble with the motor in Cairns. It kept on overheating. So the company sent a mechanic to fix the motor up … Get [south] to Gladstone, same thing again. Went and told the agent [there] and they got another mechanic down. Then we were steaming to Brisbane, outside of Double Island Point, [a] little bit north of Noosa

[on the Sunshine Coast], and the motor started heating up again. And finally it stopped.

The crew quickly realised that they were a long way from shore and were drifting in big seas in an area known for strong currents. They had few options:

> Here we are in mid-ocean, it was getting late — say about five o'clock [in the afternoon] — and the wind started to come up. So I said to the two brothers-in-law, 'We'll let her go close in to shore, as close as we can safely, in a safe position. No good sending one man to go for help [in the dinghy] and leaving two on board.' We had the radio on board but that wouldn't work. That broke down also. So I said, 'Anchor the boat here. Let a lot of anchor chain out and we'll go ashore.'

So the crew left the stricken boat behind and set out to row ashore in the dinghy:

> We took what was [on the boat that we might need] … There was about a third full of kerosene [left] in this 4-gallon kerosene can. I said, 'It's starting to get dark, we'll get some dry wood and can make a fire there until morning and we can walk along the beach. Somebody must stay along the beach here; [we can] get help.'

Such a predictable plan may have been their intention, but things worked out decidedly differently:

> We got closer to the beach and we all had our life jackets on. The wind started to come up and the sea was breaking on the beach with this big surf. As we got closer and I'm rowing, I [remembered] that what we do in the trochus vessels, when you're getting closer to a breaker, you turn your dinghy around and you put your bow into the breaker as you're rowing to the beach stern first. [To row better] as we got closer, I took my life jacket off, put it down beside me. And [then] a big breaker hit us and lifted the dinghy up and tipped the three of us out!

Amidst the chaos, luckily the kerosene tin that had been in the dinghy came to the rescue:

> It's pitch dark and the three of us came up to the surface close to each other. So I had no life jacket, the two other crew they had their life jackets on and the drum floated right in front of me and Bert he said, 'Brother-in-law grab that drum!' I dived on to the drum, grabbed it and put my hand through the handle and I hung on to it. That's what saved me from going under. So we floated right up to the beach.

When they washed ashore on the beach, they spotted a campsite not far from where they had landed:

We walked up to this camp then, explained to the people there what happened. They said, 'Oh, we'll take you up to the Double Island Point lighthouse.' They gave us a nip of Bundy [Bundaberg] rum, a pannikin full of Bundy rum to keep warm. That was our warmer upperer! Then [they] drove us up to the lighthouse and we met the lighthouse keeper. Oh, he looked after us. He said, 'All right we'll take you in. I'll report this.' And he said, 'Where's your boat?' I said, 'We had to leave it outside. It's in 6 fathoms of water, a lot of chain out.' So he drove us to Noosa, then contacted these people at Tweed Heads that I was taking the boat down for.

The boat itself was eventually wrecked: 'the surf was so big outside, [the boat] dragged anchor and it ended up on the beach too. It turned out it was insured and the owner happy the crew was safe.' In the end, Seaman and his brothers-in-law's supposedly routine voyage ended up being an adventure that could have ended badly but luckily ended well, complete with a flight home to Torres Strait.

While Seaman was working various jobs on or out from TI from the 1960s through to the end of the 1990s, he kept performing the popular music of the day on a casual basis. Sometimes it was at house parties or barbecues, and sometimes it was in the pubs on TI — the Grand, the Royal, the Federal and the Torres. TI was unique for a small, very isolated community in that the numerous hotels and pubs established in the boom times of the maritime industries kept operating as the industries waxed and waned, and TI gradually became a 'government' town and service centre. The hotels and pubs, along with the Victoria Memorial Institute, provided venues in which musicians and singers could perform — often on an unplanned basis, with the bands incorporating whoever was on the island at the time. Whereas music and dance in the outer island communities continued to emphasise traditional/ancestral styles, while at times incorporating aspects of contemporary styles, on TI the music and dance were more mainstream, modern/contemporary, and reflective of what was popular across Australia at the time.

There was ongoing entertainment on TI, and music was a strong thread binding together the community's social life as it rebuilt after the disruptions and dislocations of the Second World War and the decline of the maritime industries. The Mills Sisters, in particular, incorporated songs from many styles into their performances, and thus had a faithful following. A popular song such as 'Sad Movies (Make Me Cry)' or 'Wassa Matta You Last Night' might be followed by a traditional maritime song or a lullaby in Kala Lagaw Ya, Meriam Mir or Torres Strait Creole. Even the occasional religious *kores* (chorus) might be sung. Seaman says his favourite styles were 'blues and slow-jazz crooning'. He later wrote 'Friday Night Blues' as a tribute to the hotels, pubs and publicans on TI who gave local musicians and singers the opportunity to perform and develop their skills, as well as making a contribution

Hula dance group The Hawaiian War Chant, Victoria Memorial Hall, Thursday Island, c.1955. Top row [l–r]: Lily Shibasaki (née Bowie), Ellie Gaffney (née Loban), Ceah Seden (née Takai), Enid Matters (née Abednego), Nonya Shinjo (née Shibasaki). Bottom row [l–r]: Gertie Saveka-Levi (née Abednego), Margie Dewis (née Berola), Marian Barba, Betty Foster (née Ahboo), Carmen Nunan (née Drummond).

The Mills Sisters, c. early 1980s, Federal Hotel, Thursday Island, [l–r]: the late Rita Fell-Tyrell, Ina Titasey, Cessa Nakata.

to TI's social and cultural life as community musicians. Such homegrown entertainment was very important before the widespread advent of television, then videos and more recently computers, DVDs and portable entertainment devices.

When Seaman retired on TI from his working life in the late 1990s, little did he realise that his passion for music would unexpectedly get a chance to develop in quite unusual but very fortuitous circumstances. Not many elderly Indigenous singer-songwriters from remote north Queensland have had their musical careers flourish at the age of 70, and none other has won or been nominated for multiple ARIA Awards, a Red Ochre Award, a Jimmy Little Lifetime Achievement Award and a National Folk Recording Award, as well as performing across Australia and overseas. But that is what happened for Seaman as his life, work and adventures up to his retirement became the subject of songs and brought, if not fortune, at least a little bit of fame to a TI lad.

Part II of this book chronicles Seaman Dan's late-blooming professional career in music, and provides detailed background on the writing and recording of more than 60 songs over seven albums. His career in music provides a wonderful example of how being true to one's culture and taking life 'steady, steady' can sometimes reap unexpected rewards.

Thursday Island musicians, c.2002, [l–r] the late Raymond Wymarra, Seaman Dan, the late Hismile (Izzie) Shibasaki and Jerry Lewin.

PART II

THE MUSIC AND RECORDINGS OF HENRY 'SEAMAN' DAN

CHAPTER 7

The Opportunity of a Lifetime

In Torres Strait, we've got ailan *[island] blues,* ailan *country,* ailan *hula,* ailan *jazz,* ailan *folk. It's all just good music to us — done* ailan *style.*

– Seaman Dan

In the popular music press, stories abound about elderly musicians being 'discovered' by intrepid music researchers or producers, who then guide their discovery's career, record their music and do the festival and talk show circuit. Such notions make for a good story, but the reality is often much more matter-of-fact and less dramatic. That was certainly so in the case of Seaman Dan meeting Karl Neuenfeldt who, along with Nigel Pegrum, would work closely with Seaman for over a decade, recording, writing and performing music.

Seaman has a clear memory of that initial encounter:

> I'll never forget that day, 15 January 1999. On 14 January this [local] musician, the late Ray Wymarra, phoned me. I live on Horn Island, where the [Torres Strait's] main airport is. He phoned from Thursday Island to tell me that there is [a music researcher] from Central Queensland University and Ray said, 'He's interviewing the Indigenous artists here on TI at our local radio station, 4MW [Meriba Wakai]. I mentioned your name because you wrote 'TI Blues'. He wants to meet you and interview you.' So I said to Ray, 'Well, I can't come over today. I'm a bit tied up [doing my laundry]. I'll come over tomorrow.' So I went over Friday — on 15 January 1999 — and I met Dr Karl [Karl Neuenfeldt].

He met me at the wharf, took me up to the radio station and interviewed me. Then he asked me to sing a few songs. I said, 'Well, sorry I didn't bring my guitar. It's on Horn Island.' He said, 'That's alright, you can use mine.' So he tuned it up and I sang [a few songs]. By then I'd written more songs than 'TI Blues'. 🎵 So I sang ['TI Blues'], 'Sunset Blues', 'Little Pony' 🎵 and 'Old TI' 🎵 … He looked at his watch and said, 'Goodness Seaman, I'm sorry, it's 12.30 already. You must be hungry and thirsty. Would you like to come up to the Grand Hotel please and have some lunch?' I said, 'Yes please.' While we were eating, he said, 'You know, you have a nice voice. Would you like to make a recording?' I put my knife and fork down, took my hankie out, wiped my brow. I said, 'I beg your pardon?' he said, 'You know, make a recording, make a CD?' And I thought to myself, 'This is the opportunity I've been waiting for, for a long time.' I grabbed it with both hands, and I said, 'Yes, please.'

As this true story reveals, if Seaman had stayed home on Friday, 15 January 1999 to do more of his laundry or mow his lawn, the albums he recorded, the many concerts he performed and the prestigious music industry awards he won might never have happened. But it highlights the role of luck — or maybe more accurately serendipity — in many such musical 'discovery' stories. In reality though, luck can only present an opportunity. A singer still needs a good voice, a recognisable style, good songs and the natural ability to entertain people. Seaman Dan had all those skills ready to go at the age of 70 — especially after living the adventurous life recounted in Part I of this book — and also after decades of taking things 'steady, steady'.

CHAPTER 8
Follow the Sun

Seaman's first chance to record in a professional studio was at the now defunct Select Sound, located at 14 Water Street in Cairns. The album was called *Follow the Sun*. Nigel Pegrum was the audio engineer and he also co-produced, along with Nelson Conboy and Karl Neuenfeldt. The album was originally released in 1999, and leased to Hot Records.

The rhythm section for the original sessions was Nelson Conboy (dobro, guitar and ukulele), Denis Crowdy (guitar and ukulele), Klare Ku-Olga (bass) and Giuseppe Vizzone (drums). The musicians who added their contributions as overdubs were Yunup Benjamin (*warup* drum), Jesse Deane-Freeman (piano), Steve Gilbert (harmonica), Mat Harrison (mandolin and violin), Mark Mannock (piano), Wayne McIntosh (guitar), Nigel Pegrum (percussion), Kirk Steel (accordion), Stephen Whittington (tuba) and Margaret Willis (string arrangements, violin and viola). The professional backing singers were Jenni Clarke and Chris Lloyds, and there was also an informal male choir that included the late Yunup Benjamin, Seaman Dan, Vic McGrath, Karl Neuenfeldt, Wayne Seekee and the late Ray Wymarra.

Follow the Sun was re-released in 2011 with an additional song, Ted Egan's 'Sayonara Nakamura'. ⛵ The session musicians for that song were Will Kepa (guitar, ukulele and percussion), Giles Smith (acoustic bass), Zani (sanshin) and backing singers Dimple and Gabriel Bani, Vic McGrath and Karl Neuenfeldt.

Because *Follow the Sun* was the first time Seaman had recorded in a professional studio, and also the first time the producers had collaborated, it took some time to establish an overall style. Early on, it was decided the unique quality of Seaman's voice, and the maritime and Torres Strait Islander themes in the songs, were to be the major focus, with the recording style tending towards a folk music approach — although also including elements of blues, hula and jazz. It also took some time to establish the producers' division of labour. Generally, Nelson Conboy worked with the musicians on the songs' arrangements, Karl Neuenfeldt worked with Seaman on the songs themselves and Nigel Pegrum worked on the overall 'sound'. Once the sessions started, they and the session musicians all contributed to arrangements.

Left: Seaman Dan recording song demos at the Torres Strait Islander Media Association's Radio 4MW (Meriba Wakai) on TI on 15 January 1999.

Right: Seaman Dan during Cairns recording sessions for *Follow the Sun* album, 1999.

Based on decades of experience as an audio engineer and producer, and also a long performance career as drummer with well-known British folk-rock band Steeleye Span, Nigel Pegrum had clear ideas about both how to record Seaman as a vocalist and how to fashion a 'Seaman Dan sound':

> As soon as I heard Seaman's voice, I recognised the rich, velvety quality he possessed. But also that he sings quite quietly and in a very low register — he actually tunes his own guitar five half tones lower than normal guitar tuning. Consequently, all these factors led me to construct accompaniments that sonically complemented these qualities — such as lightly strummed or finger picked stringed instruments like ukulele, mandolin and guitar, or sometimes accordion or light piano, and on the more traditional arrangements, Torres Strait Islander percussion, all essentially sounds that would leave tonal space for Seaman's voice to be separated from the backing. In later recordings, I also created accompaniments in other genres — for instance, 1940s-style big band, or small string orchestra arrangements. However, I still always made sure never to swamp the voice, again by the subtle use of instrumentation. I also mixed the voice a little more prominently than is usually the case with pop and rock recordings.

The songs on the initial release of *Follow the Sun* were either originals by Seaman or adaptations of traditional Torres Strait Islander songs. They also focused on either what was unique in Seaman's life and work experiences, or what was unique about TI, the Torres Strait region and Torres Strait Islander culture. On his first album, Seaman was able not only to recount some personal adventures but also to incorporate the cultural, historical and musical influences of his remote home area in Australia. *Follow the Sun*'s songs were composed over several years — most after Seaman retired from an active working life. Each has its own history or inspiration, and provides insights into the processes of songwriting, arranging and producing.

'Follow the Sun'

The original idea for the title song, 'Follow the Sun', was inspired by Seaman's good friend, the late George Dewis. He and Seaman had worked together on pearling luggers and also shared a love of music. George was a talented singer and mimic, in particular doing a spot-on imitation of Louis 'Satchmo' Armstrong's gravelly singing voice. As Seaman recalls:

> I invited George for lunch one Sunday and after lunch he said, 'Oh well, we can just relax now.' So I got the guitar out and he was resting on the bed there on the porch and I said [to him], '[I'm] thinking about a new song that I would like to write but I just don't know how to start it off.' And the sun kept going down and he kept on shifting the bed away to get out of the sun. And I thought to myself, 'Well, why not!' So I started singing [and] he said, 'What are you doing?' And I said, 'Well, this is my new song and you just inspired me into naming [it] "Follow the Sun".'

The lyrics to 'Follow the Sun' evolved from that original inspiration into a love song of sorts — an imagined romance where a long separation eventually had a happy ending:

> 'Follow the Sun'
>
> *You were out there waiting for the sunrise / In your favourite chair waiting for the dawn / Right from the start you have always had this feeling / To follow your heart / To follow the sun / You went away leaving me with sorrow / Waiting each day for you to return / How can you go? / Don't you know how much I need you? / I'll wait for you / While you follow the sun / Days turn to years of longing and yearning / Too many tears now have been shed / Then you came back / You're my life / You're my sunshine / Together we will follow the sun.* (Seaman Dan)

Taken together, the song and the PNG string-band arrangement exemplify the laidback yet rhythmic and melodic style Seaman was to perfect in his music.

'Welcome to the Torres Strait'

'Welcome to the Torres Strait' also had an interesting evolution from idea to finished song. Seaman refers to it as a 'special song to welcome visitors to the Torres Strait'. Initially, the late Ephraim Bani — a significant Torres Strait Islander cultural custodian and linguist — approached Seaman:

> Monday afternoon I met him in front of this establishment and he said, 'Oh brother, there are some Cook Islanders coming over [to Torres Strait] and if you wouldn't mind I would like you to sing them a welcome song' … At that particular time all I had was 'TI Blues', and I thought, 'These people are from the Cook Islands and I could not sing "TI Blues" to

On tour in Adelaide, 2002 [l–r] Karl Neuenfeldt, Jason Troutman, Seaman Dan and Steve Gilbert.

islanders like myself. So it will have to be a special welcome song.' So I went home that night [to start writing]. Two days later, I had 'Welcome to the Torres Straits'.

Ephraim Bani suggested Seaman sing part of the song in a traditional Torres Strait Islander language. Because Seaman's ancestors were connected to the Eastern Islands of Torres Strait, he approached Bua Mabo from Mer (Murray Island) to translate part of the song into Meriam Mir, the Eastern Islands' language. Seaman recalls:

> [Bua] wrote the words out for me in language, made sure I could sing it properly in language as well as English [and then] I was in a good position to welcome the Cook Island dancers to the Torres Strait.

Seaman often sings 'Welcome to the Torres Strait' as his first song when performing:

'Welcome to the Torres Strait'

We say we say welcome /We say welcome to the Torres Strait / We're glad to have you / We extend our hospitality in good faith / You can look at the stars / Gaze at the moon / Admire our sea so blue / See the palm trees a'swaying and dance to a hula tune / So won't you come and join us? / For a happy memory / We say we say welcome / We say welcome to the Torres Strait / Ki detkarita ki detkarita maiem / Ki detkarita maiem Torres Kes em / Sere serer ki mari narpeidarda / Keriba asesered marim peike. (Seaman Dan and Bua Mabo)

In 2009, Seaman Dan was invited to perform for then Prime Minister Kevin Rudd and other delegates at the 40th Pacific Islands Forum Leaders' meeting in Cairns. To make the song more appropriate for the event, the lyrics were altered slightly to 'We say welcome to Australia'. The event was also noteworthy because Seaman got to meet delegates from his maternal grandfather Sam Savage's tiny home island of Niue in Polynesia. The event was one of many unique opportunities that arose for Seaman as a performer.

'Sunset Blues'

Seaman had loved the blues and jazz ever since hearing the African-American soldiers perform them in Cairns during the Second World War (see also Chapter 3). The song 'Sunset Blues' came about when he was sitting on a beach on the west coast of Muralag (Prince of Wales Island):

> Well, I had been bitten by the blues bug and I had just been watching that sun go down and you get that sort of sinking feeling, that blues feeling, you know. So that inspired me to write 'Sunset Blues'.

> **'Sunset Blues'**
>
> *There comes a time once in your life / When you feel that you can't lose / But there's one thing sure and certain / You're gonna get those sunset blues / The sun comes up in the morning / It's long gone when it sets / You think you're feeling great / It's that feeling that you get / There's no substitution / Whichever way you choose / There's one thing sure and certain / You're gonna get those sunset blues / Blues in the day / Blues in the night / Blues in the evening time / No place to go / No friendly hello / Still you're doing fine / When you're down and sad and blue / And she won't come to you / There's one thing sure and certain / You're gonna get those sunset blues.*
> (Seaman Dan)

The lyrics reflect Seaman's view that life has good times and bad times, so you should appreciate the good times because you know bad times might be coming too. Therefore, he says, 'what you have at hand, you should make the most of it'.

'TI Blues'

'TI Blues' became Seaman's first popular song, and has been called 'a signature tune for the Torres Strait' (Pryor 2001).

> **'TI Blues'**
>
> *I've been to Queensland / I've been to New South Wales / I've been to Queensland / I've been to New South Wales / Makes no difference where I go / I get those old TI blues / I've been to Adelaide / I've been to Darwin too / Canberra doesn't thrill me / Even Perth gives me the blues / I'm going*

back to TI / Back to the place where I belong / Ain't no dragon's gonna get me / As long as I have you / Don't need no fancy clothes wherever you may go / Folks will always greet you with a smile and say hello / Blues stay away from me / Don't know why you never let me be. (Seaman Dan)

Informed by the style of early blues recording pioneers such as Bessie Smith, 'TI Blues' evolved over many years. Musically, it dates back to his time in Cairns in the early 1940s when he first heard African-American soldiers sing the blues at house parties. Later, he emulated their style:

> We used to have parties in the backyard at Mum Dan's place in Morehead Street in Cairns, and it actually started off as Morehead Street Blues. [When] we shifted back to TI … we had a barbecue one night and a couple of my nephews, Noel Hodges and Jack Ware, [were there]. So I said, 'Fellas, how about our next barbecue I am going to write a song, we'll call it "TI Blues"?' So that's how 'TI Blues' started — at a barbecue.

'TI Blues' takes an African-American style and localises it lyrically by using Australian place names. Central to the song is the notion of returning home to TI from wherever people had to move to for personal or professional reasons. Perhaps that is one reason it became popular when TI entertainers The Mills Sisters (Cessa Nakata, Ina Titasey and Rita Fell-Tyrell) recorded it on their album, *Frangipani Land*, in 1992. It was the first recording of Seaman's songs, and its popularity encouraged him to keep writing.

When Seaman performed at the 40th Pacific Islands Forum Leaders' meeting in Cairns in 2009, a copy of the song's lyrics had to be sent to the Department of

Maritime workers coming ashore from luggers at Thursday Island, c.1920s–1930s. Courtesy Wally Woods Jnr.

the Prime Minister and Cabinet for clearance, possibly to check that they did not say anything disparaging or critical, as blues songs sometimes do. However, being critical or disparaging would be inconsistent with Seaman's apolitical approach to life and songwriting. As he has often said, 'I leave politics to the politicians.'

'Danville' 🎵

The nostalgic song 'Danville' was based on holidays Seaman took with friends at a beach camp near Bampfield Head on the western coast of Prince of Wales Island.

> 'Danville'
>
> *Bright moon shines over Danville / That's where I want to be / With Dubbo and Jamie / Bundy and D-4 / Roger and Helen too / Fine misty rain in the evening / Relax in that cool summer breeze / I see Dragan and Mina / Jessie and Crystal / Danny Kim and Jeff / All around the big log fire / Watching surf break on the beach / There's Peter and Tracy having 'debi ari' / And trying to catch reds [red emperor fish] that are out of reach / So we say farewell to Danville / As our boat pulls away from the shore / We gaze at the palm trees / Four special palm trees / Where Bundy and D-4 lie / Southern breeze clear sky / See the great mackerel leap / So there's every reason why I'll be going back to Danville / That's a promise I'll keep / Farewell.* (Seaman Dan)

The friends mentioned in the song are Helen and Roger Bolton; the late Eddie Dubbins (Dubbo); Tracy and Peter McGinlay; Dragan, Mina, Jessie and Crystal Rostoka; Danny Taafe; and Kim and Jeff (whose last names are not known). Seaman recounts a bit of Danville's background:

> It became our Easter camp, [which] used to be at Little Buttertin opposite Friday Island [near TI], where the pearl farm is. So this particular Easter we went to Little Buttertin and that place was packed out, there was no tent room … This friend of mine, Eddie Dubbins, he owned a speedboat. He said, 'What do you reckon, mate?' I said, 'Well, we got to go further around past Bampfield Head. A friend of mine, a teacher at the High School on TI, took me around there [before] and it is always deserted, we go around there crayfishing.' Dubbo said, 'Well let's have a look.' So we motored around, waded ashore and had a look. No one [was] there, [so] we set up camp.

The lyrics to the song itself came to Seaman during one holiday and are based on real people and events:

> So I'm sitting on the beach this particular Easter weekend … and had this guitar of mine. I said [to Dubbo], 'Mate, how about we write a song?' Well, he had named [the camp] Danville, so Danville it is. So I

wrote a song about Danville. [In the song's lyrics], Bundy and D4 are Dubbo's two pet dogs. One died at home on TI and the other one died at Danville so we buried the both of them there then. So when I wrote the song it was also about our friends Roger [Bolton] and Helen. Roger was the electrician at the hospital and his wife Helen, she was a nursing sister at the TI Base hospital.

When filmmaker Nancia Guivarra was producing *Hula Time: The Seaman Story* for ABC Television (2005), Seaman wanted to go to Danville to film:

It had been a while since I'd been to Danville prior to going back with this film crew. I took my guitar there too and Nancia said, 'You might want to sing a song for us.' So the camera boys sat me up on a log and I'm singing 'Danville'. It made me think of the first time that we went to Danville — the first Easter — and set up camp in 1986. It made me feel sad because Dubbo [Eddie Dubbins] had already passed on, a mate of mine, a really good friend.

For Seaman, like other songwriters, his songs tend to call up many personal memories. Some are happy, some are sad but they are always a special tribute to the people, places and events that inspired them. Also mentioned in 'Danville' is the toast '*debi ari*', which means 'good drink' in Meriam Mir.

'Black Swana'

'Black Swana' is an interesting traditional Torres Strait Islander song for several reasons: the way it was written, what it chronicles about the maritime industries of the Torres Strait region and how it was arranged musically.

'Black Swana'

Ina ngoey Black Swana sager gubanu paypa / Dhayal mathaman guba paypa / Matha lugipatalay uzarima / Guthathan maytha thayanu gar / Matha thari ulayke e / Koey koelak sageraw payaya e / This is our boat Black Swana / Sailing in the south east wind / We are sailing sailing faster / Pushed by the south east wind / Sailing in all its glory / Eastward current turn to flow / We applaud this sailing in the south-east wind. (Seaman Dan and Ephraim Bani)

The song combines lyrics in the Western Island language of Kala Lagaw Ya with an English translation. Not only is Ephraim Bani's translation into English linguistically accurate in capturing the essence of the song, it is also very singable. Singability is an important aspect of recording songs that have been translated. If the lyrics are clumsy or the meaning convoluted, it can make it difficult for a singer to sing them melodically and convincingly. Seaman was lucky that Indigenous collaborators such as Ephraim Bani and Bua Mabo were also gifted musicians

Charm (A9), also known locally as 'Black Swana', built c.1930s at TI by Japanese shipwrights for the Farquhar company. Thomas Foster and his mother, Sarah Farquhar, are standing at stern. Courtesy of Betty Foster and family.

who knew their respective languages and cultures intimately. Although not a fluent speaker of traditional languages himself, it was personally very important for Seaman to learn the pronunciations to the best of his ability, in order to sing the songs as accurately and as respectfully as he could. One line in particular stands out as a lovely turn of phrase in English, used to describe how sailors felt when out at sea working on luggers: 'We applaud this sailing in the south east wind [sager wind]'. Seaman recalls the feeling of being at sea with strong winds, clear sailing and a good crew:

> When the lugger hits a wave and the salt spray comes over you, you just stand up straight and face the sea, take it all in. Oh, it's a great feeling.

The lugger to which the song refers was actually named *Charm*, and was owned by the Farquhar family — of which Seaman's good friend, the late Tom Foster, was a member. The hulls of the Farquhar family's boats were painted a distinct black with a white circle on the bow, hence the name 'Black Swana' — although there are no swans native to the Torres Strait.

When deciding on how 'Black Swana' should be recorded, it was important to have backing singers who could sing in Kala Lagaw Ya, and also appreciate the song's maritime theme. The combination of an excellent English translation, strong-voiced backing singers and suitable instrumentation, with Torres Strait *warup* drum, mandolin and guitars, created a song that captured aspects of the traditional Torres Strait Islander music style Seaman had heard as a child.

'Isles of the Torres Strait'

When the Torres Strait region was charted during the colonial era, European names were given to many of the islands — although they obviously already had local names. Some of the islands continued to be known locally by their original names, and some modern maps now show both names. Out of respect, the song's lyrics first note the Indigenous names and then the European names. For example, Ngurapai is Horn Island, Zuna is Entrance Island and Waiben is Thursday Island:

> 'Isles of the Torres Strait'
>
> *Between the Coral and the Arafura seas / Are the isles of the Torres Strait / These are the islands of magic / Where skies of blue are calling me / Where balmy air and tropic moonlight / Shines on the golden sands of Ngurapai / Gliding along on blue waters / Pointing our bow to Zuna Isle / Then moving fast to Muralag / With flooding tide we're off to Gialag / Sailing on to Keriri / Then we go by Waiben too / Travelling with the ebbing tide / We sail home again for Ngurapai / Heading out from Horn Island / Pointing our bow to Entrance Isle / Then moving fast to Prince of Wales / With flooding tide we're off to Friday Isle / Sailing on to Hammond Island / Then we sail by TI too / Between the Coral and the Arafura seas / Are my islands of the Torres Strait.*
> (Seaman Dan)

Seaman worked in maritime industries throughout Torres Strait, and 'Isles of the Torres Strait' is a tribute to sailing the islands of the Inner Western cluster. He got to know the region very well:

> I grew up within the islands, moved around in between the islands, [fished] and dived for pearl shells … [So] you know all that area properly, it is like the back of your hand.

Musically, the song's slow pace and languid instrumentation encourage a bit of daydreaming, even though the men who worked in and among the islands were usually not sailing for recreation or pleasure, but rather as a way to support their families.

'Little Pony' ⛵

'Little Pony' came about directly from Seaman's youth, when he took part in a cattle muster on Cape York Peninsula in the early 1940s (see Chapter 2). He was only 11 years old, and his main job was to help out around the camp. However, he also got to ride horses with the professional Aboriginal stockmen and experience the bush for the first time. It was a long and arduous trip, but he learned to depend on his trusty small horse — his little pony — given to him by the Silver Plains station owner, Herb Thompson.

> 'Little Pony'
>
> *Come on little pony you just keep jogging along / Lift up your little hooves don't you fail / You're just about the end of the trail / Come on little pony you just keep jogging along / Come on little pony lift your head up high / Come on little pony don't you tire / Show you still have plenty of fire / Come on little pony you just keep a jogging along / Come on little pony eat up your*

> *crackers and corn / Tomorrow is another day / We have to go and round up all those strays / Come on little pony you just keep jogging along / Come on little pony let's get these cattle in / When mustering time is all through / There'll be no more work for me and you / Come on little pony you just keep jogging along / Come on little pony you just keep jogging along / Lift up your little hooves don't you fail / You're just about the end of the trail / Come on little pony you just keep jogging along.* (Seaman Dan)

The memory of the muster was stored away until many decades later, when Seaman had just started to write his own songs and an opportunity to perform them arose:

> I was singing at a barbecue one night [on TI] and I'm singing 'TI Blues'. And a gentleman from the Country and Western Association in Charters Towers heard me performing and said, 'You don't sound too bad. Would you like to come to Charters Towers and perform down there at our festival? We'll look after you, we'll pay your fare down and back, plus we'll pay whatever you want.' I said, 'I'm not a professional. I'm just a happy-go-lucky singer, [but] I'll come along as long as you pay my way down and back again.' I thought to myself, 'Well, I can't sing "TI Blues" all night — that was only song I had. So I thought about my little pony.

The song was recorded in a country blues shuffle, reflecting Seaman's love of both the blues and country music. Country music was very popular in the Torres Strait and Cape York because the music and lyrics were straightforward, especially for those who knew a few guitar chords and those for whom English was not their first language.

'Island Lady'

Romantic songs — or what Seaman calls 'slow jazz' — also figure in his songwriting. He says the lyrics to 'Island Lady' came to him in a dream:

> I had a dream one night when I was staying at my cousin's [Pauline Mills] place in Cairns after we started recording [the *Follow the Sun* album]. I was lying asleep and I rolled over and I was half in a daze. And I see this lady sitting on the edge of my bed with long black hair. I went to touch her and I put my hand on her shoulder and it went straight through and hit the bed and I woke up. Jumped up and I thought, 'Oh my!' [My] mind went straight for another song. [Originally] I was going to call it 'TI Lady' [but decided to] call it 'Island Lady' so that it will include all the ladies on all the islands.

Consequently, the song's lyrics incorporate a dream sequence and also tropical imagery. The track was recorded soon after Seaman wrote it:

'Island Lady'

Island lady / Flower in your hair / Island lady / No other can compare / Your sun kissed smile makes it all worthwhile / Coming home to you / When you're not around / I feel let down / And oh so blue / Island lady / Dancing cheek to cheek / Island lady / Though it's just a week / Strolling hand in hand down Parade Avenue / Under the tropic sky / You skip and you jump / Then you turn around and say 'I love you' / Island lady / Though you're far away / Island lady / Far away and out of reach / And then I awake from this magic dream / To touch you, to hold you, not so real as it seems / Island lady, Island lady I love you. (Seaman Dan)

Crooning was a very comfortable singing style for Seaman, as he preferred its laidback feel, which was complemented by the skills of the musicians and singers.

'Old TI'

Waltzes came into the Torres Strait region with European colonisation and were a common tempo in both secular and sacred songs. The musical origins of 'Old TI' are not clear, but some elderly local people associate it with Jaffa Ah Mat, a gifted musician and songwriter. The song has become an anthem not only for Torres Strait Islanders and Aboriginal people, but also the many other non-Indigenous people who have worked or lived in the region. It has also been adapted to other places in Queensland, such as 'Old PI' (Palm Island) and 'Old JI' (Jervis Island/Mabuyag). Its lilting melody and sentimentality are part of its appeal, but in addition the use of the word 'old' locates it in social, cultural and historical collective memories — a place in the past where the challenges and sometimes inequities of life on TI are muted by time and generational distance.

Thursday Island, 1934. Courtesy of the Australian Institute of Aboriginal and Torres Strait Islander Studies, Phillip Macfarlane collection, image no. N03957_14.

'Old TI'

Why are you looking so sad my dear? / Why are you looking so blue? / Are you thinking of someone so faraway? / In a beautiful place called TI? / Old TI my beautiful home / It's the place where I was born / Where the moon and stars that shine make me longing for home / Old TI my beautiful home / Take me across the sea / Over the deep blue sea / Darling won't you take me back to my home TI / TI my beautiful home / TI my beautiful home / I'll be there forever / The sun is sinking / Farewell. (Arranger Seaman Dan)

Seaman has pleasant personal memories of the song because of its links to community and his own family:

> For all of us TI [and Torres Strait] Islanders it is like a signature tune. Very old, from when Mum Dan used to play the button accordion [in the 1930s]. Dad [Henry Maynard] Dan used to rattle the bones [animal bone percussion, common in minstrel shows] and they would play it at different parties. 'Old TI' was everyone's favourite song. This is when I thought 'Old TI' must go on the album also, as a tribute to everyone around TI.

For the *Follow the Sun* album, 'Old TI' was arranged musically in the style of a small tearoom orchestra, such as could have existed on TI. In such an isolated place, a full range of instruments might not have been available and musicians would combine whatever instruments were available, such as accordion, tuba, ukulele and violin. In 2012, Seaman re-recorded 'Old TI' with the Cairns Gondwana Indigenous Children's Choir, including several young singers who had also been born on TI — just as he had been in 1929. Seaman stresses that whenever or wherever he sings the song, he thinks of his home island: 'I feel humble, very much humble.'

'Friday Night Blues'

'Friday Night Blues' is basically a pub-crawl song, listing TI's four hotels (the Grand, Royal, Torres and Federal) and some of the publicans that a community musician would encounter in search of a place to sing the blues.

'Friday Night Blues'

I started at the Grand / Lead singer in a band / Norm Shadbolt took one look and said 'It's more than I can stand' / Friday night blues / Friday night blues / I just can't seem to lose / Those old Friday night blues / So I went down to the Royal / Dave Camm was on the boil / Drinking rum and coke with Fred [Akee] / 'Get out that door' he said / Friday night blues / Friday night blues / I just can't seem to lose / Those old Friday night blues / Des Crabbe was much the same / I guess he's not to blame / The Torres has no cabaret / It's not my lucky day / Friday night blues / Friday night blues / I

> just can't seem to lose / Those old Friday night blues / To the Federal I was
> sent / To Charlie Kaz [Kazamias] I went / I asked if I could sing some blues /
> He said 'you matha loose' [just get lost] / Friday night blues / Friday night
> blues / I just can't seem to lose / Those old Friday night blues / So I packed
> my bags today / I have to get away / Ain't no use awaiting around / This old
> TI town / Friday night blues / Friday night blues / I just can't seem to lose /
> Those old Friday night blues. (Seaman Dan)

Before the advent of readily affordable home entertainment, pubs were a place to socialise and also to escape the confines of TI's often small and sweltering houses. Seaman recalls that 'basically it was a night out for everybody', particularly on Friday and Saturday nights, and meals were also served. TI had a steady stream of tradesmen and government workers coming through, as well as crews coming off luggers. Each pub had a core of local or sometimes PNG musicians to call on, for example, singers such as the Mills Sisters had a long residency at the Grand.

'Forty Fathoms'

Because the maritime industries were so crucial to the immigrant settlement and economy of the Torres Strait, they feature in many songs. Most songs are about the pearling industry, with a few about the trochus industry. One significant pearling area was the Darnley Deeps, a stretch of very deep water near Erub (Darnley Island) in the Eastern Islands. As discussed in Chapter 6, Seaman dived its rich pearl beds in the 1960s and wrote about his experiences almost 50 years later.

'Forty Fathoms'

> *Diving down to forty fathoms at the Darnley Deeps / Searching for the
> precious pearl shell / The pearls to keep / All aboard the pearling lugger /
> Grafton by name / Crews are waiting for the divers / Praying for some rain /
> Goodbye to you / Farewell my love / Soon we'll be sailing to the Darnley
> Deeps / And in your heart please think of me / For I'll come back to you from
> the Darnley Deeps / Diving down to forty fathoms / Down deep below /
> How to find a precious pearl shell / Only divers know / I can see the other
> divers / Working here with me / Getting shells at forty fathoms in the Darnley
> Deeps / Sailing home for dear old TI / Divers all asleep / So we bid farewell
> to the Darnley Deeps.* (Seaman Dan)

Like other pearl shell divers, Seaman learned his trade by starting as a deckhand or 'deckie', and eventually progressing to become a learner and then an experienced diver. As he remembers, he first 'put on the helmet' in 1948 at age 18 off the coast of northern Cape York Peninsula near Seisia:

> The head diver [of the *Yola*], George Elarde, asked my cousin, 'Would
> you like to put the helmet on and go down?' and he said, 'No, I'll stay

on deck.' [George] asked me and I thought to myself, 'Why be a deckie and get £15 a month all the time when you can put the helmet on and be a diver and you get £20 a month?' [So] when he asked me, I said, 'I'll give it a go.'

The first thing Seaman had to learn was how to use the helmet and diving equipment, and also — importantly — how to recognise a pearl shell:

> [George] put me down at 7 fathoms and he showed me how to look after yourself in your helmet. As you go deeper, the air pressure builds up in your ear. He said to me before I went down, 'You just swallow and that relieves the pressure in your head', which I did and I was okay then. So I went down but I didn't know how to recognise a pearl shell in their own environment — they are camouflaged in amongst the coral, seaweed, ferns. The only way you can recognise them is when they have their mouths slightly open to feed [so] you can see the lips. George pointed it out to me — what to look for, how to recognise a pearl shell in their own environment. After he pointed two pearl shells out to me, I knew what to look for then, how to recognise a pearl shell. I was away then.

Years later, as also discussed in Chapter 6, Seaman skippered the *Grafton* while his brothers-in-law Vincent and the late James Dorante skippered the *Floria* and *Galton* respectively. They went together to dive the Darnley Deeps and worked its pearling grounds, with each crew depending on each other for safety and support. Because they had to have utter trust in each other, Seaman says that a sense of duty to each other was 'just a given'. For example, if you were the tender on deck, a man's life down at the end of a very long lifeline and airline depended on you. Such deepwater diving was especially dangerous because divers could get the bends (divers' paralysis) if they did not ascend properly to the surface. When Seaman himself got the bends, he decided to give up diving. However, the memories stayed with him for the rest of his life.

Musically and lyrically, 'Forty Fathoms' is based on an earlier song, 'The Arafura Sea', which is of unknown origin. When the *Follow the Sun* album was played on the jukebox at its launch on TI, some older members of the community sang 'The Arafura Sea' chorus in tandem with Seaman's new lyrics to 'Forty Fathoms'. It was very common for local songwriters to adopt and adapt a good melody, either localising or indigenising a new song along with the new lyrics, and sometimes also inserting local languages.

'Farewell to the Torres Strait'

Continual departures were a fact of life in the Torres Strait, especially for the maritime workers who would leave home for extended periods to work across all of northern Australia from Broome in the west to Mackay in the east. Wherever there were pearl or trochus shells to harvest, there would be Torres Strait and Cape York people working. For pearling crews, sign-on was usually in March and sign-off in late December. Consequently, depending on the distance travelled, they might not see family and friends for many months. Thoughts of home could be especially poignant at the end of the working day, when exhausted crew-members would gather to sing a few songs or talk about loved ones far away.

> 'Farewell to the Torres Strait'
>
> *Farewell farewell to the Torres Strait / Farewell to swaying palms and golden sands / Farewell to tropic seas so blue so deep / Soft breezes blow lulls you to sleep / You can watch the seabirds flying high up in the sky / See the people sadly waving as your ship goes sailing by / When you return on that special day / You will find happiness in the Torres Strait / Nawa nawa Torres kes nawa / Pakoi pe upen bamareda / Pako zorem zorem weh / Mena nawa able tropic gul / A blu blu karem / Nade geb geb wag tide wanasig wa utem.* (Seaman Dan and Bua Mabo)

Seaman recounts how the song came about, which shows how casual remarks can stimulate a song's creation:

> After writing 'Welcome to the Torres Straits' I took my guitar and hopped in my ute and went around to an old friend of mine [the late George Bridges]. He was the caretaker at [a maritime produce factory] at Rose Hill [on TI], straight across from the Ibis store. I went around there and I told him about this new song I had written to welcome the Cook Islanders. And he said, 'That is very nice but you should also write "Farewell to the Torres Straits".' [I said], 'Ah George, thank you very much, I hadn't thought of that!' So he inspired me to write it.

'Farewell to the Torres Strait' is a musical and thematic rejoinder to 'Welcome to the Torres Strait', and provides the perfect song and sentiment to conclude the *Follow the Sun* album. Seaman also ends live performances with it, especially when entertaining tourists who visit the region.

'Sayonara Nakamura'

When *Follow the Sun* was re-released by Steady Steady Music in 2011, Seaman had the chance to add an additional song. One song he had always liked was Ted Egan's 'Sayonara Nakamura'. A story song, it recounted the tragic tale of a young Okinawan diver dying from the bends off the Western Australian coast.

> 'Sayonara Nakamura'
>
> *When the luggers all sailed away / From Roebuck Bay on that fateful day / The diver on the B19 was Nakamura / Not yet twenty-one / From the Land of the Rising Sun / His homeland was the island Okinawa / In the deepest*

holes of the Lacepede Shoals / To fulfil the pearling master's goals / Went the diver of the B19 Nakamura / His quest for the lustrous pearl / As strong as his love for the beautiful girl / He'd wed when he returned to Okinawa / But it's goodbye now farewell / Say goodbye to Okinawa / For today they'll bury you / In West Australia / And you will never be as one / With the Land of the Rising Sun / Sayonara sayonara Nakamura / From the west came a tropical squall / Then the mercury began to fall / Forty fathoms deep was Nakamura / Set sail no time to stage / For the storm began to rage / And they pulled to the surface the diver Nakamura / The agony is in his eyes / An old Malay man cries / For he knows the bends have got young Nakamura / Helplessly they cursed / As the diver's lungs near burst / And he died on the deck / The boy from Okinawa / To the divers' cemetery in Broome / Bearing gifts all deep in gloom / They walked with the body of the diver Nakamura / Headstones face the west / A thousand divers lie at rest / And they're joined today by the boy from Okinawa. (Ted Egan)

Okinawan divers also came to Torres Strait after the Second World War as possible replacements for the many deported Japanese divers who had previously dominated the industry there. The song's maritime theme was very familiar to Seaman, and his version is his tribute to all the divers and crews of the pearling luggers of northern Australia. Musically, it also included the *sanshin*, a traditional Okinawan stringed instrument.

The *Follow the Sun* album was well received in the Torres Strait, as well as Queensland generally, and then nationally. Through the support of broadcasters such as Radio 4MW on Thursday Island and ABC Local Radio in Cairns, as well as the encouragement and industry connections of Cairns-based journalist and musician Tony Hillier, it was leased to Hot Records. The album also garnered critical acclaim. In 2000, it won the National Folk Recording Award presented by the National Film and Sound Archives at the National Folk Festival in Canberra. It was becoming apparent Seaman Dan had something noteworthy to offer as a singer and songwriter. The recognition of his music was personally a big boost to his songwriting and performing. It seems Australian audiences and broadcasters were prepared to accept and appreciate a bit of 'world music' from a little-known region of Australia.

The second album, *Steady, Steady*, would continue Seaman's exploration of the music and cultures of the Torres Strait region and tropical Australia.

CHAPTER 9
Steady, Steady

Seaman's second album, *Steady, Steady* (2002), was also recorded at Select Sound in Cairns and released by Hot Records (Hot 1079). Nigel Pegrum once again was the audio engineer and he and Karl Neuenfeldt produced. Denis Crowdy (guitar and ukulele), Wayne McIntosh (guitar), Giles Smith (acoustic and electric bass) and Giuseppe Vizzone (drums) were the rhythm section. Other musicians included Mike Cooper (lap steel guitar), Steve Gilbert (harmonica), Russell Harris (flugelhorn and trumpet), Mat Harrison (violin and mandolin), Ruedi Homberger (saxophone and clarinet), Mark Mannock (keyboards), Kerry McKenzie (percussion), Karl Neuenfeldt (ukulele, banjo, bouzouki and acoustic guitar), Richie Odo (acoustic guitar), Nigel Pegrum (drums and percussion), Tristan Rich (cello), Kathryn Schenk (violin), Kirk Steel (accordion), Stephen Whittington (tuba), Megan Williams (oboe) and Margaret Willis (violin and viola). Backing singers and vocal arrangers included Gabriel Bani, Libby Brockenshire, Jenni Clarke, Rubina Kimiia, Chris Lloyds, Cygnet Repu, Sam Savage, Susan Schuurbiers and the Matha Loose Choir. Of special note was the addition of a featured vocalist, the late Jimmy Little, and a guest instrumentalist, guitarist John Nicol, both well-known Indigenous performers.

The liner notes stated: 'Steady, steady is a local sailing term meaning to sail a pearling lugger steadily into the current so divers can work safely below'. It came to be one of Seaman's favourite, and most identifiable, phrases — to the extent that once he was asked by a TI visitor and fan, 'how are you doing?' When he replied 'fine', the visitor then said in surprise, 'I thought you were supposed to say, "steady, steady"'! The album continued the production strategy begun on the *Follow the Sun* album of including songs in the musical styles Seaman loved: blues, hula, slow-jazz and traditional Torres Strait Islander songs.

Seaman Dan in the studio. Photo Kerry Trapnell.

'Somewhere There's an Island'

As a song and music production, 'Somewhere There's an Island' epitomises the Seaman Dan 'sound' (laid-back vocals and mostly acoustic instrumentation) and a familiar theme (laid-back island life far from urban hustle and bustle):

> 'Somewhere There's an Island'
>
> *Somewhere there's an island / Calling calling to me / In dreams I sail to that island / It's where I long to be / In dreams a sweet siesta is calling calling to me / In dreams I sail to that island and I find serenity / Somewhere there's an island / With palm trees and golden sand / There's sailing ships and dolphins always close to hand / In dreams a sweet siesta is calling calling to me / In dreams I sail to that island and I find serenity / Somewhere there's an island / I'll find it some sweet day / No car no phone no television / That's where I want to stay.* (Seaman Dan and Karl Neuenfeldt)

Growing up and working in the Torres Strait region meant, of course, that islands and the sea were Seaman's constant surroundings. He recalls the memories triggered by the song:

> It reminds me of the sea because I used to swim in the Great Barrier Reef for trochus shells when I was a young fella, started diving there when I was 16 years old. I honestly do dream of an island, a secluded island with a lot of water around [it] and a nice sandy beach. Yes, I often dream about that island. And I always say I belong to the sea.

The song — with its combination of 'sound', theme and performance — clearly had an appeal because it was used in several film and documentary soundtracks. Hot Records released the *Steady Steady* album in the United Kingdom, and the song was chosen for the soundtrack of the Emmy and BAFTA nominated television movie *Girl in a Cafe* (2005), written by Richard Curtis and starring Bill Nighy and Kelly Macdonald. The film was released internationally, although the connection of the song to the movie's setting of a Group of 8 (G8) political and economic meeting in Iceland was arguably a bit tenuous. Another somewhat odd use was in the American movie *Jack Satin* (2011), about a washed-up lounge entertainer in search of a new lease on life and music who is hiding out in a desert town while on the run from Las Vegas criminals. A rather more understandable use of the song was in the documentary *Blue Horizon* (2004), by world-renowned surfing cinematographer Jack McCoy. It follows well-known surfers to different locales for big waves, and at least had an obvious maritime link. Similarly, it was an appropriate addition to David Bridie's eclectic soundtracks for the SBS television series *RAN (Remote Area Nurse)* (2005) and ABC TV's *The Straits* (2012), both set in the Torres Strait region.

A BBC radio announcer in Great Britain, who loved the song, interviewed Seaman while he was on tour in Adelaide. He recalls:

> She phoned me personally from Newcastle and commented about 'Somewhere There's an Island'. Whenever she plays that over the air, she always imagines she is sitting on the beach on a secluded island.

When a song appeals to broadcasters and makers of such stylistically diverse movies and documentaries, it clearly has a greater appeal than was apparent when it was being recorded. The production team knew it was a good song, but it is only after completion that some songs take on a life of their own. For whatever reason, they literally strike a chord with listeners, but they also highlight the importance of the contributions of the collaborating musicians and singers because it is they who help flesh out a song. 'Somewhere There's an Island' is an example of one of Seaman's songs with wide appeal — perhaps because islands are often idealised as places of simplicity, escape and reinvention, especially in tourism and literature — even if sometimes unrealistically.

'Mena Menali'

There is a popular genre of secular songs from the Eastern Torres Strait known locally as love songs, and 'Mena Menali' is a well-known example. Seaman's cousin, the late George Mye MBE, OAM, wrote many such songs, and 'Mena Menali' is one of his most popular. It is sung in Meriam Mir and English.

> 'Mena Menali'
>
> *Mena Menali / Au muris ge kari alam / Ko takomer ko takomer karim / Mena ika nali mari naukaili / Oh my love I need you / Honest I do / Now that you leave me / My every thought will be of you / Remembering our love that used to be / Please come back to me / Darling I want you / Oh my love I need you honest I do.* (George Mye)

Seaman has a very clear memory of when, where and how he first heard the song:

> George Mye lived at Darnley Island, and he wrote that song for his girlfriend — his future wife — Jenny. I used to be on a pearling vessel working at the Darnley Deeps and he was a store manager [at Mer (Murray Island)] so I sailed over to visit him, as I hadn't seen him for a few years. He sang the song to me and I quite liked it.

Seaman often combined languages in a song because:

> Well, me being a Torres Strait Islander, those sorts of [different] languages you hear all the time and it is in your head all the time. It sort of comes out naturally when you have to use it [singing].

His mother was multilingual, so he grew up hearing different languages. It was also commonplace for Torres Strait Islanders to sing songs in different languages. Many are multilingual, perhaps speaking a traditional language such as Meriam Mir or a dialect of Kala Lagaw Ya, along with Torres Strait Creole/Yumpla Tok and English.

'Mena Menali' was also used in the David Bridie soundtracks for *RAN (Remote Area Nurse)* (2005) and *The Straits* (2012), and when Seaman first heard it on television he remembers: 'It really inspired me and it makes me sit up straight, [with a] big smile on my face. And then I am thinking, "is that really me?"'

'Ailan Kwiktaim'

The title of 'Ailan Kwiktaim' is in Torres Strait Creole/Yumpla Tok, and means 'go to the island quickly' — that island being Thursday Island. In the context of the song's theme and dialogue, it refers to the crew members being anxious to return home to see their girlfriends after a long time away at sea.

> 'Ailan Kwiktaim'
>
> *Islander boys are always happy / Thinking of those island girls / Now we have met and we have parted / So please don't mention TI's name / Islander girls Islander girls lovely little Islander girls / If you spoon down the beach with a nice rosy cheek / You can bet she's an Islander girl / Islander boys have gone to sea dear / Diving in the Coral Sea / Soon they're sailing off to Darwin / Then they work their way to Broome / Islander girls Islander girls / Waiting with their sun-kissed smile / For the boys to come home, never to*

roam / Those lovely little Islander girls / Dialogue: Crew member — Skipper which way? Sail 'em home kwik taim? Skipper — Wa! TI kwiktaim! Up the jib sail! Crew member — Jib sail up, skipper. We go island now! (Composers/authors unknown, arranged by Seaman Dan, Karl Neuenfeldt and Nigel Pegrum)

'Ailan Kwiktaim' started as two separate songs that Seaman heard from his good friend and fellow musician the late Hismile 'Izzie' Shibasaki. It was unclear where the songs originated, but they were combined for the recording, with one becoming the verse and the other the chorus of the new song. Seaman says he found the arranging process interesting:

> It took some doing, but for me it was really good. I had never done anything like that before, to bring two songs together to make the one song. After the recording was finished and we played the songs over and over again I thought, 'Well, that's great!' It hadn't been done before.

Seaman Dan and the late Hismile (Izzie) Shibasaki making music on the veranda at Seaman's home on Horn Island, c.2002.

'Ailan Kwiktaim' encapsulates two features of maritime work that Seaman himself lived: men working far from home on pearling luggers travelling from TI to Darwin and Broome; and their loved ones — including girlfriends — remaining at home. He reminisces:

> It takes me back to my young days when I was on the pearling vessels. [When] you go out to work, you work [but] when you come back into port the girls are already there, waiting for you. And they put on a party for all the boys that work out at sea. So you bring your guitar ashore, your ukulele ashore, and you have a dance. They usually hire the old town hall on TI [Victoria Memorial Hall] and they make a dance for all of us lugger boys.

Some crew members of the TI luggers that worked across northern Australia never returned to Torres Strait because they married and raised families elsewhere, but TI was still considered home — at least in song.

'Ailan Kwiktaim' received substantial radio airplay due to its lightheartedness, catchy chorus and up-tempo rhythms. It was also used in the soundtrack of *The Straits*.

'Pearly Shells'

'Pearly Shells' is a very well-known popular song, and is associated with hula dancing, in particular the generic kind of hula that can be attempted, often in a lighthearted manner, with no knowledge of the culturally rich aspects of traditional

Polynesian hula. The song itself is credited to Webley Edwards and Leon Prober, although segments of it clearly are based on a Hawaiian song, 'Pu'u o Ewa'. Seaman had always admired Hawaiian music, having grown up listening to Sol Ho'opi'i and other Hawaiian artists whose early recordings circulated in the Torres Strait. Seaman recalls 'Pearly Shells' as a popular song on TI:

> That was one of our favourite songs when we would go to a party. Jerry Lewin, another one of my mates, an ex-pearl diver, he used to play the Hawaiian slide guitar. Then someone would play the ukulele and I would get on the acoustic guitar and we would have a ball. I think it is a really nice song, the words are nice and it is a natural for a hula song.

'Pearly Shells' is such a well-known song that it lends itself to being adapted and added to. As well, dancers — even untrained ones — feel comfortable attempting a bit of hula (usually with some hip wiggling and hand swaying), even if only in a vague approximation of the traditional dance's intricate and culturally meaningful movements. In 2005, Seaman was a featured performer at 'House Party Hula', an event in Cairns recreating Torres Strait Islander house parties of earlier eras. An overflowing audience enjoyed the music of Seaman, Cindy Drummond, Jerry Lewin and John Nicol, along with a backing band. They also got to enjoy some featured hula dancing by a friend of Seaman's, Sarina Ah Mat (née Adams), then in her late seventies, and also some spontaneous dancing by women in the audience. Seaman notes:

The late Jimmy Little and Seaman Dan at the National Museum of Australia's Tracking Kultja festival, 2001.

> When we did 'Pearly Shells', quite a few women in the audience jumped up and started doing the hula to it. They came to the front of the stage and it was just like automatic: '[If you play] "Pearly Shells", we're going to dance.' We had them on the floor [dancing].

Seaman is a long-time admirer of the late Jimmy Little, one of the first Indigenous singers to gain widespread recognition in Australian popular music, and recounts the first time he saw him perform:

> He came with Col Joye and the Joy Boys in 1960, up to Cairns. I was living [there] at the time and they put on a show at the old Hibernian Hall so me and my wife [Clare] went along to see them. It was great! That was the first time I had heard him sing [live], and I have been a fan of his ever since — and still am.

Years later, when Seaman had just started recording, he had his first chance to meet Jimmy personally:

I went to another one of [his] concerts [in Cairns] and was sitting in the third row. That is the closest I could get to the stage, and he saw me there. Then he asked over the [sound system] before he started to sing 'Pearly Shells', 'Is Seaman Dan in the audience? If you are there, would you like to come up and sing a duet with me?' Well, that was a big buzz for me so I walked up to the stage, proud as one thing, and we both sang a duet of 'Pearly Shells' on stage.

In 2001, Seaman met Jimmy again at a concert they were doing at the National Museum of Australia, 'Tracking Kultja', and they agreed to collaborate on a recording if the opportunity arose. Jimmy's performance schedule eventually took him to Cairns, and he recorded a duet of 'Pearly Shells' with Seaman, with Indigenous guitarist and singer John Nicol also adding his unique instrumental skills. Unbeknown to everyone, Jimmy was then suffering from a serious kidney illness. Although ill, he added his distinctive vocal style to the recording, which blended perfectly with Seaman's crooning style. Jimmy also had additional lyrics to 'Pearly Shells' that he had sung for many years, but they were deleted from the recording because of copyright concerns. Seaman was later to receive the Jimmy Little Lifetime Achievement Award at the 2009 Deadly Awards (the National Aboriginal and Torres Strait Islander Music, Sport, Entertainment and Community Awards) at the Sydney Opera House — a venue a long way from the verandas of TI or the backyard of a country pub on Cape York Peninsula.

Seaman Dan at Tracking Kultja Festival 2001. Courtesy National Museum of Australia.

'Steady, Steady' 🎵

'Steady, Steady' was one of the first songwriting collaborations with co-producer Karl Neuenfeldt, who had recorded three singer-songwriter albums in Australia, Canada and the United States before embarking on a career as an academic. As noted earlier, the phrase 'steady, steady' itself is a common Torres Strait maritime term. Seaman explains its maritime origins:

> It's about [working on] a pearling lugger. If the current is too strong and the seas are too big and the boat is drifting too fast away from the diver, you turn around. You just make your boat run upwind, up against the sea, steady steady. Face up against the sea, the motor going slowly, the prop turning slowly and it drifts backwards to make the boat slower. Drifting backwards, so the diver can walk along steady, steady to follow the boat.

Although 'steady, steady' is a Torres Strait maritime term, as a metaphor it can also be applied to the dynamics of a romantic relationship, such as 'going steady'.

> 'Steady, Steady'
>
> *Won't you tell when / The time when you are ready / Must be pretty close / What say we go steady steady / I can see it in your sky blue eyes / All your love for me / Though we're far apart you are always in my heart / Whether rain or shine I'll be yours you'll be mine / Until then through stormy seas / Steady steady we'll be / I can see the rainbow through the drifting cloud / Lots of happiness / Tears are not allowed / I see fields of flowers just for you and me / So much joy you will see / Steady steady we'll be / Won't you take my hand / Then you will understand / Knocking at your door / Just can't wait to tell you more / Until then you will always be steady steady with me.*
> (Seaman Dan and Karl Neuenfeldt)

The evolution of the song from a maritime phrase to a complete song was a bit convoluted. Seaman had originally wanted to call his first album *Steady, Steady*, but had not yet written a song with that title. However, after the release of the first album — named after the song *Follow the Sun* — he did write a song using the title. It was based on the slow-drag dance style popular in the Torres Strait. Seaman defines slow drag as 'like a slow fox trot. We just call it slow drag, like a boat drifting backwards. Like you and your dancing partner on the dance floor.' The song was produced and arranged musically in a 1940s fashion, including a string arrangement and brass. Seaman admits he loves the slow-drag style, as it fits his crooning vocal style and also because 'being a teenager in that period [the 1940s], I always go back to that period'. Similar to how a boat needed to be handled steady steady, so too did a dance partner — or, for that matter, a potential romantic partner: 'If you are lucky she goes steady steady with you. You've got to start somewhere!'

'Barron Delta Blue'

Andy 'Sugarcane' Collins, a Cairns-based singer-songwriter, wrote 'Barron Delta Blue'. The Barron River comes cascading down from the nearby highlands and runs through the sugarcane-growing coastal area of Cairns to the Coral Sea.

> ### 'Barron Delta Blue'
>
> *As the sun settles down on the Barron Delta / Up in sugarcane land / I don't understand why I'm feeling blue / Gets under my skin in Freshwater when the cane's ablaze at night / The cool star light and I'm feeling blue / When I see the shimmer on the Barron River / As the moon's rolling slowly by / If I'm feeling ragged coming through Stratford / I'll stop for a while and say hi / I'm still feeling blue / And I'm telling you / I'm not going down south again / Here comes that rain / I'm Barron Delta blue.* (Andy Collins)

When Seaman first heard the song broadcast on ABC local radio in Cairns, he liked it because, as he says:

> I grew up in Cairns during the war years and I have been to the places that were named in the song. And it had a nice tempo too, it very much appealed to me.

The song was arranged in a bluesy and slow traditional jazz style, with clarinet and banjo ukulele helping to set it in a particular musical era. Unlike many other Torres Strait Islanders who migrated to the Australian mainland after the Second World War, Seaman never worked in the sugar industry. He chose to work at sea if possible, finding it a healthier and cleaner lifestyle than cutting sugarcane by hand in the hot, humid and snake-infested lowlands of north Queensland.

'Running Aground'

Like 'Steady Steady', another song with a maritime theme is 'Running Aground' by Alistair 'Azo' Bell. He is one of Australia's foremost ukulele players, performing solo and with the ukulele, tea-chest bass and snare drum trio Old Spice Boys. Seaman first heard the song on an album Azo recorded with Sarah Tindley. Musically, it lent itself to a harder-edge production style with the addition of horns and electric guitar.

> ### 'Running Aground'
>
> *What a life / Just rolling on the beach / But there's a hard rocky little reef / And my heart is like a wooden boat / If it runs up on the reef / It's never gonna stay afloat / Give it time / Maybe one day some sweet wave might wash this rock away / But for now there's broken water all around me / And we better hang on / We're navigating desperately / Looks like we're running aground / Running aground / We're running aground / Navigating desperately / In the*

> dark trying to find a way ashore / There's a storm brewing / I can hear the ocean roar / When the morning sun comes shining on down / Don't know if we'll be swimming or if we'll be drowned. (Alistair 'Azo' Bell)

During his years working at sea, Seaman had a close call once, and almost ran aground:

> 'Running Aground' reminded me of [when] the lugger that I was skipper on touched bottom. I sort of misjudged and you never make the same mistake twice, you may not be so lucky the second time. And [I've] never done it again, once bitten twice shy. Just as well it was just a sand bar and not a reef. We didn't damage the boat at all.

Although, on a surface level, the lyrics are about sailing, the song could also be interpreted as applying to the trajectory and challenges of a romantic relationship. Seaman thinks people like the song partly because of its energy, but also because it says that a relationship can run aground: 'You know, it hits a reef, an obstacle.'

'Return to Me'

One reason Seaman loves the blues as a musical style is that it allows the expression of personal feelings — real or imagined. The blues style has wide appeal because it is accessible. Listeners can project their own lives and life experiences on to the often straightforward and repetitive lyrics. 'Return to Me' is one such accessible blues song.

> 'Return to Me'
>
> *You have gone away from me / Far away across the deep blue seas / You have gone away from me / Far away across the deep blue sea / Don't know where you've gone to / You're always on my mind / This world is such a big place / You'll be hard to find / Please return to me / Feeling blue as blue as can be / Don't have no one to care about me / Another bar and misery to follow / A new head I wish I could borrow / Bartender he says 'Joe you better go real slow / You're wasting all my gin / That's a mortal sin' / Please return to me / Lord I wish I could die / Aim to catch me that big bird and fly / Lord I wish I could die / Aim to catch me that big bird and fly / Come tomorrow morning won't be waiting around / Have to make that plane-boat / Leaving this lonely town / Please return to me.* (Seaman Dan and Karl Neuenfeldt)

The lyrics were written out of Seaman's personal experience:

> I had a relationship that ran aground. It was a very good relationship, [but] she left TI to go south again. So I am sitting on the wharf on TI and I'm looking out to sea, thinking of her, and that is when I started to write [it].

The plane-boat mentioned in the lyrics refers to the passenger ferry running between TI and Horn Island where the airport is located. As Seaman says, unfortunately for travellers (both with and without the blues), 'If you miss the plane-boat, you miss the plane!'

'A Song for Leilani'

This song was more or less written by accident. Musically, it started as a chord pattern for a Charlie Rich song that Seaman wanted to record. However, after Denis Crowdy had created a lovely guitar part, it was decided that it could be used as the basis for a new song by adding original lyrics and a melody. Seaman kept a notebook full of lyrics, phrases and stories, and when he looked through them he found some that might be suitable. A rough mix of the guitar part was done, and Karl Neuenfeldt then worked on connecting Denis's chord pattern and Seaman's words via a melody. Luckily, Seaman has always been able to learn melodies with ease, and the song was finished quickly.

> 'A Song for Leilani'
>
> *When love has gone away / Far away from you / You will realise that love was not true / Try not to cry / Don't look so sad / Memories left with you / Could never be bad / Always look to the future for what tomorrow may bring / Each day could bring you joy / Then once more your heart will sing / Don't run away / Just make new friends / Hold on to what you have / Let your heart mend / That's when you'll find someone to share / You'll share your happiness with someone who cares / You'll find happiness with someone who cares.* (Seaman Dan, Denis Crowdy and Karl Neuenfeldt)

The Leilani named in the title is Leilani Binjuda, who is the daughter of one of Seaman's godchildren, the late Frances Binjuda (née Hodges). The song is not about Leilani Binjuda personally, but rather about an elderly person giving advice to a younger person who has experienced a failed relationship, or one that may have run aground. Leilani had been very supportive of Seaman's music when she worked on TI for the Torres Strait Regional Authority, and later when she moved to Canberra to work for the Department of Foreign Affairs and Trade. Using her mellifluous name in the title was a small gesture of thanks for her encouragement.

'Thank You for Saying Hello'

The style Seaman calls slow-jazz refers to medium- or down-tempo songs that use more complex chords and structures than those found in blues, hula or more traditional Torres Strait Islander songs. Its roots lie in the jazz he heard from African-American soldiers in Cairns during the Second World War, and also from recording artists he idolised, such as Nat King Cole, Ella Fitzgerald and Frank Sinatra.

'Thank You for Saying Hello'

I want to thank you for saying hello / I want to hold you close and never let you go / You came to town to visit with your friend / I'm hoping that your stay will never end / You turned and I saw tears in your eyes / It was then I felt we could never say goodbye / You smiled at me and suddenly it seemed / This can only happen in my dream / Why does this have to happen? / To people like you and me? / Why does the world keep turning? / Spins and churns like a stormy sea / Right from the start when we said our first hello / You held my hand / I can never let you go / From afar and with all my heart / I want to thank you for saying hello. (Seaman Dan)

A chance meeting inspired the lyrics. Seaman remembers:

> Yes, there was a girl and we both said 'hello'. And I thought, 'What a lovely girl.' She wasn't actually my girlfriend, just a girl that you could admire from a distance, you know. And I thought, 'Oh, she said hello to me.' So I said, 'Well, thank you for saying hello!' That's how the song started.

Slow-jazz is a natural fit with Seaman's voice, and it also added variety and space to his albums by giving the instrumentalists a chance to stretch themselves musically and display their talents.

'Gubaw Paruka'

'Gubaw Paruka' means 'sailing into the wind', and this is a traditional Torres Strait Islander song in Kala Lagaw Ya from the Western Islands. The English translation is by the late Ephraim Bani. When Seaman sang in a traditional language, it was usually privileged in the sequence of a song's lyrics, coming first before an English translation. Traditional songs are very meaningful to him:

> I like singing [them] because it is my heritage and I must keep in touch with my heritage at all times.

'Gubaw Paruka'

Gubaw paruka / Inur napayki e / Kaziw ngulaymaya e eya e / Ngath nginu paruka / Wakaynthoemayma / Towards the south-east wind / Storm is rising / My son is caught in the storm in the storm / I am thinking of your face / Thinking of you / Your beautiful face is in my mind. (Composer/author unknown, arranged by Seaman Dan and Ephraim Bani)

The song arises out of the region's long maritime tradition, where workers and travellers would sometimes go missing and families and friends had great concern for their welfare. In this case, a parent realises their child is lost at sea and imagines their face before them. Before the advent of airplanes, helicopters and Emergency

Pearl boats *Harold*, *Kismet* and *Kailag*, from Yorke [Masig] Island escort Reverend WH MacFarlane and Mrs MacFarlane on the mission boat Herald as they leave for the last time after 17 years in the Torres Strait. Courtesy the Australian Institute of Aboriginal and Torres Strait Islander Studies, Phillip Macfarlane collection, image no. N04026_02.

Position Indicating Radio Beacons and Personal Locator Beacons, searching for them was much more difficult because the Torres Strait is an extremely complex labyrinth of strong currents, open seas, coral reefs and shallow cays. Tragically, workers and travellers in the region still go missing at sea, never to be found.

'Are You from TI?'

Because the Torres Strait was a commercial and cultural crossroads, it was also a musical crossroads. Its Indigenous peoples and immigrants all had their musical traditions, but music also arrived through popular culture via recordings, sheet music, movies and touring performance groups. One such example is 'Are You from TI?'

'Are You from TI?'

Up in the sky so far away / There is a place for everyone / The moon and stars that always shine / Out on the ocean waves / And as the lazy waves roll by / Breezes blowing memories / Yes yes somewhere there's joy / Somewhere there's sorrow / Out on the sea / It's always the same to me / Are you from TI? / Are you from TI? / Where the wild wild wongai tree grows? / Are you from Torres Strait or any place including St Paul way? / Any place that's just around by Mabuyag way? / Are you from TI? / Are you from TI? / Well I'm from TI too / Pleased to meet you / Well I'm from TI too.
(Arranged by Seaman Dan)

The first part of the song's lyrics, 'up in the sky', and its melody are of unknown origin. The lyrics could be interpreted in many different ways, including suggesting sailors can leave behind the responsibilities of life on land by going to sea and being out in the natural world, where 'it's all the same to me'. The second part of the song's lyrics and its melody are clearly based on 'Are You from Dixie?' by George Cobb and Jack Yeller and copyrighted in the United States in 1915. It became an early bluegrass favourite, and was also recorded much later by major country artists such as Jimmy Dean, Jerry Reed and Grandpa Jones. The original lyrics are:

Are you from Dixie? / Are you from Dixie? / Where the fields of cotton beckon to me? / I'm glad to see you / Tell me how be you / And those friends I'm longing to see / Are you from Alabama Tennessee or Carolina? / Any place below the Mason Dixon Line? / Are you from Dixie? / I say from Dixie / 'Cause I'm from Dixie too. (George Cobb and Jack Yellen)

Seaman was alerted to the partial origins of what he performed as 'Are You from TI?' by an audience member at the National Folk Festival in Canberra in 2001, who told him about the origin of the chorus. Seaman remembers hearing the version he sang in the 1940s:

> When we used to go to parties, us young fellas, the older fellas they'd sing 'Are You from TI?' so we would join in too. That was where I learnt that song, from the older fellas. They would have probably learnt it the same way too. There were always visiting ships coming through the port of TI, so it could have come from one of the passing ships. But we [also] had movies [on TI]. I used to go on Saturday night when I was six years old, so movies were there before I was born. [The song] might have been on screen.

Whatever its origin, 'Are You from TI?' has become an iconic Torres Strait song. Possibly because many people who lived elsewhere in the region or on the mainland were born at the regional hospital on TI, they technically could say, 'Well, I'm from TI too.' A regional airline used Seaman's version of 'Are You from TI?' for on-hold music, a suitable up-tempo musical accompaniment while waiting to book a flight.

'The Torres Strait Hula'

A hybrid form of hula dancing — more akin to 'Hollywood hula' based on movie depictions — was and still is popular in the Torres Strait. Hula groups were active both on TI and on the outer islands, and also among the Torres Strait Islander evacuees on the mainland during the Second World War. Torres Strait hula is still danced today at social occasions and community events. Historically, other versions of the hula were also danced in Cape York Aboriginal communities, as Seaman encountered when touring there in 2003.

What could loosely be termed hula-style music was historically also very popular. It was based on a mixture of Hawaiian styles from recordings and movies, and also styles that came into the region with pre-Second World War immigrants from what is now Indonesia. Perhaps the best-known proponents of the style were the Mills Sisters: Cessa Nakata, Ina Titasey and the late Rita Fell-Tyrell. As mentioned in Chapter 1, Seaman had known Cessa and Ina from the 1930s when they were also in TI's Sacred Heart Convent boarding school. Rita was a younger sister so he did not meet her until he returned to the Torres Strait in the late 1940s. Seaman felt it was a good idea to 'write a tribute song to the Mills Sisters … because they did a lot of publicity for the Torres Strait'. In the song's lyrics, the phrase 'hello cockie' refers to an Australian parrot, the cockatoo. Whereas many ukulele players tune to the 'my dog has fleas' intervals, the Mills Sisters' musical mnemonic device was 'hello cockie'.

'The Torres Strait Hula'

Way up north among the Islands / Way up in the Coral Sea / Two things always go together / The Mills Sisters and memories / Cessa plays the ukulele / Ina taps the tambourine / With Rita's guitar all together / They sing island harmonies / Hello cockie is how they tune the ukulele / It just might be perfect island harmony / Making me smile with their island style / Singing the songs we love to sing along / Doing the Torres Strait hula / Each one a story to tell / The beauty of music in motion / And that sweet sweet frangipani smell / Cessa Ina and Rita / Swaying as they sing along / From TI to Sydney and Europe / Travelling with a smile and a song. (Seaman Dan, Wendy Rattenbury and Karl Neuenfeldt)

The song's lyrics, and the ukulele-based musical accompaniment, summarise the accessible, upbeat and eclectic performance style the Mills Sisters perfected when playing first in the pubs of TI and later on national and international tours. Referred to by some fans as the 'Hula Grannies', they did not start performing publicly until they were grandmothers. Their music reflects the cultural, linguistic and musical mix typical of the Torres Strait region. They were the first Torres Strait Islanders to take what was essentially very local music to a wider audience, and gain respect as unique performers and cultural ambassadors. When Seaman performs the song live, it is common for the audience to start to do the Torres Strait hula, and thereby also to pay indirect tribute to the Mills Sisters as musical pioneers who paved the

Seaman Dan with the TI Mills Sisters, [l–r]: Ina Titasey, the late Rita Fell-Tyrell and Cessa Nakata at Select Sound Studios in Cairns, c.2000. 'Torres Strait Hula' was written as a tribute to them.

way for other Torres Strait Islander recording artists. And how did the Mills Sisters react to the song? Seaman asked Cessa and Ina, and says 'they were very, very much happy'.

The *Steady Steady* album had a larger budget than *Follow the Sun*, as it received generous funding from the Australia Council for the Arts. That allowed more production scope and recording time, but it did not alter the basic 'sound' — or Seaman's desire to present his culture in all its musical diversity. Because the album presents songs Seaman had known for many years, along with some new ones, Seaman still says that, although he likes all his albums, '[*Steady, Steady*] is my favourite album'.

CHAPTER 10

PERFECT PEARL

In 2003, Seaman's third album, *Perfect Pearl*, was recorded at Select Sound in Cairns and released by Hot Records (Hot 1094). Nigel Pegrum was the audio engineer and he and Karl Neuenfeldt again co-produced. The song 'Veiga, Veiga' was co-produced by Denis Crowdy in Australia and the late Tony Subam in PNG. Steve Gilbert's harmonica was recorded in the United Kingdom at The Music Farm studio in Cumbria. The Seaman Dan 'sound' that had been established on the first two albums was broadened further by the addition of different musicians and singers. Additional musicians were Ben Hakalitz (drums), Robbi Jib (guitar and bass), Ric Montgomery (slide guitar and dobro), Tom Seepoy (piano), Andree Baudet (saxophone), Jason Fox (trombone), Stella Massey (viola), Tristan Rich

Seaman Dan with his 2004 Australian Record Industry Association (ARIA) Award for Best World Music recording for *Perfect Pearl* with co-producers Nigel Pegrum (l) and Karl Neuenfeldt (r). Courtesy Amanda Feher and Giuseppe Vizzone.

(cello) and Shakimra (bamboo flute). Additional singers were Gabriel Bani, Tony Ghee, Cessa Nakata, Charles Passi, Laura Pegrum, Gere and Gima Rupa and Ina Titasey. Art design was by Jon Watkins. The album title came from the song 'Perfect Pearl', which proved to be prophetic: the album won the prestigious Australasian Recording Industry (ARIA) Award for Best World Music recording in 2004. By the time of the third album, Seaman was also touring with a small band, and his skills as a singer, songwriter and entertainer continued to develop.

'Going Back Home'

The album begins with a song originally recorded by the popular Indigenous band the Pigram Brothers and featured in the *Bran Nue Dae* play (1990) and later in the movie of the same name (2010). The Pigram Brothers come from Broome, Western Australia, where Seaman had worked as a deep-water pearl-shell diver. It was also where he got to enjoy one of his favourite fruits, mango, and one of his favourite meals, fish soup and rice made from fish bones, fish heads and tails.

Similar tastes in food were one of the many things familiar to maritime workers coming to the Broome area from Torres Strait. Like TI, Broome was a centre for maritime industries, and it was also very multicultural. That meant a lot of different music could be heard, and songs in Malay, English and Aboriginal languages were played, exchanged and enjoyed, and the TI lugger crews added theirs to the mix.

When Seaman first heard 'Going Back Home', it made him nostalgic. It brought back pleasant memories of the importance of music in the social life of the itinerant lugger crews who worked a long way from home for extended periods:

Seaman Dan performing in Darwin, c. mid-1950s, [l–r] Peter Cardona, Seaman Dan and Div Collinson. Courtesy Joy Cardona.

> People had heard us singing at a party one night at a hotel [in Darwin] and they introduced us to some of the Broome people [there]. So I met some of the divers in Darwin before we went to Broome. Then, when we got to Broome, we met their families and they invited us to their parties whenever we were in port. I always had a guitar on board so I would take the guitar along and sing a few songs with the people in Broome. And they would get up and they would entertain us with their songs too, which was very good of them.

It was interesting to Seaman that, 50 years later, he was able to reconnect with Broome music — but from a younger generation of musicians, such as the Pigram Brothers, who took great pride in presenting their version of tropical north Australian Indigenous music. Like Seaman Dan, the Pigram Brothers also relied on ukulele, guitar and harmonica to create a tropical ambience, which made their music a natural fit for Seaman's vocal style, and his maritime and tropical themes.

'Waiting for the Ice Man'

'Waiting for the Ice Man' was mostly written on a long, uneventful drive from Darwin to Jabiru in the Northern Territory in 2002 while on the 'Steady Steady Backroads Tour'. It is a good example of how Seaman's songs could arise in mundane circumstances that nonetheless triggered memories, which then inspired lyrics and music.

> 'Waiting for the Ice Man'
>
> *Waiting for the ice man to come around / In the heat and the dust of old Darwin town / When you heat up oh yeah you gotta cool down / Working all week in the tropical sun / Weekend time you wanna have fun / When you heat up you gotta cool down / Saturday night at the Sunshine Club / Doing the waltz and the jitterbug / Rock'n'roll hula string-band too / Do any dance that you wanna do / Saturday night at the Sunshine Club / Jumping around with the one you love / Doing the Twist or singing the blues / Do any dance that you wanna do / When you heat up you gotta cool down / Waiting for the iceman comes around / In the pouring rain of old Darwin town / When you heat up oh yeah you gotta cool down / Working all week on a railway line / Party time you dress up fine / When you heat up oh yeah you gotta cool down.* (Seaman Dan and Karl Neuenfeldt)

Seaman and his band (Steve Gilbert, Karl Neuenfeldt and Jason Troutman), together with road manager Vic McGrath and a support crew comprising Will Kepa and Tibau Oui, were touring to remote and regional communities in Queensland and the Northern Territory. The 'Steady Steady Backroads Tour', with special guest Peter Brandy, visited Thursday Island, Mapoon, Aurukun, Coen, Wujal Wujal, Cooktown, Cairns, Burketown, Doomadgee, Mt Isa, Tennant Creek, Elliot,

Katherine, Darwin, Jabiru and Nhulunbuy. Artback NT, Arts Queensland, the Australia Council for the Arts and the Torres Strait Regional Authority supported the tour. It was a chance for Seaman to both take his music to new places and revisit places he had not seen for many decades, including Darwin.

'Waiting for the Iceman' was begun after Seaman had played the prestigious Darwin Festival, which in 2002 presented the themed event *String Bands and Shakehands: The Days of Old Darwin*. It featured dance troupes, singers and even a large rondalla band recreating the music of Darwin's multicultural communities. Seaman's old friend and entertainer Ted Egan compered the event, which was very well organised and attended. However, the next day's performance at Jabiru was a reality check — and an ego equaliser. As Seaman recalls:

> [At the] main festival in Darwin that previous night, there were about 20,000 people. The next day we were invited to go to Jabiru. It is a uranium mining town, so we rocked up there at the swimming pool [where the gig was] and there were six people! [Karl Neuenfeldt] said 'Uncle Seaman, there are only six people here.' And I said to him, 'Mate, if we can perform for 20,000 people we can perform for six people. Set 'em up!'

The song itself was written to the shuffle rhythm of a vehicle travelling at speed through open country. Cal Williams, the former guitarist with Yothu Yindi, was driving, which meant the band was free to relax, sleep or write. The song's lyrics were thematically based on Seaman's time in Darwin in the mid-1950s (discussed in Chapter 5), when he worked delivering ice for Koolpinyah Cool Stores. According to Seaman, 'My customers always greeted me with, "Here comes the Ice Man, Seaman Dan the Ice Man."' The lyrics also mention the Sunshine Club, a social club established by some Indigenous and non-European people because the Northern Territory's restrictive race laws barred or discouraged some of them from frequenting hotels and pubs. The lyrics to the song's chorus go: 'Saturday night at the Sunshine Club, doing the waltz and the jitterbug, rock and roll, hula, string-band too, do any dance if you wanna do; Seaman recollects: 'That's exactly what it was like.' The music and dancing had great variety, and the musicians had a crucial role in orchestrating the entertainment. Seaman also remembers the Jabiru performance because it was his seventy-third birthday, which was celebrated at the crocodile-shaped hotel, Gagudju, at Jabiru.

'Perfect Pearl'

The album's title track can be interpreted as a maritime-based metaphor for the rarity of a perfect romance.

'Perfect Pearl'

Diving in the deep blue sea / Searching for you / Searching for the perfect pearl / My perfect pearl / And when I find you in this sea so blue / I'll never let you go / My perfect pearl / In all this deep blue sea / Where the water runs free / There's lots of shells down there / To find a pearl so rare / Now that I found you / My perfect pearl / We'll share our dream for two / Do what we want to do / There's just you and me and the endless sea / Sailing peacefully to where we want to be / Diving in the deep blue sea / I was searching for you / Searching for the perfect pearl / Then I found you.
(Seaman Dan)

The song was inspired by a chance remark by Indigenous filmmaker Donna Ives, another example of how Seaman Dan's songs could arise out of everyday situations and conversations:

> [Donna] came up to interview me at Thursday Island from Townsville and she found out that I was an ex-pearl shell diver. So she started talking about my diving experiences and she asked me did I ever find any pearls at all? And I said, 'Well, [one season] me and my four young divers, out of 15,000 pearl shells we picked three second grade pearls.' Then she said to me, 'How about the perfect pearl?' I said, 'That is very rare.' And I also said, 'You know, you have just inspired me. One day I am going to write a song and I am going to call it "Perfect Pearl".'

Pearls from Thursday Island, 1921. Frank Hurley, National Library of Australia, image no. 3314159.

It comes as a surprise to many people that pearls are comparatively rare in nature, partly because nowadays pearls are artificially farmed and thus quite common, and also potentially much more uniform in shape and size. Today there is a successful pearl farming industry across tropical Australia, including in the Torres Strait; however, there is limited demand for the pearl shells themselves, and the divers required to harvest them are no longer needed to the extent they were in Seaman's working time.

Seaman admits that it had not occurred to him to write a song about pearls because they were secondary to the primary work of gathering pearl shells that he and other divers did as a matter of course. To them, it was not necessarily a romantic occupation, as often misportrayed, but a rather dangerous one that required mental focus and physical fitness. He says:

> Finding the perfect pearl … it had never occurred to me before. When you are working pearl shell, you are just thinking about pearl shell all of the time and nothing else.

Like romance, finding a pearl — let alone a perfect one — was uncommon but that did not stop the quest to do so.

'Frangipani'

'Frangipani' was written and composed by Alistair 'Azo' Bell — who had contributed 'Running Aground' to the *Steady Steady* album — and Billy Milroy. They both played in the Old Spice Boys band as the ukulele player and bassist respectively. Seaman liked the song because it was lyrically and musically interesting, but also because he likes the flower:

> Frangipani is one of my favourite flowers; it has a beautiful perfume. And I was very pleased that [the songwriters] gave us the opportunity to sing that song. I really appreciated that and I liked that song very much.

'Frangipani'

We're dancing in the early dawn / And walking beside the silver sea / And living in a bamboo house / With the sweet sweet scent of frangipani / Summer sun on endless waves / That come and go like all my days / Brown-skinned girls in their island home / Call me back from where I roam / As day turns into night / We're getting ready for that early morning flight. (Alistair 'Azo' Bell and Billy Milroy)

The song's tropical and maritime themed lyrics and its laidback musical style were a perfect fit for a natural crooner such as Seaman Dan. However, the song did present a musical challenge: Azo's original idiosyncratic ukulele part underlying the Old Spice Boys' version proved virtually impossible to replicate. It took several guitarists and many takes, and the aid of some judicious ProTools digital edits by Nigel Pegrum, to finally approximate Azo's unique instrumental style. 'Frangipani' could easily have been written and composed about life and love on TI, and that is one reason why Seaman found it so attractive.

'Red Shirt Day'

The song 'Red Shirt Day' came directly out of a casual conversation Seaman had at the Torres Hotel on TI with Rachel, a bar attendant. As mentioned in Chapter 6, he lives on Horn Island, a short ferry ride from TI that takes about 20 minutes. The ferry normally runs during daylight hours, which means that if the last ferry is missed, you have to find a place on TI to stay overnight. Seaman explains:

> On a Saturday I was invited to go to a barbecue on Thursday Island. We had a good barbecue, I sang a few songs there and it was late when we finished and I missed the ferry [back to Horn Island] completely. So I stayed at a friend's place [on TI] Saturday night. Sunday morning, I thought I better go down early to catch the ferry, but after that barbecue I woke up late and I got a taxi down[town]. The Torres Hotel was open and I thought I may as well dive in there and catch the next ferry back to Horn Island. The Torres is one of my favourite hotels on TI so I walked in and [Rachel] is behind the bar and I said, 'Morning, Rachel.' She said, 'Good morning, Uncle Seaman.' She said, 'I feel sad today.' I asked, 'Why?' She said, 'When I work on a Sunday I feel sad, so I wear this bright red shirt.' And I said, 'Yes, you have a nice bright red shirt on, Rachel.' She said, 'That is to put a smile on my face so I can put a smile on the patrons' faces.'

The conversation itself may have been short and quite unremarkable, but it inspired Seaman to start writing immediately:

> The Torres Hotel also has a TAB [Totalisator Agency Board betting outlet] in the bar, so I got a ticket and started writing away … And Rachel said, 'Uncle, you're writing a song. What's it about?' I said, 'My girl, it is about your bright red shirt, your pretty red shirt, but I haven't got the middle part, just the verses, the first and the last verses. When I go back home to Horn Island, I'll finish the song and Tuesday I'll come back. I have a little tape recorder so I'll tape it and bring it back and I'll play it for you, the full song.' She said, 'What are you going to call it?' I said, 'Oh well, it is about your bright red shirt so I'm going to call it "Red Shirt Day".' So that's how 'Red Shirt Day' started.

The final song incorporated the original inspiration but also broadened out into a song about staying optimistic even if life can sometimes seem restrictive or sad:

'Red Shirt Day'

Put on your brightest colour it's a red shirt day / Be cheerful and be happy and enjoy your stay / Please don't feel down-hearted put a smile on your face / Today is a red shirt day / Today it could be sunny tomorrow rain / If your loved one calls you honey you can smile again / No matter where you are reaching for that falling star / Today is a red shirt day / Look at all the people around you / Jumping up and down with glee / Everyone's singing and dancing / So why cannot we? / When you think you want to travel / To go from A to B / To Brisbane or to Sydney or maybe overseas / Cross over you rover you have your destiny / Today is a red shirt day. (Seaman Dan)

The song also had a unique performance at the National Folk Festival in Canberra in 2006, when the festival declared a Red Shirt Day. Seaman performed it live on national radio and when he went over to the sports oval there in the grandstand were hundreds of choir singers all wearing red shirts — something totally unimaginable when the song was inspired during a pub conversation on TI in far north Queensland. And what did Rachel think of the song when she heard it? Seaman says with pride: 'I played it for her at the bar and she was all smiles!'

'TI Taxi Driver'

As described in Chapter 6, among the many jobs Seaman did during his working life was taxi driving on TI, a very small town with only a few kilometres of road that encircles most of the island. Because of the shortage of public transport such as buses and the relatively large population, taxi drivers got to know many people in the community, and also found out a fair bit about their personal lives and activities, and also what went on behind the scenes. The song's lyrics mention some of his taxi-driving friends (Alan Filewood, Victor Joseph, Ron Laifoo, the late Raymond Pau and the late Ron Viti), and also allude to the kinds of fares they might have in a normal working week.

'TI Taxi Driver'

[Taxi talk: 'Seaman Dan here. Can I get a taxi to the Mangrove Hotel please?'] TI taxi driver going round and round / A giant traffic circle in a tiny town / Knows everybody's business / What's going on / TI taxi driver going round and round / Ronny's parked under the almond tree / Eating kaikai *[food] from Mary's Bakery / Waiting for another call to come / Just enough time for a sweet cream bun / Victor's doing a late pub run / Friday night and everybody's having fun / But he knows he's got to work late / And get up in the morning in the taxi by eight / Raymond likes to sit and play his guitar / Loves to play music more than driving that car / Then before he knows it the car phone rings / Boss says 'hurry up! You come pick up dis ting, wa' [yes]*

/ Alan's working hard on pension day / Then he hears 'hey driver you going our way? / We only live across the street but your cool taxi sure beats the heat / [Taxi talk: 'This is Seaman Dan again. Can I get a taxi to the Mangrove Hotel please?'] [Taxi talk: 'This is Seaman Dan here. I'm gonna walk home.']
(Seaman Dan, Steve Gilbert and Karl Neuenfeldt)

Much of the song is factual. On TI, there is an Aunt Mary's Bakery and a shady almond tree on the foreshore near the Ken Brown sports oval. With four pubs, Friday nights were very busy, and sometimes shoppers with very many bags would take a taxi for just a few blocks, especially during the hot and humid summer months. What is not factual is an actual Mangrove Hotel. That was a term for the mangroves where Indigenous people would go for a few drinks in earlier eras when they were barred from the pubs because of the restrictions on who was, or was not, allowed in a hotel or pub.

Seaman enjoyed recording the song because it came out of his own working experiences and was also a tribute to his taxi-driving friends. It was also fun recording the song's dialogue, which was done after the musical parts were completed. The owner of several TI taxis, Ron Laifoo, helped out by letting Seaman sit in one taxi parked downtown right next to another with co-producer Karl Neuenfeldt in it with a microphone and tape recorder. Then the two talked back and forth on the taxis' phones and recorded different bits of dialogue. As it was midday, the taxis were still open for business, so several incoming calls were also received. One caller actually hung up their phone as it probably sounded to them as if something odd was going on with the taxis because of Seaman's and Karl's dialogue going on at the same time as their call. The sound of that phone being hung up was inadvertently recorded too, and its 'beep, beep, beep' can be heard at the very end of the song. The song's other dialogue by Seaman's old friends Cessa Nakata and Ina Titasey as 'passengers', and by actor and musician Charles Passi as the 'boss', was recorded at another time, when backing vocals were recorded on TI by co-producer and audio engineer Nigel Pegrum. 'TI Taxi Driver' has proved to be one of Seaman's most popular recorded songs: it is up-tempo, musically varied, funny, full of local people and a real slice of life about taxi drivers and their clients 'going round and round [on] a giant traffic circle in a tiny town'.

'Watching the Weather'
'Watching the Weather' came out of stories Seaman told about life at sea for the men working on pearling luggers. A small lugger crew commonly had two experienced divers, two divers' tenders, an engineer, a deckhand, a cook and maybe one or two learner divers. It was part of everybody's job to watch closely for signs of what changes the weather might bring.

'Watching the Weather'

Divers down getting shell / Tender watches the ocean swells / Out on the reef / Frigate birds flying high / Captain sees and gives a sigh / Out on the reef / Watching the weather / Day in day out / Watching the weather / As we come about / Seven men out on the sea / Work as one quietly / Watching the weather / The sun is up / The moon is low / The wind is rising time to go / From the reef / Heading south upon the tide / The rigging creaks as we glide / Shoreward bound / Home again with family / Getting ready to go to sea / Out on the reef / Sail again when tide is slack / Take our chances going back / Out on the reef. (Seaman Dan and Karl Neuenfeldt)

Seaman explains further the importance of watching the weather, such as the winds:

> When you are down below and the sea grass on the bottom just stand straight up and down, [then the winds at the surface are calm]. But when the wind starts to get stronger and the current starts to run stronger, you can see the seaweed on the bottom as it starts to sway backwards and forwards. And you can feel that sideways surge underneath; you are moving sideways, backwards and forwards. You know there is going to be a change in the weather then and they notice it up top there [on deck]. And they watch the clouds if they are moving fast.

The crew members also look for signs from the natural world, such as birds — especially frigate birds:

> They are way up high when the weather is fine. [With] better vision up top they can dive directly on to that fish. But when the weather is [getting] strong it starts up the top there, then they come down closer to the surface [and] you know there is going to be a change in the weather.

The luggers could be working out of sight of land sometimes far from shelter, leaving few options if caught in bad weather. But, as Seaman notes, the skipper would know where you could run to if you needed to get shelter: 'You have a chart there and you know your navigation and you use your compass and you can use your stars too.' Safety was of paramount concern, both above and below the sea, and 'Watching the Weather' recounts the obligations crew members had to each other and the trust they had to have in each other — after all, their lives and livelihoods depended on it.

'Veiga, Veiga'

'Veiga, Veiga' was recorded and produced in three locations in Australia and one in Papua New Guinea (PNG). Relatively inexpensive digital recording technology and the internet now allow music production to take place in different locales and with comparative ease compared with previously, when quality recording was usually limited to fixed facilities such as dedicated studios. The original song is in the Hula language from PNG's Central Province.

> 'Veiga, Veiga'
>
> *Avu rigo pie rigo omarai / Oi pene lavu mau mu / Oi ao mu uga magi maparara / Wau ne e pie rawa ali / Veiga veiga ge kamuna ao nai / Ao mu pane paru lele / Veiga veiga ge kamuna ao nai / Gima mu paa ne kala ro wau / E raka kala ka ge wala na / Alu maguli ra ge irau irau na / Gera kala ina ina ao rai / Avu ra nama ra pie gia ra.* English translation: *There are days when sea breeze is blowing / It can lull you off to sleep and so / All the good thoughts you may have within you now / Try and let them calm you down / If something goes wrong or bad things happen / Our lives are changed but we must carry on / And through our good deeds and through our kind words / We will gain much more than we may give / Memories memories when they come back to me / There's no need to be angry / Memories memories sweet ones I've been waiting for / I want them to stay with me a while.* (Denis Crowdy, Gere Rupa, Gima Rupa and Karl Neuenfeldt)

The song was brought to the *Perfect Pearl* album sessions by long-time musical collaborator Denis Crowdy, whose wife Gima Rupa and brother-in-law Gere Rupa are from the Central Province. Co-producer Karl Neuenfeldt had first heard the original song in 1996 in Port Moresby while working on a project with Denis. He recalled it when choosing songs with Seaman for the *Perfect Pearl* album. Seaman liked the original song because he had heard string band music on the PNG national radio network and in the villages when working in PNG decades before (as discussed in Chapter 6):

> I had been up to [PNG] with a mining company [prospecting for gold] in the Eastern Highlands, at Kainantu in the Goroka [area]. I spent six weeks up there, met up with the local people. We had four local carriers and you would talk Pisin [Pidgin] to them. It took a bit of understanding because we have a different pidgin language in the Torres Strait [Torres Strait Creole / Yumpla Tok] to what they have over in Papua New Guinea. But you get to learn it and you understand it. And when this song 'Veiga, Veiga' came along, I thought, 'Well, it is a challenge but I will accept that challenge.' I liked the tune and I put all my effort into it to make it sound the way it sounded [when completed].

The basic rhythm tracks were recorded in Cairns at Select Sound, with Denis Crowdy playing open-tuning guitars and an electric bass with muffled strings to approximate the sound of a PNG string-band. He had done a Masters degree in ethnomusicology on guitar tunings in villages in the Central Province, so he knew the string-band style very well. Seaman then did his lead vocals in English, translated from the Hula language. The recording was then sent to Denis at Macquarie University in Sydney to add his wife Gima's vocals. Next the recording was sent to Port Moresby PNG to have the late Tony Subam add Gere Rupa's vocals. Then it went back to Cairns and Nigel Pegrum took the recording to Thursday Island to add Torres Strait Islander backing vocals there. When all the parts came back to Nigel to mix, they required a bit of editing because there were different microphones and recording techniques used and the quality varied. However, the end result was worth the effort put into post-production. 'Veiga, Veiga' is unique: a multilingual and musically hybrid song conveying a positive message about trying to move on from hardship and personal disappointment.

'The Ukulele Waltz'

Although the *Perfect Pearl* album contains many pleasant iconic images of the tropics and maritime industries, it is not all sepia tinged — pretending there were not serious social and economic issues facing Indigenous people such as Seaman living in the Torres Strait region. Before they were abandoned in the 1970s, Queensland's race-based laws affected not only day-to-day life but also personal relationships. This could be problematic within a community such as TI, with its large population of people of mixed heritage — some Indigenous, some not. 'The Ukulele Waltz' addresses those issues, but in an indirect way.

> 'The Ukulele Waltz'
>
> *The ukulele waltz at the mangrove hotel / I remember remember the music so well / We'd all be ashore when the spring tide arrived / Instead of the ocean the dance floor we'd ride / There was a bass man and mandolin / Two beach guitars and a sweet violin / Playing and singing and doing so well / Ukulele waltzing at the mangrove hotel / There was music and dancing until half-light / Then we'd sit on the beach and laugh with delight / Each of us had our own story to tell / About ukulele waltzing at the mangrove hotel / Birds and the bees they fly through the trees / Chirping and buzzing as free as the breeze / Everyone's happy at the sound of church bells / While ukulele waltzing at the mangrove hotel.* (Seaman Dan and Karl Neuenfeldt)

Seaman recalls what inspired the song's underlying legal contexts, one about age and another about race:

> You had to be 21. Then you can go into the hotel. One of our mates on board, he was 21 and I am 18 and the other boys are 17 or 18. We were on £15 a month so when we come into port after six weeks out at sea we get an advance of £5 so we would all dob in and get our [21-year-old] mate to go into the hotel and get some refreshment for us. So, we would have to go somewhere else, secluded, away from the public eye. The only place that we could get out of everyone's vision was in the mangroves.

> That was it; we were in the mangroves. That was our hotel! There was sand flies and there was no mosquito repellent in those days so we just kept on drinking refreshments until you are numb, you can't feel any bites at all!

The other legal restraint was race. Some people on TI were allowed in pubs and some were not, depending on whether they were classified 'under the Act'. Technically, Indigenous people were not allowed in pubs, which created a dilemma for people of mixed heritage — including Indigenous heritage. For example, with which heritage would a person identify? What was the situation for maritime crews who worked together for months at sea, yet were unable to socialise while ashore on TI? Seaman recalls:

> We call it [being] 'under the Act', mainly the Torres Strait Islanders that live up in the islands and the Aborigines. Growing up, you're still a child and you don't worry about the alcohol part of it. It doesn't make any difference until you get about 17 or 18 … You're working on a pearling vessel … You take all those risks [when] you go down for the pearl shells but it's an entirely different situation when you're ashore and you want to go into the hotel for a drink.

Regardless of the discrimination and humiliation encountered by Torres Strait Islander and Aboriginal people, Seaman acknowledges that overt racism such as that which existed 'under the Act' has diminished over his lifetime. The imaginery Mangrove Hotel, along with all it symbolised, is now a memory recounted in song. By way of contrast, in 2010 he performed at a large-scale display of Torres Strait Islander culture, *The Torres Strait Islands: A Celebration*, in Brisbane. It was presented simultaneously at the Queensland Gallery of Modern Art, the Queensland Museum and the Queensland State Library from 2–8 July 2010. He not only felt honoured to perform at the event, but was delighted that his culture was actually the focus of celebration rather than a culture on the fringes of Queensland and Australian societies:

> I was moved and very much appreciated how far we've come. And we had an appreciative audience from all walks of life [and] generations. There was Europeans, Indigenous [and] everyone was smiling. It was a happy day, a really happy day, and it really moved me. I thought to myself, 'Well, we are getting there.' [When I was younger], I had no idea it would come to that, that particular [kind of] day.

'Magic Carpet of Pearls'

Seaman has a large extended family, including many grandchildren and great-grandchildren. He admits: 'I've lost count of great-grandchildren. Last count was 14. It was 20 grandchildren, could be more now. I love them all. 'Magic Carpet of

Pearls' is a children's fantasy song about travelling on an imaginary carpet of pearls through the magnificent night skies of the Torres Strait.

> **'Magic Carpet of Pearls'**
>
> *On a magic carpet of pearls / Let's say we go for a whirl / Fly up to Mars / All through the stars / Then on to Venus / Let no meteors come between us / Visit the Milky Way / Say hi to a falling star / See the man-in-the-moon / Must get home pretty soon / Just remember where you are / When eating rainbow candy bars / On a magic carpet of pearls / I can see the sun will soon be rising / Must be nearly time to go home / Little teddy bears are still sleeping / No more outer space will we roam / On a magic carpet of pearls / On a magic carpet of pearls / We immensely enjoyed our whirl / We say farewell to Mars / All the other stars / Farewell to Venus / No meteor came between us / On a magic carpet of pearls.* (Seaman Dan and Karl Neuenfeldt)

Because it was a children's song, a group of youngsters was invited into the studio to sing along. They included Emily Bonham, Vicky Gray, siblings Stacee, Franceen and Thomas Ketchell, Royce Mau, Courtney Plasto, Natasha Springer and Brandon Winship. Producing youngsters can be a challenge, because they generally have a very short attention span and recording can be a repetitive and at times boring process. However, Nigel Pegrum had recorded many children's groups, so with a bit of prompting they gave a spirited performance that is certainly authentic in the context of a children's song.

'Minna Murra Moon'

Between the mid-1880s and 1941, there was a steady stream of passenger boats stopping at TI when travelling between Australia and the Orient, including destinations such as the Dutch East Indies, Malaya, the Philippines, China and Japan. The boats also brought with them performance troupes. Consequently, from the colonial era, TI had a steady influx of entertainments mirroring the popular culture and technologies in circulation. These included bioscopes, lantern shows, light opera, clairvoyants, dancers, skaters and intriguing cultural fare such as the touring 1903 *Land of the Maori*, complete with music, song and scenery. One romanticised image of travel by sea was the potential for shipboard romances, and 'Minna Murra Moon' recounts one such imagined scenario.

> **'Minna Murra Moon'**
>
> *Minna minna murra moon / Midnight on the ocean / Minna minna murra moon / Dancing in slow motion / We were on a slow boat bound for China / And we met each other just by chance / Now you come to me with a smile in your eyes / You say you love me and from me the same applies / Minna minna murra moon / Midnight on the ocean / Minna minna murra moon /*

MV *Marella*, a Burns Philp passenger boat servicing TI and other ports in Australia and South-East Asia, undated c.1920s–1930s. Courtesy of Torres Strait Historical Society.

Dancing in slow motion / We see islands shimmer in the distance / And tiny boats along the shore / Some day we'll remember / The thrill of it all / You and me in the moonlight is what we'll recall / Minna minna murra moon / Midnight on the ocean. (Seaman Dan, Denis Crowdy, Karl Neuenfeldt and Wendy Rattenbury)

'Minna Murra' was the name of a property owned by Chris Lawe-Davies and Dinah Hall at Iluka on the north coast of New South Wales; it incidentally also means 'many fish' in the local Aboriginal language. The song also includes an oblique reference to a well-known song from the late 1940s, 'I'd Like to Get You on a Slow Boat to China'. Written by Frank Loesser, it was a hit record in Australia in 1949. Seaman remembers seeing large passenger boats at TI as a child, such as the MV *Merkur*, a Burns Philp boat servicing Australia and Hong Kong, and the MV *Marella*, also a Burns Philp boat but servicing Australia, Java and Singapore. He also recalls that sometimes passengers on the boats would visit the convent school on TI:

> The nuns they gave us music lessons [at the school] and we would all get on the front veranda and sing for the visitors.

Up to the start of the Pacific war in 1941, the local TI newspaper was advertising trips to the Orient. Sadly, some TI people with Asian family connections went for visits there and were caught in occupied Japanese territories for the war's duration, with some having problems later trying to return to Australia. Over TI's history as a port, passenger boats played a key role in maintaining it as a cosmopolitan place with a steady inflow of goods, ideas, people and popular culture, such as music. TI is once again a destination for passenger boats, and occasionally Indigenous entertainment is arranged for them, including Seaman and a local dance group.

'Islander Drums/Warraber'

Occasionally a song in its simplest form — maybe just voice and a guitar — can suggest a particular setting that can be built upon musically with fuller production. 'Islander Drums/Warraber', by Father Dalton Bon, is one such song. Seaman first heard Father Bon play and sing it in Canberra at a National Museum event, and it immediately joined the list of possible songs for the *Perfect Pearl* album. Seaman liked it because, 'It's got that nice rhythm to it and I really like the island words in there, Torres Strait Islander words [in Meriam Mir].'

> #### 'Islander Drums/Warraber'
>
> *Wa [Yes] / I'd like to take a trip to an island in the sun / To the island of blue lagoons / And from the waters it can be heard / The sound of Islander drums / I know my brown-skinned girl is waiting for me / On the pearly beaches of TI / When she sees me come-in she do the hula-twist / And I cuddle her up in my arms / Wai Warraber keriba ged e / Wai Warraber keriba ged e / Mari debe sager wag gi de na mulie / Warraber keriba ged e / Sik tedimrida / Zeuber / Boomer / Mari / Breaka ge tabarapeda ge / Summary translation of Meriam Mir lyrics: Oh Warraber our dear home land / You are being entertained by the southeast wind / Oh Warraber our dear home land / The sweet smiles of the seas and their laughter caresses your beautiful shores.*
> (Father Dalton Bon)

Before becoming a cleric, Father Bon had worked at Warraber Island, also known as Sue Island, in the Central Island cluster of Torres Strait. He was inspired to write the song when he was returning to the island after going fishing on the reefs, and could hear the island drums — the hourglass-shaped *warup/buruburu* drums — from far out at sea. Seaman remembers visiting many of the islands in the Torres Strait region, including Warraber, while working on the pearling luggers. The crews would occasionally 'come-in' to a community if they needed supplies, or the weather was bad, but there were protocols to observe when visiting:

> We would go ashore, just for a visit. Show your respect to the councils there, the people there. They appreciate you going ashore so you say hello. You do not want to be standoffish, [such as] 'I am this and I am that'. No, no, it don't happen up there.

Seaman also recalls that some crew members met their future girlfriends and even wives on those short visits:

> My engineer [at the time], Tony Tardent, an ex-croc shooter in the Northern Territory, [and I] were working the Darnley Deeps. [It was] spring tide so you can't anchor out at the work area, it is too deep, 30 fathoms. So we [would] always run in to Darnley [Erub] and anchor

there. When it is work time, nobody goes ashore, everybody stays on board. When it is the spring tide you can go ashore. So this particular weekend, Saturday after work we race in … and we are invited to go to this school dance. Tony is a white boy and I introduce him to my cousin, Wasie (née Kiwat), and they got on famously together. This was 1963. [Then] we signed off, got paid and finished [for the season]. The next thing I hear they both got married and they are still together today!

Nigel Pegrum recorded the song's backing vocals on TI, and recalls that Gabriel Bani, Tony Ghee and Charles Passi were very concerned to sing and pronounce the lyrics properly. Consequently, they consulted with Seaman Dan's songwriting collaborator Bua Mabo, a fluent Meriam Mir speaker. Just what kind of dance the 'hula-twist' was might not be clear — how would you combine the hula and the twist? — but nonetheless it conjures up an image of a unique dance. 'Islander Drums/Warraber' combines solo and ensemble voices with Torres Strait Islander percussion (*warup/buruburu* drums, *kulap/gor* rattles and *lumut/thram* bamboo slit drums), ukuleles and guitars. It also includes a wooden flute emulating a traditional flute historically played in the Eastern Islands of Torres Strait. The song recreates the kinds of local music and instruments Father Bon and Seaman would have heard many decades before across the Torres Strait region.

Building on the successes of the first two albums, *Follow the Sun* and *Steady Steady*, the *Perfect Pearl* album received widespread circulation and promotion through the efforts of Hot Records and Seaman's live performances. As noted earlier, it also received critical acclaim by winning the 2004 ARIA Award for Best World Music Album. It was a great honour for an elderly Indigenous singer-songwriter from remote Australia, and especially noteworthy because Seaman was the oldest Australian to win such a prestigious award. Starting his recording career at 70 years of age was not a drawback, as he had a full lifetime of experiences and adventures to draw upon — and, importantly, retained his unique singing voice. In fact, it got richer the more Seaman recorded, as was displayed on his next album, *Island Way*.

Seaman Dan receiving his 2004 ARIA award from then Premier of New South Wales and current Australian Foreign Minister, Bob Carr.

CHAPTER 11
Island Way

By his fourth album, *Island Way*, Seaman was well seasoned as a studio singer. The producers, Nigel Pegrum and Karl Neuenfeldt, were able to embellish his voice with full arrangements, courtesy of funding support from the Australia Council for the Arts and the Aboriginal and Torres Strait Islander Arts Board. The album's nomination for an ARIA Award for Best World Music Album (2005) validated their support of Seaman's talent.

The album was recorded at Nigel Pegrum's new recording facility, Pegasus Studios in Cairns, in 2005, and released by Steady Steady Music (TI1001), distributed by MGM/Planet. The core musicians from previous albums remained, but with the addition of Rick Cunha (lap steel guitar) and Dale Diefenbach and Jason Fox (trombone). Additional singers included Norah Bagiri, Cindy Drummond, Geoffrey Lui, Patrick Mau, Amelia and Carmel Pegrum, and Harry Rivers. Art design was by Louise Cook.

Island Way had two main themes. One was Seaman's musical links to the heritage of some of his ancestors. He is not at all unusual in having different heritages to draw upon. Many Torres Strait Islanders and TI people are descended from immigrants from Polynesia, Melanesia, Asia, Europe and the Caribbean, as well as from New Guinea and Cape York. The region has been truly multicultural since the 1870s, as a result of the maritime industries and colonial settlement patterns and governance. Traces of the various heritages can still be found in current cultural practices, such as the kinds of food eaten, the dance styles and the musical styles that Seaman in particular absorbed and adapted in his recordings. Another theme was the notion of how islands develop distinct cultures, and how they can exert a lifelong influence on a person. This sentiment is well expressed by Indigenous author Terri Janke in the following passage from *Butterfly Song* (2005):

> They say if you live on an island for too long, you merge with it. Your bones become the sands, your blood the ocean. Your flesh is the fertile ground. Your heart becomes the stories, dances, songs … They say when

you leave, the sounds of the waves stay with you … The island calls to you, and your children, and their children. It will beg for you to dream it, and know it, forever. No matter where you or your children travel, the island is home.

The *Island Way* album used the music of different Oceanic islands to celebrate not only their cultures, but also their influence on Seaman's life and music and the people of Torres Strait.

'Kapa Roa'ia Se Laloga'

Melanesian and Polynesian migrants from Oceania have had a strong influence in the Torres Strait region. The original migrants came mainly from what are now New Caledonia (the Loyalty Islands), the Solomon Islands, Vanuatu, Niue, the Cook Islands, Tonga, Samoa and Rotuma (now part of Fiji). One of the larger groups of migrants in the colonial era was the Rotumans, who came firstly to work in the maritime industries. They also brought with them their cultural practices, such as dance styles — adaptations of which still survive today — and their music — fragments of which also survive. To make a musical connection with the music of Oceania, an opportunity arose to record Seaman singing with a Rotuman choir that Nigel Pegrum and Karl Neuenfeldt had recorded in Fiji. They had done a collaborative project with the 40-member Rotuman Churchward Chapel Choir of Suva and the Oceania Centre for Arts and Culture at the University of the Pacific, then under the direction of the late Epeli Hau'ofa. Samuela Taukave was the choirmaster, and the late Reverend Iveni Fatiaki and Rotuman academic Makereta Mua were the liaison persons. One of the secular chants recorded, known as a *sua*, proved suitable for adaptation to Seaman's style.

'Kapa Roa'ia Se Laloga'

Kapa roa'ia se laloga / Ale poto koroa hiutug / Fakväre ne huag 'os Kunohoga / Fakanonoa Iova he'oa / My people came from Oceania / Across the sea I hear them call to me / Their voices sing of Oceania / So far away but they are family / My people came from Oceania / Across the sea I hear them sing to me. (Reverend Iveni Fatiaki, Seaman Dan and Karl Neuenfeldt)

Seaman recalls his emotions on hearing the original recording when it was under consideration as music to which he could add new lyrics: 'It really sort of stirred me up; my emotions were running high. It went right back to the Pacific and it made me think a lot about my heritage.'

The process of Seaman recording his vocals to the already recorded and mixed choir recording was a challenge for several musical reasons. First, the choir used no instruments so it was a capella, meaning Seaman had to get his pitching from the choir's key. Second, he has a very low voice and at the beginning of the song he

Performing at Central Queensland University, Bundaberg, 2002. Courtesy Tim Peek.

was at the very top of his vocal range. However, as the song progressed the singing got easier for some reason. It turned out the members of the choir had gone down together in pitch from the original pitching. Consequently, it was more comfortable for Seaman to sing by the end of the song because it was in a lower key.

The end result of the collaboration was interesting musically because of the juxtaposition of a large, trained choir and a solo voice — a musical format Seaman had never recorded before. But it was also interesting culturally because the song combined a communal chant in Rotuman with English-language lyrics from the personal perspective of one of the many descendants of Oceanic migrants to the Torres Strait region. The combination of the musical and cultural perspectives was one possible reason David Bridie used 'Kapa Roa'ia Se Laloga' in his soundtrack for the Australian Broadcasting Corporation's television series *The Straits* (2011).

'Let's Get to Where We Ain't'

'Let's Get to Where We Ain't' arose out of one of Seaman's conversational sayings: 'I only use that phrase when me and my friends get together and we have got to go to visit somewhere. So we look at each other and we say, 'Let's get to where we ain't!''

> #### 'Let's Get to Where We Ain't'
>
> *Every time I start to roam / Oh so glad to get back home / Let's get to where we ain't / On the Cape York highway / Let's get to where we ain't / Are you going my way? / Corrugations on the road / Shake and break my heavy load / Learn to love the taste of dust / Black and white and red as rust / Let's get to where we ain't / On the Tassie [Tasmania] railway / Let's get to where we ain't / Are you going my way? / Gig at night was freezing cold / Frozen fingers feeling old / Ten days we did the best we can / Warming up that Apple Island / Let's get to where we ain't / On the Tokyo subway / Let's get to where we ain't / Are you going my way? / Cherry blossoms on the ground / Everywhere urban sounds / Packed like sardines on the train / But I'd love to go back again.* (Seaman Dan and Karl Neuenfeldt)

The lyrics recount some of the traveling Seaman did with his touring band and the fact that TI was always home — a place to return to after some musical adventures. First, it recounts driving the length of Cape York Peninsula on the 'Steady Steady Backroads Tour' in 2002. The main roads on the Cape are mostly unimproved, and on gravel surfaces corrugations build up, making for a very bumpy ride at times. The Cape roads also have lots of dusty stretches, and when travellers arrive in Cairns it is easy to tell where they have been travelling by the colour of the dust on their vehicles, clothing and shoes. Some dust is also very fine, and seeps into a vehicle no matter how well sealed it appears to be. Being on the Cape was special for Seaman because he had lived and worked there: 'It was really great to see the people, to visit the place again as an entertainer. Everyone was happy to see me and likewise, me to see them.'

Second, the lyrics recount Seaman and his band performing in Tasmania for the Ten Days on the Island Festival in 2005. While doing performances across northern Tasmania (Flinders Island, St Marys, Hobart), he saw railway lines on a drive from Launceston to St Marys, where the performance was outside. It was a very cold night — so cold you could see the musicians' breath as they sang and played. Being from the tropics, it was particularly cold for Seaman: 'It was cold [which made it] hard singing, but I got through it.'

Third, the lyrics recount travelling to the 2005 World Expo at Aichi in Japan for Queensland Week at the Australian Pavilion. The cherry trees were in blossom so it was a beautiful time to be in Japan and meet people from all over the world. Travelling on the trains was something new for Seaman, as they were very crowded compared with Australian trains. However, people were also very polite in the confined and congested space, and tried not to stare too much at some of the Torres Strait Islanders in the delegation, who literally stood heads above the crowd. Because Seaman had many friends from Torres Strait with Japanese ancestry, it was a chance to appreciate their home country and culture. Seaman remembers:

> For me [Japan] was an eye opener ... the people were so friendly and the city we were in, Nagoya, is so clean. There's not a matchstick or a piece of paper on the footpath, so clean. Entertaining there, you might not speak the same language, understand each other conversation-wise but through music, we both understand each other. And I was happy to see the people crowding around the stage and taking photos, the cameras were clicking! When we would finish a performance they would get us together, us performers, and take photographs. Oh, it was very nice to see people like that.

At the 2005 World Expo, Seaman also got the chance to perform for the then Premier of Queensland, Peter Beattie, and his wife, Heather. Coincidently, her father, David Scott-Halliday, had been an Anglican clergyman at St Paul's community in the Torres Strait. Wherever Seaman travelled, he was surprised at how many people had connections with the region, and also how many relatives — close and distant — he had across Australia. Through his performing, he also had the chance to meet Australian national politicians such as ex-Prime Minister Kevin Rudd, ex-Premier of Queensland Anna Bligh and ex-Premier of New South Wales and now Foreign Minister Bob Carr, as well as many state and local politicians and dignitaries, which was exciting for someone from a very remote part of the country. Having a recording career provided Seaman with a chance not only to have his music heard, but also to learn about the wider world in which he had always been intensely interested.

'Ailan Man'

Like 'Veiga Veiga' on the *Perfect Pearl* album, 'Ailan Man' — 'island man' in Torres Strait Creole/Yumpla Tok — was another song with an international connection. It was co-written and co-composed by Seaman, Bernard Fernandes (a West Indian-Canadian musician and educator living in Vancouver, Canada), Seaman's grandson, Patrick Mau (also known by the hip-hop moniker Mau Power), and Karl Neuenfeldt. The idea arose from Seaman's desire to link the generations of his extended, and very international and multicultural, family via music, and also via their maritime connections to 'treasures from the sea'.

Seaman Dan with his grandson, Patrick Mau (also recording as Mau Power), on the cover of the single release of 'Ailan Man', their song about their family's heritage.

'Ailan Man'

Great grand-dad came from Jamaica / He was a black man Jamaican black man / He came sailing on the seven seas / Hard of hand a sailor man / Taking treasures from the sea / Great grandma came from the Loyalties / A woman fine of a chiefly line / Sad goodbye to her family / Urgent need many mouths to feed / With treasures from the sea / Many many ships came sailing to the Torres Strait / Many many men went diving down below / They could see women and children / Watching from the shore / Wondering if the men came back once more / My grand-dad came from Polynesia / From Niue he came to stay / Tahega Toa was his island name / Light of hand dancing music man / With tales of treasures of the sea / My ama [mother] Dan was an [island] gel / Strong and kind of a single mind / Taught me how to work and play / Cooked and cleaned / Raised me 'til eighteen / I gave her treasures from the sea / Many many smiling faces / Shining in the Torres Strait / Many many yumpla family close to me / I can see my ancestors / Sailing on the seven seas / So many many yumpla family just like me [Patrick Mau] / This is the story of this one blood / Yupla ai go lessen prom dis ailan man / Sa here's a story 'bout a long long journey / A story of my ancestors my grand-dad told me / How they sailed across the deep blue seas / Warrior chiefs it was told in my history / Bringing treasures of unknown waters to the world / Like mai athe [grandfather] ai bin spik wi ol perfect pearls / So that quest found its way to the perfect place / Wa [Yes] this paradise called the Torres Strait. (Seaman Dan, Bernard Fernandes, Patrick Mau and Karl Neuenfeldt)

The lyrics provide a brief overview of some members of Seaman's extended family, and also recount their migrations to the Torres Strait region. Seaman considers the song a family song, a 'family get-together'. As noted earlier, his great-grandfather, Douglas Pitt Snr, was an African-American from Kingston, Jamaica; his great-grandmother, Sopa, was a Melanesian from Lifou Island in the Loyalty Islands of New Caledonia; and his grandfather, Sam Savage, was a Polynesian from what is now called Niue, but was then known as the Savage Islands (also see Chapter 1).

In the lyrics, Seaman's grandson, Patrick Mau, also cleverly links the new song to another song of his grandfather's, 'Perfect Pearl', which was the third album's title song. As well as being a hip-hop artist and radio broadcaster, Patrick also knows the sea well from his work as a crayfish diver and on the barges servicing Torres Strait. Seaman was very proud to have Patrick involved in the song:

> It was something different and much more personal for me because he is my grandson, number two grandson. And out of 20 grandchildren, he is the only one that takes after me in music, even though it is rap. But it is still some kind of music to me and I like it too. I am very proud of him.

Family connections in the Torres Strait regions can be complex, given the often-large families of previous generations and also the mingling of people from all over the world, and Seaman's family is a good example. Now that the majority of Torres Strait Islanders live outside the region, even more complexity has been added to all-important family, island home and ancestral connections.

'Blues on a Ukulele'

Although Seaman himself was not a ukulele player, the instrument was a part of his musical heritage growing up on TI, where it was played and enjoyed by many people because of its simplicity and affordability. It also had a strong connection to the Hawaiian music and dance that was popular in Seaman's youth. When he started his recording career, it became one of the instrumental signatures of his 'sound', and figured prominently in many of his recordings and live performances. The ukulele itself was developed in the 1880s, and combines features of the rajoa and the cavaquinho, little guitar-like instruments that were brought to Hawaii by Portuguese Madieran migrants. Interest in the ukulele had had several revivals, the most recent one being in the 1990s. A major figure in that revival was Jim Beloff, a musician, songwriter and marketer of ukuleles on the fleamarketmusic.com website. Along with the virtuosic Hawaiian ukulele player Herb Ohta Snr, he provided two songs for the *Island Way* album. 'Blues on a Ukulele' asks whether it is possible to play blues on a ukulele. Because of its small size and stereotypic image as a simple instrument with a light-hearted sound, it is not usually associated with the blues — except perhaps for the blue skies and seas of its Hawaiian homeland.

> 'Blues on a Ukulele'
>
> *They say you can't play blues on a ukulele / But there they are wrong / You went away / And this is all I play / My ukulele sad song / They say you can't cry and play a ukulele / Well what do they know? / I start to strum and soon the tears will come / And then the blues just follow / They say that there's no happier sound / That's not the case when you're not around / They say you can't play blues on a ukulele / But since we're apart / Oh from that day / I can only play the strings of my broken heart.* (Jim Beloff and Herb Ohta)

Seaman has always liked the laid-back ambience established by the ukulele because it complements his crooner vocal style and is often associated with tropical environments. 'Blues on a Ukulele' is a fine example of the melding of the versatility of the instrument and Seaman's rich, velvety voice.

'Old Men and the Sea'

Friendships have always been very important for Seaman, and with 'Old Men and the Sea' he pays tribute to three of his lifelong friends, all of whom worked in the maritime industries of the Torres Strait region. Ali Drummond was a fisherman, Tommy Nakata was a boat-builder and Budden Ah Mat was a stern-tender on a pearling lugger.

> 'Old Men and the Sea'
>
> *Old men young again / Old men young again / Ur ma iguseda peibri pekem iguseda / Ali had the arms of a fisherman / The legs of a sailor / For so long a time he lived from the riches of the sea / Working sunrise to sunset on the turn of tides / With hooks and lines and nets he made his living / Once he was a young man / Now he is an old man / But his eyes shine bright when he talks about the sea / And he caught with his hands / The fish that fed the islands / Ali Drummond is a young man when he talks about the sea / Tommy had the arms of a fisherman / The legs of a sailor / Sunburnt brown from hard work on the sea / Sailing the waters of northeast Australia / From the islands of New Guinea to the coast of Queensland / Once he was a young man / Now he is an old man / But his eyes shine bright when he talks about the sea / And he built with his hands / The ships that sail the islands / Tommy Nakata is a young man when he talks about the sea / Ur ma iguseda peibri pekem iguseda / Old men young again / Old men young again / Budden had the arms of a fisherman / The legs of a sailor / Stern tender on a TI pearling lugger / From daylight to dusk / He's a man they can trust / As*

his divers walk the ocean in perpetual motion / Once he was a young man / Now he is an old man / But his eyes shine bright when he talks about the sea / And he held in his hands / The lives of many a diver / Budden Ahmat is a young man when he talks about the sea / Old men young again / Ur ma iguseda peibri pekem iguseda. (Seaman Dan, Karl Neuenfeldt and Kyana-Lili Neuenfeldt Pearson)

For Seaman, as he and his friends reach old age, getting together is important for the companionship and also the memories: 'Yes, [it is] good to get together and talk about our early days, our young days out doing what we used to do and sort of memorising all of the good times that we had.' While getting together provides an opportunity for old men to feel young again, it can also be bittersweet — both sad and happy. Even though Seaman and some of his friends are, as he says 'still on deck', when they meet up they recall 'all of those friends that we have lost, that have gone and just a few of us are left. And we always get an instrument out and we try to forget about things. You know, the sad part [of life]. We just carry on because we're still on deck, so we just keep on.'

Regardless of his old friends ageing and slowing down physically, Seaman emphasises that they learnt to trust in each other when out at sea working:

> You had to trust each other, for the safety of everyone on board. And as a skipper, you are responsible for everyone on board so you've got to think of everyone's safety. The ship has got to be right and your running gear, your sail, your rigging, everything has got to be checked every day, nothing left unchecked. That is for safety because when you are out at sea, if something goes wrong, there is nowhere to fix it. You have about a 50 or 60 miles [80–95 kilometres] sail back into port again, against the heavy seas. So any spare time that you have, everything has got to be checked.

Not only did many lives depend on trust, but social cohesion did too, because of the interrelatedness of some crews. A tragedy for any one of them would have had repercussions throughout extended families and the wider community.

'The Hawaiian Turnaround'

Along with 'Blues on a Ukulele', Jim Beloff and Herb Ohta Snr also provided 'The Hawaiian Turnaround', a musical tribute to Honolulu and Hawaii but also a musical riff common in some Hawaiian music.

'The Hawaiian Turnaround'
When you arrive at Honolulu there's an unmistakeable sound / Everywhere that music is found / It's the Hawaiian turnaround / Kind of a vamp / You'll hear it at the start and end of many a song / And you'll find you're humming

Seaman Dan at the Society for Ethnomusicology's 2006 Honolulu conference event, 'Honoring our Elders: A Concert by Hawai'i's National Heritage Fellows'. He had brought Torres Strait pearl shells as gifts, and was invited on stage to present them to the elders. [l–r] Seaman Dan, Barbara B Smith, Uncle Richard Ho'opi'i, the late Auntie Genoa Keawe and the late Seisho 'Harry' Nakasone.

along / Beautiful views every direction / Tropical hues / Picture perfection / Paradise found each time you turn around / When you get home the moment that your feet are finally touching the ground / In your heart you're paradise bound / It's the Hawaiian turnaround. (Jim Beloff and Herb Ohta)

Seaman liked the song when he first heard it, partly because he 'always liked Hawaiian songs', but also because he got a chance to travel to Hawaii in 2006 to attend the Society for Ethnomusicology conference at the University of Hawaii (Manoa) in Honolulu. In particular, he remembers fondly how Hawaiian music was associated with hula dancing on TI:

> Before the Second World War on TI, my cousin, Florence [Flo] Kennedy [née Savage] she used to do a lot of hula. And they had a windup gramophone and they had Sol Ho'opi'i playing Hawaiian songs and she used to do the hula to that, to the records. And Ketchell Anno, another [TI musician of] Malaysian ancestry, he used to play the slide steel guitar. He would play that [and] she would do the hula to that music [too]. And there would be others with acoustic guitar and the ukulele and she used to perform at the old town hall on TI [the Victoria Memorial Institute Hall]. Oh, it was really good and that was what made me [familiar with Hawaiian music]. You know, you grew up with that sort of music and it is in you all the time.

When Seaman got to Hawaii, he also had the good fortune to meet accomplished Hawaiian musicians such as the falsetto singer Richard Ho'opi'i. He recollects,

'I was thinking to myself, now I am seeing and hearing the real thing. It's not on record anymore. It's alive. And I was very much pleased and proud to be there.' As a visiting Indigenous elder, Seaman was also invited on stage at the ethnomusicology conference's major concert, and presented other music elders there with gifts, including the Hawaiian music legend the late 'Aunty' Genoa Leilani Adolpho Keawe-Aiko. Then 86 years old, she was still an excellent entertainer and singer. Seaman remembers: 'I gave her a pair of pearl shells from the Torres Strait … I've still got a photo, it is on my feature wall [at home on Horn Island].'

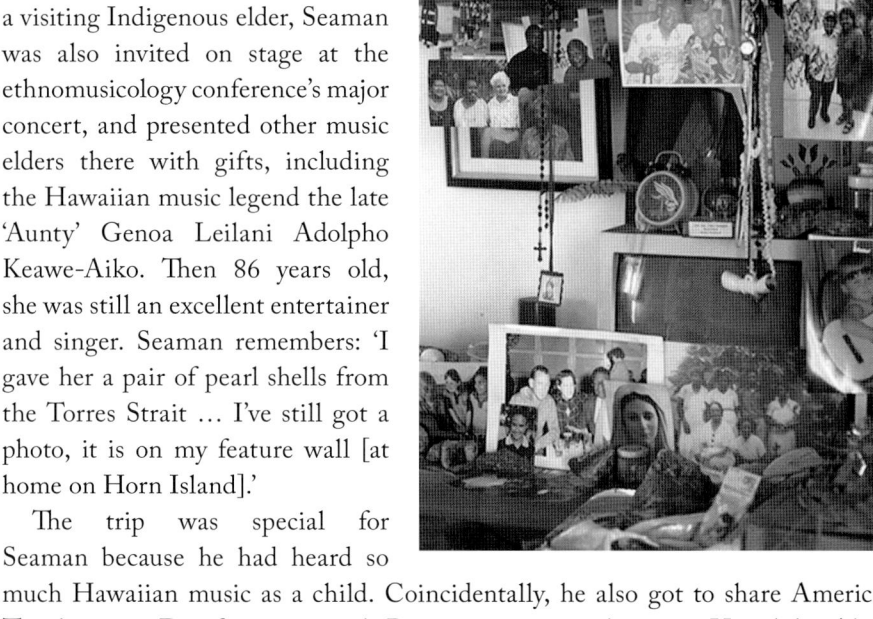

Seaman Dan's feature wall of memorabilia at his home on Horn Island. Courtesy Polly Hemming

The trip was special for Seaman because he had heard so much Hawaiian music as a child. Coincidentally, he also got to share American Thanksgiving Day festivities with Rotuman migrants living in Honolulu. Along with the traditional meal of roast turkey, cranberry sauce and pumpkin pie, he also got to sample a traditional Melanesian drink: kava. Perhaps kava and turkey dinner is an odd combination, but travelling as a well-regarded musician led to many new and unexpected experiences for Seaman.

'Rhythm of the Hula'

In its various localised forms, hula is ubiquitous across Oceania, as well as elsewhere such as Japan, North America and Europe. Although not traditional hula as in its natal Polynesian cultures, it is perhaps popular because of its inherent grace but also its association with tropical tourist destinations: warm weather, white sandy beaches and deep blue seas. Norfolk Island singer-songwriter George 'Toofie' Christian is a descendant of Fletcher Christian, the HMS *Bounty* mutineer. By way of tribute, he wrote 'Rhythm of the Hula' after returning home from seeing diverse hula styles at the 1992 Pacific Festival of the Arts in Rarotonga, in the Cook Islands. The Norfolk Island version of hula reminded Toofie of terns flying in synchronised movements along the rocky cliffs of Norfolk Island.

'Rhythm of the Hula'

Let d' rhythm fe de hula / Go out through d' Pacific / From Hawai'i to New Zealun' / Let et flow orn through / Hula hula hula / Let et flow orn through / Beat it out irn a drums / Guitar en a ukulele too / Sem as two tern play'n / How gud fe woach it moowe / Woach wun palm when swayen / Yu ort tu get d'rhythm in you / In de cool fe d' evening / Under wun palm tree / Darns dara hula rhtym / Let it flo through yu [translation of keywords: darns-dance; moowe-move; ort-ought / should; swayen-swaying; woach-watch; wun-one].
(George 'Toofie' Christian)

Some of the lyrics are in the unique Norfolk Island language, which is a mixture of 18th-century English and Tahitian. Seaman enjoyed singing in another language and also the languid and lovely slow-waltz rhythm.

'Jymeekah'

Seaman was inspired to create 'Jymeekah' after a chance encounter with Torres Strait Islanders living in Gladstone in Queensland. He recalls:

> We went to a meeting in this hall, and I met [a relative who] was married to my cousin and she had her daughter there called Jymeekah, a pretty little girl … Then we started to write this song as we were driving along and that is where that song started.

The name was unusual, but also lilting and rhythmic, so it triggered a song about a fictitious Jymeekah, the 'queen of the hula'.

'Jymeekah'

Everybody's dancing by the coconut tree / Everybody / Jymeekah the queen of the hula / Jymeekah with her Islander eyes / How she can dance / How she can sing / How she can make me forget everything / Jymeekah the queen of the hula / I was on a sailing ship heading for Fiji / When I went ashore awhile to see what I could see / Friday night at the Bula Bula Club / She was standing all alone / So I introduced myself / And I've never gone back home / So we stayed in Suva Town with laughter love and smiles / Then I said to her one day 'Let's try another isle' / Maybe French Tahiti or New Caledonia / We can roam the island homes of Oceania / Me and Jymeekah the queen of the hula / Jymeekah with her Islander eyes / How she can dance / How she can sing / How she can make me a Singapore Sling / Jymeekah the queen of the hula / Oh my sweet Jymeekah / So matha nais [very nice] to me / Oh matha nais / Matha matha nais. (Seaman Dan and Karl Neuenfeldt)

The lyrics are a fantasy about a sailor travelling Oceania (Tahiti, New Caledonia) after meeting someone special in Fiji at the fictitious Bula Bula Club — perhaps a fantasy entertained by sailors no matter where they roam. In Fijian, the word *bula* has many meanings — usually positive ones — but often means 'welcome'. There is also a song, 'Bula Malaya', which is sung to welcome tourists to resorts. The wave sound effects were recorded in the Torres Strait region, and add a bit of audio authenticity to the tropical imagery of the lyrics.

'Thirsty Work'

Although many of the songs on *Island Way* drew upon a wider geographic frame of reference than the Torres Strait region, one song was a slice-of-life recollection for a community musician performing there. The title of 'Thirsty Work' comes from one of Seaman's sayings:

> 'Thirsty work' means that after a round of singing you got to sort of wet your throat again. You get thirsty so you've got to have a *debi ari* [good drink]. You've got to have a refreshment.

The song also includes imagined dialogue, the kind that might be heard in a hotel bar, pub or TAB [Totalisator Agency Board betting outlet]:

'Thirsty Work'

[Spoken Dialogue] Hear the pennies dropping / Bala [brother] you got anything jingling in your pocket / Sisi [sister] you got / Give gar / Please gar / Give please give / Ai no gad baker bala wiswei yu / Ai no gad luk em der bambai next time / [Sung] On the outer islands / Waiting for the sun to go down / Mr Steve Foster was passing the guitar around / He said 'hey old fella can you sing us a song' / I ended up singing all night long / That's okay I love to play / But understand the message when you hear me say / It's thirsty

Seaman Dan and his friends worked in maritime industries and also played music together. It was 'thirsty work' entertaining at the Federal Hotel on TI. [l–r]: the late George Dewis, Jerry Lewin, the late Hismile 'Izzie' Shibasaki and Seaman Dan.

work / Thirsty work / You can blame it on the heat / Blame it on the rain / It's thirsty work all the same / We're on Thursday Island waiting for the gig to begin / Russell [Barkus] is ready Izzie [Hismile Shibasaki] is wearing a grin / Then we heard 'Hey Three Amigos sing us a song' / So we ended up singing all night long / That's okay we love to play / But understand the message when you hear us say / It's thirsty work / Thirsty work / Blame it on the heat / Blame it on the rain / It's thirsty work all the same / Thirsty work / Debe ari [good drink] / Thirsty work / Kapu wana / Blame it on the heat / Or blame it on the rain / Thirsty work all the same / [Spoken dialogue] Henry wanem yu mekem / Kam ya kai / Henry yu lesen a / Seaman / [Sung] Tonight on Horn Island / Everybody's having a ball / Horses are running / Greyhounds cover the wall / Cessa says 'hey you balas can you sing me a song?' / We ended up singing to her all night long / That's okay she knows we love to play / Understands the message when she hears us say / It's thirsty work / Kapu wana / Thirsty work / Debe ari / Blame it on the heat / Blame it on the rain / It's thirsty work all the same / Thirsty work / Matha loosely / Thirsty work / Absolutely / You can blame it on the heat / Or on the rain / Thirsty work all the same / [Spoken dialogue] Henry yu lesen ai singaut yu a / That's it / Henry I'm coming to you / Whew hot in here tonight / Think I'll step outside.
(Seaman Dan and Karl Neuenfeldt)

The people mentioned in the lyrics all live in or are from Torres Strait. Steve Foster is an educator now located on TI but previously based at Badu Island. His father, the late Tom Foster, and his mother, Betty (née Ah Boo), had known Seaman since childhood. When Seaman went to perform for the Badu schoolchildren, Steve kindly arranged a barbecue at beautiful Gaubuth Beach and Seaman was glad to sing a few songs. Russell Barkus and the late Hismile 'Izzie' Shibasaki performed with Seaman in the Three Amigos as the bass and ukulele players respectively. They performed at community events and local hotels, presenting a wide range of popular songs. Cessa Nakata (née Mills) is an old friend of Seaman's and is always happy to contribute to his recordings. The spoken dialogue is by the Torres Strait Islander actress and comedian Norah Bagiri, along with Wayne Seekee and Vic McGrath. Singer and entertainer Cindy Drummond also added musical interjections. Part of the setting for the song is the Wongai Hotel on Horn Island, where Seaman performs regularly. It happens to have a TAB outlet with many television screens, so racing greyhounds literally do 'cover the wall'. Seaman enjoys performing live locally because, as he says, 'The people enjoy our music and it's a great audience … They are clapping and they are very much happy, it puts smiles on people's faces.' But for the musicians in a tropical climate, it ends up as 'thirsty work'.

'Magic Island Moon'

Sometimes a song will appear that has a special appeal because, while it may be a good song, it also has a good story behind it. One such song recorded by Seaman was 'Magic Island Moon', written by the late Loftus Dun in the late 1930s. Loftus had passed through Torres Strait during active duty in the Second World War, and held fond memories of its natural beauty. Many decades later, his son, Ken Dun, taught in the Torres Strait region at Moa Island and met co-producer Karl Neuenfeldt. Ken said his father wrote songs and Karl, always keen to hear new songs, told Ken to have his father send some song demos as Seaman was recording an album. When Loftus sent several songs for consideration, Seaman instantly liked 'Magic Island Moon'. He says, 'When I heard the song for the first time I thought, "Well, this is a very nice song." I thought, "yes, please, I would very much like to [record it]."'

> **'Magic Island Moon'**
>
> *Magic moon / Swinging high above / Take me to my love / Magic island moon / Far apart / We're so far apart / Take me to my heart / Take me magic moon / The night will bring its own melody / With stars to light the way / Our joy will live in all memory / Tell me what more I can say / Magic moon / Will you help me now / Take me back somehow / Magic island moon.* (Loftus Dun)

Because 'Magic island Moon' had been written in the late 1930s, it had the musical structure and lyrical nostalgia of the pre-Second World War era of Seaman's youth. That suited not only his vocal style but also the album's romanticised Oceanic theme. Loftus was very happy to have his song recorded, even if there was a gap of almost 70 years between it being written and finally being recorded. Like Seaman, Loftus was not too old to make a memorable musical contribution.

'Island Way' ⛵ (Reprise: 'Kapa Roa'ia Se Laloga')

As noted earlier in the passage from Terri Janke's book *Butterfly Song*, islands can have a profound effect on those who live on them or come from them. It may be part geography and part isolation, but being an 'islander' is especially very important to a Torres Strait Islander such as Seaman Dan, whose very name is tied to an island way of life. Culturally, there can also be an 'island way' of doing things. As Seaman states:

> If we are going to do something we say, 'Oh well, let's do it "island way".' It's the way that we know how to go about what we're going to do. We do it our way. We know it's going to be all right because we do it properly.

'Island Way'

Goodbye my friends / It's time for leaving / But not time for feeling sad / Just listen to the music / Remember all the fun we had / I will always be here with you / Though my ship may sail away / You will hear me in the west wind / And in the children as they play / Goodbye farewell yawo / Tell me that more need I say / It's time to take my leaving / I'll do it in the island way / Yawo [Farewell]. (Ernest Ahwang, Seaman Dan and Karl Neuenfeldt)

The song's original music came from a ukulele-based instrumental written and recorded by the late Ernest Ahwang for a music project funded by the National Museum of Australia for its *Paipa/Windward* Torres Strait Islander exhibition. As a very young child, Ernest had been evacuated along with his family from TI at the beginning of the Second World War, and he remained on the mainland. His extended family was well known for its fine musicians. Like many other Torres Strait Islander musicians, they played hybrid music, mixing their own and other styles including South-East Asian styles such as *krongchong*. It is a style that provides the musical and rhythmic underpinning for 'Island Way'. When Ernest passed away, Karl Neuenfeldt attended his funeral in Mackay. On the long drive north to Cairns for the *Island Way* album's recording sessions, he repeatedly listened to the beautiful but also now melancholy instrumental Ernest had recorded. Seaman decided that they would add lyrics as a tribute to Ernest, both as a composer and as a Torres Strait Islander community musician who was always willing to perform for his community.

The *Island Way* album and the title track end with a reprise of 'Kapa Roa'ia Se Laloga', which began the album. The musical journey across Oceania included stops along the way at the islands of Fiji, Rotuma, Hawaii, Norfolk Island, Tasmania and the Torres Strait. It helped Seaman to reconnect with the diverse cultural heritages of his ancestors, recount some of his music-related travels and reaffirm his personal view of himself as a man of the islands. The next album, *Sailing Home*, would focus on his diverse and geographically dispersed maritime connections.

CHAPTER 12
Sailing Home

In 2009, Pegasus Studios in Cairn was once again the site for recording *Sailing Home*, Seaman Dan's fifth album. Like *Island Way*, it was released by Steady Steady Music and distributed by MGM/Planet. The production team remained the same, with Nigel Pegrum as audio engineer and also co-producer along with Karl Neuenfeldt. The core of studio musicians remained similar to the lineup for the earlier albums, with the addition of Andree Baudet on saxophone, keyboards and string arrangements, Malcolm Cole on violin and viola, Christine Jackson on cello and Will Kepa on guitar, bass, keyboards and ukulele. Additional singers included Danny Benjamin, Libby Brockenshire, Brett Charles, Jacob Pilot, Kay Pilot, Cygnet Repu and Moses Warusam. All but one of the songs on *Sailing Home* was a new recording, and the theme was the maritime industries of tropical Australia — their dangers and delights. The maritime theme was reflected in the song choice and the original artwork of Vic McGrath. Design was by Nadene Jones at Nova Graphics, and incorporated archival photographs of maritime industries. Seaman had spent many years at sea, and he had many stories to recount arising from that phase of his working life. The album contained songs in English and Torres Strait traditional languages. With *Sailing Home*, Seaman won his second ARIA Award for Best World Music Album (2009), an unprecedented achievement for an 80-year-old Indigenous singer-songwriter.

'Sailing the Southeast Wind'

'Sailing the Southeast Wind' chronicles in song what life was like for men working the trochus and pearl shell industries out from TI along the coasts of Queensland. Their working lives were spent at the whim of the winds and tides, and the turn of the seasons, with each season having a specific wind and overall climate associated with it. TI's Gab Titui Cultural Centre's website provides a good summary of the seasons of the Torres Strait region:

Kuki (pronounced *Cook-ee*): North-West winds (strong winds) — Blow from January until April — Wet Season (monsoon)

Sager (pronounced *Sa-gerr*): South-East trade winds — Blow from May until December — Dry season

Zey (pronounced *Zay*): Southerly winds — Blow randomly throughout year

Nay Gay (pronounced *Nai-gai*): Northerly winds — Blow from October until December — Season when both heat and humidity are at their highest.

The original recording of 'Sailing the Southeast Wind' was made on TI for a project funded by Central Queensland University, where Karl Neuenfeldt is employed as an Associate Professor. It was the title song for an album featuring maritime music from the Torres Strait region, all written and sung by Torres Strait Islander community musicians. The late Raymond Wymarra brought the original core of the song to Seaman. They had a maritime connection because Seaman had worked on pearling luggers with Raymond's father, Nicholas Wymarra, a very experienced engineer who taught him a lot about working at sea. Raymond had also performed with Seaman in a TI band called The Ramblers. Other members included Raymond's brother, Ted Wymarra, Hassan Bin Awel, Karim Bin Awel, George Dewis, Bob Dunbar, Jerry Lewin and Neville Newman. Many of the musicians on TI had worked in the maritime industries, so when it came time to record the song's backing vocals, it was natural to include some of them. Consequently, Jerry Lewin, Bua Mabo, Vic McGrath and Hismile 'Izzie' Shibasaki added their voices.

Postcard of Torres Strait trochus divers, undated.

'Sailing the Southeast Wind'

Oh the southeast wind will blow all around us / And the winter wind can chill us to the bone / We will sail the Torres Strait and east coast waters / In working time we have to sail about / Oh oh sailing the southeast wind / Oh oh sager gubanu / Oh oh sager wag wamli / We are sailing we are sailing / Sailing home / We are working men but sometimes we miss family / Who wait for us far away at home / As we sail the Torres Strait and east coast waters / Our teardrops kiss the waves upon the reef / Let the southeast wind blow around us / Let the winter wind chill us to the bone / We must sail the Torres Strait and east coast waters / We are working men and this is working time. (Seaman Dan, Karl Neuenfeldt and Raymond Wymarra)

Seaman recounts how the song reminded him of his time free diving for trochus shells as a young man with just a face mask and no compressed air. He says it is also an honest portrayal of the effect itinerant work could have on crew members:

> It's mainly about sailing through the Great Barrier Reef, working out from Cairns [and] out from Mackay. You had your friends on board and you are away from home say four or five weeks at a time. When you are diving for trochus, it is work time but when you are back on board after a day's work and you are having your break, your thoughts drift back to your family at home then.

Seaman recalls the original recording sessions on TI as great fun because he was able to sing with his friends: 'Oh, it was really great! We all grew up together on Thursday Island. So it was like one big happy family.' Even today, it is easy for him to pick out who sang what part because 'you are used to each other's company and sing along together, so it is easy to pick them out'. However, hearing the recordings years later for him is 'both happy and sad also. Some of them are not here with me anymore, it's really sad. I miss them.'

The original recording of 'Sailing the Southeast Wind' was later updated for the *Sailing Home* album, with a few instrumental overdubs, but it remained essentially the same version. It provides a good introduction to the album by capturing a bit of the human element of the otherwise strictly commercial maritime industries.

'Lighthouse'

One of the many maritime jobs Seaman did was to work on a lighthouse tender vessel, MV *Wallach*. It was based on TI, and he recalls how he and his friend, Thomas Sabatino, were employed as ERAs — engine room assistants — on board:

> [The MV *Wallach*] used to do maintenance on the islands around the Torres Strait and way over to Daru on the Papua New Guinea coast … We would go down to Cairns every six months to do the lighthouses

the MV *Cape Moreton*, the bigger lighthouse tender vessel, did not have time to do. We would do that right down to Grafton Passage outside of Cairns.

He found it an interesting job:

You learnt something apart from diving for pearl or trochus shells. You're still out at sea, which is good for us boys, you know, but you are doing something different.

Seaman first heard the song 'Lighthouse' being performed by Snake Gully, a band that used to play regularly at the now defunct Johno's Blues Bar in Cairns, where many local musicians honed their skills backing touring professional overseas musicians and also in amateur local talent shows. Josh Cunningham of The Waifs, a popular Australian group, wrote the song, and its imagery was a natural fit for both Seaman's voice and the maritime theme of the *Sailing Home* album.

'Lighthouse'

Lighthouse tall and grand / Standing on a cold headland / Shine your light across the sea / For a wayward sailor boy like me / Lighthouse man / Guide this sailor back to land / Steer my ship on through the storm / Back to water safe and calm / Sometimes I need a lighthouse for my own / It gets so dark I can't see which way I'm going / Lighthouse man I'm all at sea / Shine a little lighthouse light on me / Lighthouse man can't help us all / Some are saved and some will fall / He'll show you where the danger lies / But he can't help it if you capsize / He'll light your way but that is all / You steer your own ship back to shore / Oh won't you light my lonely way back home / This sea is full of misery and woe / Woe betide those that say / They don't need no light to light their way / They think they're safe enough on their own / But they'll drown in murky depths below / We all need a lighthouse for our own / It gets so dark I can't see which way I'm going / Oh lighthouse man I'm all at sea / Shine a little lighthouse light on me. (Josh Cunningham, reproduced by permission of Josh Cunningham and Three Little Fish Pty Ltd)

It is always a challenge to record a well-known song such as 'Lighthouse' — especially when it is associated with a very popular group like The Waifs. However, Seaman took a different, quasi-Cajun musical approach to the song. Josh Cunningham has said, 'I really love Uncle Seaman Dan's version of the song' — which is a great compliment to all involved.

'Mango Rain'

Growing up in the Torres Strait, Seaman instinctively absorbed the rhythms of the natural environment, including when certain birds would arrive or fish would flourish or certain fruit would ripen. Mangoes are very common in the tropics, and one of the fruits that is acclimatised to the region's heat, humidity and pests. Mangoes also help mark the seasons when they flower and ripen, and also when they get nourishing rains. Seaman notes that around September, 'Rain brings on and ripens the fruit. So we call it the mango rain. So we thought we'll write a song about mango rain and it is quite a catchy tune also.'

December is when the fruit fully ripens, and also when the lugger crews would return home before the cyclone season began in earnest in Far North Queensland. So if someone in the crew had a girlfriend he had met earlier in the year, he might not get to spend much time with her until December.

> 'Mango Rain'
>
> *I met you in the mango rain / The sun would hide then come back again / You would smile then you'd wave good bye / I would have to wait until the tide was high to see you again / Mucka tuka teah toka / Mucka tuka teah toka / Mucka tuka teah toka in the mango rain / In my heart I knew our time would come / And you came shining through just like the sun / Chased away the rain / Wait until the season's over I'll come back for you / Come December we'll remember love in the mango rain.* (Seaman Dan and Karl Neuenfeldt)

Seaman recollects that maritime work was intermittent at times because of the tides and winds:

> You don't come in until it is dirty water outside that you cannot recognise a pearl shell — you come in to offload then. You take advantage of the dirty water, slip into port, do what you have to do as regards offloading your shells and get a new supply of food, water, fuel. And if it is still dirty water, well you have a couple of days' rest in port before it starts to clear and you steam out again then. You do have about two or three days in port to socialise and meet your family.

Due to the itinerant nature of maritime work, personal relationships could be interrupted, and it also could affect communities if many of the working-age men were gone for extended periods. Consequently, it was the women who often kept the communities going, especially on the outer islands. They shouldered the burdens of not only raising families but also taking care of the myriad other duties necessary to keep small, isolated communities functioning.

'Mango Rain' was fun to record in the studio because it afforded an opportunity to invite a group of Cairns-based Cook Islander singers and musicians to add their unique style. The members of the Hakaora family, College, Taki and Terina, were experienced entertainers who presented Polynesian-themed shows at casinos, conventions and nightclubs. Their high-energy show includes an impressive array of singing, dancing and drumming, so their cultural and musical skills were perfect to embellish the song's already tropical atmosphere.

The song's repetitive phrase 'mucka tuka teah toka' sounds like it could possibly be in a Polynesian language, but is actually made up — it has no meaning. Co-producer Karl Neuenfeldt had heard the phrase somewhere and written it down and kept it in his wallet, planning to some day use it in a song. When he first sang it to Seaman as a possible addition to the song, Seaman was a bit puzzled. But he was also aware of the use of 'play song' words in Torres Strait Islander songs and dances. Even though the words were made up, it was important they did not accidently actually mean something. So Karl asked several Polynesian language speakers to vet them. Coincidently, some of the individual words were recognisable. However, luckily they were neither rude nor derogatory. The fun and energy captured in 'Mango Rain' made it an appropriate balance to the album's sometimes more sobering maritime themes.

'The *Floria* Sails Again'

The pearling luggers used across northern Australia varied by region. For example, those in the Torres Strait region were built differently from the ones used in the Broome region (see photo page 35). Due to frequent cyclonic weather along the north-western coast of Western Australia, the round-bottomed luggers could enter the mangrove creeks, where they could safely shelter or sit on the mud until the cyclone season had passed. Torres Strait was not as cyclonic; however, the region's strong winds required a deeper-keeled vessel, which in turn needed deeper water for moorage. The luggers built for Torres Strait evolved over the decades, with some built locally at TI and others built elsewhere. Seaman had the opportunity to work on some well-built and well-regarded luggers as both a diver and a skipper.

The *Floria* is one historic lugger with which he was associated indirectly. It is still around today. Seaman's brother-in-law, Vincent Dorante, skippered it in 1963. It was one of three Burns Philp boats working out of TI, where Japanese shipwrights had laid its keel in 1914. It was a sister ship to the *Grafton*, which Seaman skippered then, and also the *Galton*, skippered then by his brother-in-law the late James Dorante (see Chapter 6). Seaman remembers the practicality and the beauty of those luggers:

> They were built especially to take the seas, to handle the seas. We had three sails on board. The jib sail that is in the bow, the fore sail that is the big one in the centre and the mizzen that is in the stern. You direct your boat by using your mizzen sail and you've got your tiller there under what we [in the Torres Strait region] call the main mast … that is the mizzen. The [Torres Strait luggers] are built especially to work out in rough weather. Even if the water is rough [but] the water is clear, you are still out there. No matter how high the seas are, your closest land [might be] about 20 miles away. And you have to steam up against a 25-knot south-easterly wind. We just anchored out there, leave your mizzen

Model of the *Floria* by George Mosby. It was a sister ship to the *Grafton* skippered by Seaman Dan. Courtesy National Museum of Australia.

up and you flatten your sheet straight up and down with the waves and no matter how big that sea is [you are safe]. They were good sail boats, good sea boats.

The larger pearling luggers would have a crew of 12 or 13 men, and Seaman stresses that it was very important to have a hard-working and cooperative crew:

> We all know each other and we all sort of grew up together. When you are skipper you've got to be wise [when] you select your crew. You know their temperament, happy disposition, you can talk with each other, sing, [enjoy] music … and that is how you select your crew. You have a happy ship then.

However, when the boats were out at sea working, there was not much time for fun. As Seaman often emphasised:

> When you are out there, you cart water from different islands, cut firewood. You leave all of your enjoyment and pleasure for when you come back to TI, come back into port again. Your time off is your time then and then you go looking for pleasure.

After the *Floria*'s working life as a pearling lugger, she was sold into private hands, but eventually sank at Cairns. However, she was raised up from the seabed, and local enthusiasts and the Cairns Maritime Museum began a restoration project, which is still incomplete. Seaman got the chance to visit the boat when she was being restored, and recalls that 'it took my mind back to when I was on board the *Grafton*, the sister ship … brought back good memories of being out on the sea again'.

'The *Floria* Sails Again'

The Floria *sails again / Back in all her glory /* Floria *sails again on the Coral Sea / Travelling with the tide all her sails unfurling / The* Floria *sails again with a cargo of memory / She worked the pearling grounds from March to January / Tacking through the reef to dive the Darnley Deeps / From TI down to Cairns and back before the rains came / No matter where she roamed the* Floria *came back home / And the crew would sing about the sea / While the seabirds circled endlessly / The* Floria *sails again back in all her glory /* Floria *sails again on the Coral Sea / Facing wind and wave in every kind of weather /* Floria *sails again oh so majestically / And the crew would sing about the sea and seabirds circled endlessly.* (Robert Campbell, Seaman Dan and Karl Neuenfeldt)

Given the many hundreds of pearling luggers that have worked out of TI since colonial times, it is sad that so few have survived. Work, weather and the climate certainly took their toll, but the restoration and upkeep of a lugger like the *Floria* are very expensive and beyond the resources of most individuals — and even public museums. The luggers now live on mainly in the songs and stories of a diminishing generation of maritime workers, and memories are the only cargo they can still carry.

'Dock of the Bay'

As with The Waifs' song 'Lighthouse', it was a challenge to take an iconic song such as 'Dock of the Bay', written by Steve Cropper and Otis Redding, and do something different with it. Its lyrical setting was certainly suitable for the album's maritime theme, but arranging and recording it proved to be a challenge — partly because, as a crooner, Seaman's natural tendency is to sing the melody and words smoothly, often with a laid-back feel. However, arranging the song with a light reggae feel meant reggae's off-beat accents made it a challenge for Seaman to sing in his usual style. Singing against the syncopated bass, drums and guitars was not working well, so a smooth arpeggiated guitar was recorded so that he could sing to a more comfortable rhythm. That worked out fine, and he was surprised to hear the end result when he came from the studio into the control room, because when he was doing his vocal he only heard the smooth guitar in his headphones and not all the other accented instruments.

Seaman also remembered working on the wharves at TI's harbour, so the song had special resonance:

> I used to work for Torres Strait Industries, fuel the boats up and fill the empty gas cylinders up also to supply the island. When you are down at the wharf and the ships are coming in, you get the feeling that you want to go back pearling again — to get back on board a boat and go to sea again.

Crowd on the wharf, Thursday Island, c.1928. CM Yonge, National Library of Australia, image no. 4179597.

When maritime industries were still active on TI, it was not uncommon for men who had worked on the luggers to move to onshore jobs when their careers as divers or tenders ended. They had years of experience, and loved being close to the sea.

'Shimmering Blue'

'Shimmering Blue' was written from an unusual confluence of a dance style, a dream and a couple of guitars. As noted earlier, slow drag historically was a favourite dance style in the Torres Strait. It allowed some physical contact and also did not require great skills as a dancer because the couple could simply cling to each other and slowly sway to the down-tempo music. The style itself had its origins in the United States in the 1890s, and originally was danced to ragtime music. It later was featured on Broadway and was associated with African-American popular culture, which had a very innovative and often imitated dance scene. How it got to Torres Strait is unclear, but it was especially popular after the Second World War. Seaman remembers it being danced by African-American soldiers stationed in Cairns when he was there, as noted in Chapter 3. They frequented parties in the Malay Town area and some dated young Torres Strait Islander women whose families had evacuated from TI in early 1942.

Like the song 'Island Lady', 'Shimmering Blue' came to Seaman in a dream: 'I dreamt about a blue guitar, so I started to write that same night.' He always had a cassette recorder handy so snippets of melodies or lyrics could be remembered and worked on the next day.

> 'Shimmering Blue'
>
> *I've got a funny feeling in my heart / I don't know much about you where do we start / Let's take it one step at a time / Each precious moment that I spend with you / Let's spend each moment at our rendezvous / Keep smiling and everything's fine / I love you my shimmering blue / There's no other like you on the ocean so blue / Or the sky way up on high / Let your heart sing forget everything / All your charms I hold in my arms / When you and I are dancing I look into your eyes / I see a certain sparkle burning with desire / A flame that sets me on fire / I love you my shimmering blue / Keep on smiling, everything's fine / Each precious moment, just me and you / We'll spend each moment at our rendezvous / Keep on smiling and everything's fine / I love you my shimmering blue / Keep on smiling everything's fine / My shimmering blue / You know I love you.* (Seaman Dan and Karl Neuenfeldt)

Seaman later bought a blue acoustic guitar and eventually a blue electric guitar, which he still uses for local performances. The song was arranged to mirror the musical style of the late 1940s and early 1950s, when crooners and big bands still dominated popular music before the onslaught of rock'n'roll. The opening string arrangement is the 'dream sequence', similar to how film music of the era would use ephemeral, shimmering string arrangements to suggest a dream before reality intruded.

'Water'

Once the theme of the album was decided upon, songs were sought that would thematically and musically complement Seaman's own songs. One that struck an immediate chord was 'Water', by the well-regarded Australian singer-songwriter Shane Howard. The imagery in the abridged lyrics encapsulates much of what Seaman recalled of life at sea and the challenges of men making a living from the sea, rather than just the sea as a place of recreation.

> 'Water'
>
> *I was standing on the ocean / On a boat to uncertainty / I was dreaming / I was drifting / Deep into infinity / All I see is water / Salty water / This old boat has seen better days / But at least I can call it mine / Changing fortunes changing weather / It's all the same to me / All I see is water / Salty water / Then I'm dreaming / Drifting / Far beyond where I have been / There is air and there is water / And just this little boat in between / All I see is water / Salty water.* (Shane Howard © 1994 Big Heart Music/Mushroom Music)

Seaman reminisces that work was always the main priority, and there was little time to be sentimental or reflective. However, some images remain:

> Especially when the water is fine and you are steaming along doing about 8 or 9 knots, then the dolphins would come and swim alongside you. And they would race up past you and dive, some in front of your vessel, to follow you across the Gulf of Carpentaria. It's a huge expanse of sea, endless miles upon miles. I always just looked up to the sky and just shook my head.

Although the luggers had compasses and charts, sometimes they would navigate only by the stars:

> You would look up and you would see the stars. I would line a star up with the full rigging. With the compass, it is on course. You would forget about the compass, just line that star up to your rigging. It's very accurate.

He also remembers it as very peaceful at times:

> You hit a wave and you hear 'chuurr, chuurr, chuurr', like that and you know the boat is steaming along and punching into the waves. It's a peaceful, satisfying feeling. It also had a thoughtful dimension at times because [the sea] is something big and [the boat is] very, very small.

Memorial to Japanese maritime workers at Thursday Island cemetery, 2008. Courtesy Liberty Seekee.

Perhaps Shane Howard's evocative lyrics — 'there is sea and there is sky and just this little boat in between' — best summarise Seaman's recollections of the immensity of the seas off the coast of northern Australia.

'Full Fathom Five'

There were tragedies at sea — some because of weather, others because of equipment failure or misuse, and still others because of encounters with sharks or gropers. The impact of weather was exemplified by the tragedy of Cyclone Mahina, which struck the pearling fleet at Princess Charlotte Bay on Eastern Cape York in March 1899. It devastated the fleet, with the loss of schooners and many luggers. It also killed hundreds of people, who either drowned at sea or were swept away on land by the storm surge and flooding.

Deep-water diving was also consistently a very dangerous part of the pearling industry in its early decades, when underwater breathing apparatus was introduced. Some of the luggers with early motors were under-powered for the Torres Strait's strong currents, and the procedures for decompression were also not well understood. A visit to the cemetery on TI attests to the substantial toll taken by diving, especially among the Japanese divers. There also were attacks by sharks and gropers, which although not common were a constant concern for divers and crew members.

Around 2007, Seaman heard a local story about some crayfish divers in Eastern Torres Strait recently finding a very old diving helmet wedged under coral in the Darnley Deeps, where many diving deaths had occurred. That story triggered a song about the dangers of the occupation, and also its effects on the people left at home. The song's scenario is fictional, but such tragedies were not fictional in Torres Strait.

'Full Fathom Five'

Emelina is standing on the shore / In her heart she knows he'll come no more / Pearling luggers sailing in a line / Tribute to a diver left behind / Full fathom five her lover does lie / In the deep endless ocean / Full fathom five where seabirds cry / Salty tears never dry / Emelina scarce believes the sight / Like her dreams had whispered in the night / Pearling luggers sailing in a line / Tribute to a diver left behind / Full fathom five her lover does lie / In the deep endless ocean / Full fathom five where seabirds cry / Salty tears never dry.
(Seaman Dan, Will Kepa and Karl Neuenfeldt)

Seaman had his own memory of a death at sea that stayed with him when he eventually became a skipper himself:

> This particular time we were diving at an area [west of Badu Island] called the Old Grounds. This is my first year of diving, I was 18 years old. And the other young diver that was lost, he was 18 years old also. We were using just the helmet and corselet. This is the reason you wind the air hose close to your helmet under your arm so you don't slip out of your helmet, because you can slip out of your helmet. And this is what happened to this young fella. He must have blacked out. It's only 7 fathoms of water and there were about 30 pearling vessels in this area, [but] it's a huge area.

> The tender [on the missing diver's lugger] pulled the helmet up and there was no diver in the helmet. Immediate panic straight away. Then word was passed from lugger to lugger that one of the pearling vessels had lost a young diver … I was one of the divers that went down to look for him. And my skipper, George Elarde — who taught me how to dive — he said, 'When you find him, careful how you hold him because if they are just about to go, to die, they will grab you and give you that death grip. You can't release yourself from him and you might drown too.' So I was really scared then, 18 years old, so I am looking and looking — none of us found the body. There were three helmets and three divers from each vessel searching for the body. [He] must have gone with the tide. The tide was running west then, very strong.

It was cultural protocol within the fleet that when such a tragedy happened, all the luggers would proceed back to the home port:

> The body wasn't found so the vessel that he was with they put the flag at half-mast. That is when there is a dead diver on that vessel. So then [the skipper] started to sail towards TI, so we all followed him in a funeral procession. We were about 35 or 40 miles [55–65 kilometres] away from TI and we all sailed in a line back. Then the lugger that had that flag

at half-mast [went in first]. As soon as it turned the corner at Hospital Point to go into harbour, the whole township knew straight away that there was a fatality on that pearling vessel with that flag at half-mast. The word spread right around Thursday Island then.

There was also a strict legal protocol to follow after a death at sea because there would need to be an investigation into the circumstances of the accident:

> The skipper would row ashore to the pearling station that they worked for and tell the pearling master. Then they would contact the authorities and the authorities would contact the family. They would go through the gear and go through all of the safety procedures that you do to look after the lives of all of your crew on board. Your skippers are responsible so they go through all that.

However, such a tragedy so early in his diving career impressed on Seaman the duties of a skipper and the need for persistent attention to safety:

> After that experience you are always [alert]. You always look after your crew, your divers, everything must be done right. There's no half measures.

In the song's lyrics, the title and phrase 'Full Fathom Five' is from Shakespeare's *The Tempest*. The following excerpt is a reminder of the universality of tragedies at sea:

> Full fathom five thy father lies / Of his bones are coral made / Those are pearls that were his eyes / Nothing of him that doth fade / But doth suffer a sea-change / Into something rich and strange.

'Baba Waiar'

The Torres Strait region has a highly valued tradition of sacred Christian music. What are called language hymns have been popular since the colonial era and more recently contemporary sacred songs, known locally as *kores* (choruses), have gained widespread popularity. Many Torres Strait Islanders write and compose them, and many *kores* also incorporate traditional languages, as well as English. One of the best-loved *kores* in Kala Lagaw Ya is 'Baba Waiar', written and composed by the late Miseron Levi from St Paul's community on Moa Island.

'Baba Waiar'

Baba waiar ninu Maygi Mari / Baba waiar ninu Magi Angela / Ngoelmuniya kaymel / Inub kubilnu / Inub kubilnu / Kurusika goeyga / Father we ask you / Please send your Holy Spirit / Father we ask you for your holy angels too / To come and stay with us all through the night / All through this night until the morning light. (Miseron Levi)

Miseron and Seaman were friends, and when Seaman was choosing songs for the *Sailing Home* album, he thought it would be respectful of Miseron's memory to record 'Baba Waiar'. Not only is it a beautiful song, but it also brought back many personal memories for Seaman. He recalled from his years at sea:

> When you are out at sea you are always praying because there is no church there, the church is in your heart. And when I hear the song, it is very religious to me.

Seaman wanted to sing it in English as well as Kala Lagaw Ya — in part to make it accessible to a wider audience — so Miseron's own English translation was used. The song has become very popular across Australia, especially with community and children's choirs, as well as its common use in Torres Strait Islander church services. The version Seaman recorded for *Sailing Home* was kept simple instrumentally (ukulele and accordion), and the all-male voices were specifically reminiscent of how he remembered lugger crew members singing. Seaman felt Miseron would be very proud of his recording of 'Baba Waiar'.

'Mak Taim'

Dance is an integral part of Torres Strait Islander culture, and its energy, spectacle and music make it unique. However, it is hard to capture all those characteristics in a recording. 'Mak Taim' was an attempt to create a soundscape that blended traditional languages and live recordings of dance music into Seaman Dan's tribute to such an important part of his culture.

> 'Mak Taim'
>
> *Narbit teter / Keimer teter / Dancing man from the stingray clan / Dance all night if he can / Frontline backline everybody in time / Midnight daylight everybody turning right / Mak taim / Dancing gel [girl] from the stingray clan dance all night if she can / Kuki kuki in gar / Zugubau kuki / Ngoeymunia in gar lumadhuya asin / Garbuthuya / Redinsia pudhiz / Bombaya / Gebarya / Maubaya / Kadaipa thapuriz.* (Alfred Aniba, Seaman Dan, Bua Mabo and Karl Neuenfeldt)

Mak Taim means 'mark time', a technique for coordinating dancers' movements on the dance field. The term is perhaps analogous to the military term 'marching in time', which could have come into the Torres Strait region with troops garrisoned at TI originally during the colonial era. It also could have been from the Second World War era, when many Torres Strait Islanders served in the Australian military and also danced for entertainment and recreation. In translation, Bua Mabo's Meriam Mir lyrics (*narbit teter, keimer teter*) mean 'right foot, left foot'. Alfred Aniba's Kala Kawaw Ya lyrics from Saibai Island (*Kuki kuki in gar / Zugubau kuki / Ngoeymunia in gar lumadhuya asin / Garbuthuya / Redinsia pudhiz / Bombaya / Gebarya / Maubaya*

/ *Kadaipa thapuriz*) mean 'the north-west wind blows through our village, along Garbuthu, Redlynch, Bombey, Gebar and up along Mawb'. In order to incorporate some traditional dance music into the recording, 'Mak Taim' includes live recordings from Badu Island during celebrations following several tombstone unveilings in 2003. Bua Mabo sang in Meriam Mir and Wilfred Aniba, the cultural custodian of his late brother Alfred's song 'Kuki Kuki', sang in Kala Kawaw Ya.

Seaman recollects how crew members of a trochus lugger on which he worked in the Whitsunday Islands north-east of Mackay used to go ashore occasionally and dance for their own entertainment during breaks in the diving. He says they performed 'mainly dances from their home islands. It was good fun for young fellas, somewhere to relax.'

Seaman grew up on TI, and in his youth traditional dancing only took place occasionally. Outer island people who were 'under the Act' were not allowed on TI except on special occasions, such as civic events (e.g. Royal coronations or community anniversaries), or for health or legal reasons. He notes: 'If you lived out on the outer islands, then you learned how to do the traditional dancing.' He did, however, do a bit of jitterbugging when he was in Cairns during the Second World War. Like many other musicians, though, he spent most of his time and energy making music, not dancing to it. That was an important role for community musicians: they provided entertainment so others could dance — and also possibly romance.

'Saltwater Cowboy'

On the *Perfect Pearl* album, Seaman had recorded one of his favourite songs by the Broome-based Pigram Brothers, 'Going Back Home'. But they also had written and recorded perhaps the best-known Indigenous Australian song about the pearling industry, 'Saltwater Cowboy'. Although its lyrics are mainly in English, it also includes Malay, Aboriginal and Japanese words, in keeping with Broome's multicultural maritime history.

> 'Saltwater Cowboy'
>
> *Lend me your body tonight my blue water lady / This salty wind is getting to my bones / These lugger sails are moving too slowly / For this saltwater cowboy sailing home / This ol' copper hat is aching my shoulders / These lead weight boots don't need any spurs / To ride these waves and bare back mermaids / Ah this saltwater country is my home / Stand back you shallow water man / Let a deep sea diver through / Selamat tingal nakula jarndu / Sayonara slo'n' gallow nyundu / These lugger sails are moving too slowly / For this saltwater cowboy sailing home.* (Alan, David, Gavin, Philip and Stephen Pigram and Paul Mamid, Pigram Music Publishing)

Seaman Dan with his 2009 ARIA award for Best World Music Album for *Sailing Home*. Courtesy Colyn Huber/Lovegreen Photography.

Although the song is set in Broome, it is also relevant to the Torres Strait region. So, for the recording, a section in Kala Lagaw Ya was added by singer-songwriter Cygnet Repu from Mabuyag Island: '*Koey maluw mabayg kuniya tidi koey malungu*', which translates as 'Deep sea man returning from the deep sea'.

For Seaman, the lyrics reminded him of how tired the divers would get after numerous dives to great depths:

> You do get weary; you do get tired. You can't sit up straight all the time for long periods, especially if you are sailing home. You get that expectant sort of feeling. You know [that] just around the corner you will see the headland. Oh yes, it's a great feeling!

As well as dealing with exhaustion, another concern for a lugger skipper was the health of crew members. Even though all divers had to pass a medical examination to get their licence, there were very limited provisions for illness. Skippers had to:

> Make sure there is no sickness on board. Most times — well, a lot of times — [concerning] medical supplies, we would make sure there was four or five jars of Vicks on board. And we would have cotton wool, sticking plaster and Band-Aids and Irish Moss for coughs and sore throat. That is all our medical supplies used to be … and Bex powders.

The pearling luggers of northern Australia created a world among themselves, and also had a code of etiquette. Seaman recalls one incident with a laugh:

> I am a guest at this pearling vessel that is alongside of mine. And I go on board and the cook wouldn't light the fire or make a cup of tea for the visitors. This was a breach of etiquette, and one of the other divers that was invited too, he said, to the skipper, 'You get a heap of firewood, [put it on the beach] and give [the cook] a blunt axe to cut firewood, that should civilise him!'

'Saltwater Cowboy' closed the album, and its final lyrics — 'these lugger sails are moving too slowly for a saltwater cowboy sailing home' — express a sentiment similar to the lyrics of the album's opening song, 'Sailing the Southeast Wind': 'we are sailing, sailing home'. The *Sailing Home* album won Seaman his second ARIA Award for Best World Music Album (2009), which was a great honour. But perhaps equally important was his knowing that the album was a fitting and heartfelt tribute to a working life he loved and had shared with many good friends. At his advanced age, he knew he would never again 'put on the helmet', but he still cherished his memories of when he was a deep-sea diver and not a shallow-water man.

CHAPTER 13

Sunnyside and Still On Deck: Personal Favourites

Sunnyside

Seaman suffered a serious bout of pneumonia in 2008. He had caught a chill on a flight from Horn Island to Cairns that was diverted to Weipa. Unfortunately, the passengers were left on the plane there for hours in the air-conditioning. By the time he arrived in Cairns, he had developed a cough. He was booked to appear at the 2008 'Big Talk One Fire' Indigenous cultural event for Umi Arts at the Cairns Civic Centre. As a professional entertainer, he wanted to honour his commitment so he sang, but shortly afterwards was admitted to the Cairns Base Hospital. At the age of 79, pneumonia is a serious illness, and the coughing and general weakness took a heavy toll on him, and on his voice. After several months, he was released from the hospital and returned home to Horn Island, but his overall health had been affected and it was unclear whether he would be able to sing, let alone record, again.

After an extended period of not singing or performing, Seaman's health slowly improved, and miraculously so too did his singing voice. Because music has always been such an important part of his life, he was keen to continue performing and recording, so it was decided that he would go into the studio and see whether his voice had recovered. It was instantly apparent it had — and had even deepened and become richer, rather like a very mellow cello, so the next step was to decide what to record.

Since his time performing in Darwin in the 1950s, Seaman had always loved the music of Nat King Cole, so he decided to record a personal tribute. The title,

Sunnyside, echoes his personal sentiment that looking on the sunny side of life is preferable to looking on its dark side. Cole had recorded a vast repertoire of popular songs on his many albums and for his television shows. Therefore, it was a challenge to pick the songs that best suited Seaman's voice and vocal range. The songs chosen were: 'It's Only a Paper Moon', 'Dream a Little Dream of Me', 'On the Sunny Side of the Street', 'I'm Gonna Sit Right Down and Write Myself a Letter', 'Autumn Leaves', 'Is You Is or Is You Ain't My Baby', 'Makin' Whoopee', ⛵ 'Sweet Embraceable You', 'Ain't Misbehavin', 'Stardust' and 'What a Wonderful World'. Cole had recorded all of them except 'What a Wonderful World', which Seaman wanted to record because it is a personal favourite from his live performances.

The songs chosen include popular songs from Seaman Dan's own lifetime, written by some of the world's greatest English language songwriters. They are also songs that had found their way to Torres Strait and into the musical memory banks of several generations of local music lovers and performers. Since he is a crooner like Cole, the songs and Seaman's singing style meshed effortlessly.

In keeping with the 'Seaman Dan sound' that Nigel Pegrum had fashioned, most of the instrumentation was kept acoustic and in line with the kinds of instruments used historically on TI. Most of the songs started off with just a ukulele and a guide vocal. A drum machine was recorded to set an initial tempo, which was later erased. Once Seaman's final vocals were completed, the other instruments, percussion and singers were added. Musical stalwarts from other albums, such as Dimple and Gabriel Bani, Denis Crowdy, Steve Gilbert, Ben Hakalitz, Russell Harris, Ruedi Homberger, Will Kepa, Rubina Kimiia, Chris Lloyds, Vic McGrath, Wayne McIntosh, Tom Seepoy, Giles Smith and Kirk Steel provided the backing with the addition of Nikki Doll, Peter Ella and Simon McMenamin. Several songs also lent themselves to duets, so Cindy Drummond was called on for 'On the Sunny Side of the Street' and 'Ain't Misbehavin' and John Nicol for 'Is You Is or Is You Ain't My Baby'. Both are artists Seaman has always admired, and they both came out of the tradition of Indigenous community music performed on verandas for family and friends.

Sunnyside was released by Steady Steady Music and distributed by MGM/Planet, with art design by Nadene Jones. It proved to be a fun album to record, and Seaman had definitely returned to his old form as a singer. Released when Seaman was 83 years old, it is a fitting tribute both to a great singer, Nat King Cole, and also an excellent interpreter of popular songs, Seaman Dan.

Cindy Drummond and Seaman Dan dueted on two songs on the Sunnyside album: 'Sunnyside of the Street' and 'Ain't Misbehavin'.

Still on Deck: Personal Favourites

When the opportunity came to do this book on Seaman's life and music, preparing a compilation CD of some of his personal favourites made sense. The first part of the title, *Still on Deck*, is a maritime-based allusion to the fact that, as noted earlier in Chapter 11, many of Seaman's close friends and co-workers have passed away, and he is one of the few still active — 'still on deck', so to speak. Luckily, after the *Sunnyside* album was released, Seaman had continued to record. He re-recorded several of his signature tunes, including what he terms a 'jumped up' version of 'TI Blues'. It has bluesy electric instrumentation, with rhythm guitar from Ryo Montgomery, and also a horn section. As well, it features a guest vocal from Nikki Doll. She sings the verse the Mills Sisters had written for their popular version of 'TI Blues' to add a female perspective on the blues:

> *When a woman gets the blues she hangs her head and cries / when a woman gets the blues she hangs her head and cries / when a man gets the blues he hops on that big bird and flies away.*

Seaman also revisits 'Forty Fathoms' from his days as a deep-water pearl shell diver at the Darnley Deeps, in a solo-voice version that instrumentally features accordion, mandolin and violin. A previously unreleased ukulele-based version of his tribute to The Mills Sisters, 'The Torres Strait Hula', was included, along with Ted Egan's 'Sayonara Nakamura', which had been released on a reissue of Seaman's first album, *Follow the Sun*.

Perhaps most importantly for Seaman, he had the opportunity to record with the Cairns Gondwana Indigenous Children's Choir. They recorded the iconic 'Old TI' and Miseron Levi's *kores* 'Baba Waiar'. The songs feature the unique combination of 30 very young voices and one very old one. Seaman has always encouraged younger generations to consider music as a hobby, and perhaps even a professional goal. After all, they are the next generation of Torres Strait Islander musicians and singers, and they now have a substantial body of recorded music to draw upon — something Seaman did not have available when he was starting out in music. Seaman's own albums and those of The Mills Sisters, Rita Mills, Christine Anu, Danny Bani, Fred David, Dave Dow, Tim Gibuma, Toni Janke, Fred and Richard Kiwat, Patrick Levi, Patrick Mau/Mau Power, Andrew Namok, Aven Noah, Cygnet Repu, Lexine Solomon, Kura Stephens, Northern Xposure and the Torres Strait Regional Authority's community music projects contain many recorded examples of the richness and variety of Torres Strait Islander secular and sacred music, and the importance of music — be it traditional/ancestral or modern/contemporary — to Torres Strait Islander culture.

In 2012, Seaman Dan and the Cairns Gondwana Indigenous Children's Choir recorded 'Old TI' and 'Baba Waiar'. Singers included [l–r]: Sade Bingarape-Minniecon, Desiree Bingarape, Salu Messa, Jenetta Dorante-Lyons and Brianna Durante.

Epilogue

Trying to determine what a musician's music means or has meant to individuals or communities is always an imprecise exercise because music and its effects are very subjective — different for every listener. As the music critic Alex Ross (2007) observes: 'Music is always migrating from its point of origin to its destiny in someone's fleeting moment of experience.'

In a sense, the music that Seaman Dan has recorded, written and performed has had exactly that kind of varied effect. Some listeners might enjoy the evocation of an era of sailing ships and pearl diving; some might enjoy a musical introduction to a beautiful but isolated part of Australia and its culture; others might enjoy a unique voice and a laidback musical ambience; yet others might enjoy the way it celebrates being an Indigenous Australian. But part of the appeal of his music arguably is that it is open to interpretation. It can mean what listeners want it to mean and it can be enjoyed on different levels — be they musical, aesthetic or cultural. Importantly, like Seaman himself, it lacks artifice. It does not claim to be greater than it is, but rather is an honest and heartfelt effort to document, circulate and celebrate Torres Strait Islander music — or at least one Torres Strait Islander's perspective on it.

On a personal level, Seaman has always wanted his music to be about more than just him and his life. It has also been the music of those in his generation and what they experienced, the social and economic challenges they faced, the momentous political changes they witnessed, and the lessons they hope to pass on to subsequent generations — and how music can carry and strengthen those lessons. As well, Seaman himself remains humble in the ego-obsessed music industry, and is genuinely grateful about his accomplishments and opportunities. As he is wont to say, 'My hat still fits!'

On a broader level, perhaps Ted Egan's words best sum up what Seaman has accomplished by taking his life and his music 'steady, steady': '[Seaman Dan's] musical career, his entire life since, has been nothing short of remarkable. Australia is indeed a lucky country!'

Seaman Dan performing at Thursday Island hotel c.2012. Courtesy Kim Wirth.

REFERENCES AND FURTHER READING

Baker, J 2003, 'Better late than never for Uncle Seaman, *Australian Associated Press General News*, 28 March.

Beckett, J 1972, *Traditional Music of Torres Strait*, booklet accompanying LP recordings, with musical analysis and transcriptions by TA Jones, AIAS, Canberra.

—— 1981, *Modern Music of Torres Strait*, booklet accompanying audiocassette, with translations and transcriptions by E Bani, S Townson, K Mabo & D Ober, AIAS, Canberra.

—— 1987, *Torres Strait Islanders: Custom and colonialism*, Cambridge University Press, Melbourne.

—— 2001, '"This music crept by me upon the waters": recollections of researching Torres Strait Islander music, 1958–1961', *Perfect Beat: The Pacific Journal of Research into Contemporary Music and Popular Culture*, vol. 5, no. 3, pp. 75–99.

Beloff, J 1997, *The Ukulele: A visual history*, Backbeat Books, Milwaukee, WI.

Carroll, M 2011, *The Man Who Loved Crocodiles and Stories of Other Adventurous Australians*, Allen & Unwin, Sydney.

Connell, J 1999, 'My island home: the politics and poetics of the Torres Strait', in R King & J Connell (eds), *Small Worlds, Global Lives: Islands and migration*, Pinter, London, pp. 195–213.

Corfield, J 2010, *String Bands and Shake Hands: A tribute to the life and music of Val McGinness*, Jeff Corfield, Townsville.

Costigan, L & Neuenfeldt, K 2002, 'Torres Strait Islander music and dance in informal and formal educational contexts in Australia', *Research Studies in Music Education*, no. 19, pp. 46–55.

—— 2004, 'Negotiating and enacting musical innovation and continuity: how some Torres Strait Islander songwriters are incorporating traditional dance chants within contemporary songs', *The Asia-Pacific Journal of Anthropology*, vol. 5, no. 2, pp. 113–28.

—— 2007, '"Doing the Torres Strait hula": the adaptation and perseverance of "hula" in an Australian performance culture', in R Moyle (ed.), *Oceanic Encounters: Essays in honour of Mervyn McLean*, Research in Anthropology and Linguistics series, University of Auckland, Auckland, pp. 97–108.

—— 2011, 'Kapua Gutchen: educator, mentor and innovator of Torres Strait Islander music, dance and language at Erub (Darnley Island)', *Australian Journal of Music Education*, no. 2, pp. 3–10.

Crowdy, D & Neuenfeldt, K 2003, 'The technology, aesthetics and cultural politics of a collaborative, transnational music recording project: "Veiga, Veiga" and the itinerant overdubs', *Transformations*, no. 7, viewed 20 January 2013, <http://www.transformationsjournal.org/journal/issue_07/article_06.shtml>.

Cunningham, J 2012, Personal communication, 22 October.

Dan, H 2007, Interview by Karl Neuenfeldt, 799453, National Film and Sound Archives: Canberra.

—— 2011–12, Interviews by Karl Neuenfeldt, various dates, Central Queensland University, Bundaberg.

Davis, R (ed.) 2004, *Woven Histories Dancing Lives: Torres Strait Islander identity, culture and history*, Aboriginal Studies Press, Canberra.

Donovan, V 2002, *The Reality of a Dark History: From contact to conflict to cultural recognition*, Arts Queensland, Brisbane.

Dunbar-Hall, P & Gibson, C 2004, *Deadly Sounds, Deadly Places: Contemporary Aboriginal music in Australia*, UNSW Press, Sydney.

Edwards, R 2001, *Some Songs from the Torres Strait*, Rams Skull Press, Kuranda.

Eyken, T 1896, *Parts of the Pacific*, Swan Shonnenschein, London.

Faulkner, S & Drummond, A 2007, *Life B'long Ali Drummond*, Aboriginal Studies Press, Canberra.

Foley, J 1982, *Timeless Isle: An Illustrated History of Thursday Island*, 4th edn, Torres Strait Historical Society, Thursday Island.

Fuary, M 2000, 'Torres Strait and Dawadhay: dimensions of self and otherness on Yam Island', *Oceania*, vol. 70, no. 3, pp. 219–30.

Gab Titui Cultural Centre website, <http://www.gabtitui.com.au>.

Gaffney, E 1989. *Somebody Now: The Autobiography of Ellie Gaffney, A Woman of Torres Strait*, Aboriginal Studies Press: Canberra.

Ganter, R 1995, *The Pearl-shellers of Torres Strait: Resource, development and decline 1860s–1960s*, Melbourne University Press, Melbourne.

—— 1999, 'The Wakayama triangle: Japanese heritage of North Australia', *Journal of Australian Studies*, vol. 23, no. 61, pp. 55–63.

Haddon, A (ed.) 1901–35, *Reports of the Cambridge Anthropological Expedition to Torres Straits*, 6 vols, Cambridge University Press, Cambridge (reprint 1971, Johnson Reprint Corporation, New York).

Hayward, P 2001, 'A glad round of melody and song: Frank Hurley's account of music and dance on Erub (Darnley Island) during summer 1920/21', *Perfect Beat: The Pacific Journal of Research into Contemporary Music and Popular Culture*, vol. 5, no. 3, pp. 66–74.

Hayward, P & Konishi, J 2001, 'Mokuyo-to No Ongaku: music and Japanese community in the Torres Strait (1890–1941)', *Perfect Beat: The Pacific Journal of Research into Contemporary Music and Popular Culture*, vol. 5, no. 3, pp. 46–65.

Herle, A & Rouse, S (eds) 1998, *Cambridge and the Torres Strait: Centenary essays on the 1898 Anthropological Expedition*, Cambridge University Press, Melbourne.

Hodes, J 2000, 'Anomaly in Torres Strait: living "under the Act" and the attraction of the mainland', *Journal of Australian Studies*, no. 64, pp. 166–72.

Hurley, F 1924, *Sun* newspaper reports, Hurley Newspaper clippings, 833 Series 2, Item 30, National Library of Australia, Canberra.

Janke, T 2005, *Butterfly Song*, Penguin, Ringwood.

Kidd, R 2005, *The Way We Civilise: Aboriginal affairs – the untold story*, University of Queensland Press, Brisbane.

Lance, K 2004, *Redbill: The amazing story of an Australian pearling lugger*, Fremantle Arts Centre Press, Fremantle.

Lawrence, D 1998, 'Customary exchange in the Torres Strait', *Australian Aboriginal Studies*, no. 2, pp. 13–25.

Lawrence, H 1998, '"Bethlehem" in Torres Strait: music, dance and Christianity in Erub (Darnley Island)', *Australian Aboriginal Studies*, no. 2, pp. 51–63.

—— 2005, '"The great traffic in tunes": agents of religious and musical change in Eastern Torres Strait', in R Davis (ed.), *Woven Histories, Dancing Lives: Torres Strait identity, culture and history*, Aboriginal Studies Press, Canberra, pp. 46–72.

Lawrie, M 1970, *Myths and Legends of Torres Strait*, University of Queensland Press, Brisbane.

—— 2006, *Sound Recordings Collected by Margaret Lawrie, 1968*, AIATSIS, Canberra.

Loos, N 2005, 'Mabo, music and culture', in F Magowan & K Neuenfeldt (eds), *Landscapes of Indigenous Performance: Music and dance from Torres Strait and Arnhem Land*, Aboriginal Studies Press, Canberra, pp. 51–56.

Lui, L & York, F 2003, 'Torres Strait Islander traditions', in J Whiteoak & A Scott-Maxwell (eds), *Currency Companion to Australian Music and Dance*, Currency House, Sydney, pp. 662–5.

Mabo, E 2005, 'Music of the Torres Strait', in F Magowan & K Neuenfeldt (eds), *Landscapes of Indigenous Performance: Music and dance from Torres Strait and Arnhem Land*, Aboriginal Studies Press, Canberra, pp. 46–50.

MacFarlane, W (Rev.) 1927, Diary Entry, 18 October 1927, AIATSIS MS2616/1/3.

Maugham, S 1936, *Cosmopolitans: Very short stories ('French Joe' and 'German Harry')*, William Heinemann, London.

Mosby, T & Robinson, B 1998, *Ilan Pasin This is Our Way: Torres Strait art*, exhibition catalogue, Cairns Regional Gallery, Cairns.

Mullins, S 1995, *Torres Strait: A history of colonial occupation and culture contact 1864–1897*. Central Queensland University Press, Rockhampton.

Mullins, S, Bellamy, M & Moore, C (eds) 2012, *Andrew Goldie in New Guinea 1875–1879: Memoir of a natural history collector*, Queensland Museum, Brisbane.

Mullins, S & Neuenfeldt, K 2005, 'Grand concerts, Anzac Days and evening entertainments: glimpses of music culture on Thursday Island, Queensland 1900–1945', in F Magowan & K Neuenfeldt (eds), *Landscapes of Indigenous Performance: Music and Dance from Torres Strait and Arnhem Land*, Aboriginal Studies Press, Canberra, pp. 96–118.

Mullins, S & Wetherell, D 1996, 'LMS teachers and colonialism in Torres Strait and New Guinea, 1871–1915', in D Munro & A Thornley (eds), *The Covenant Makers: Islander missionaries in Oceania*, Institute of Pacific Studies, Suva, pp. 186–209.

Nakata, M 2007, *Disciplining the Savages: Savaging the disciplines*, Aboriginal Studies Press, Canberra.

Nakata, M & Neuenfeldt, K 2005, 'From Navajo to Taba Naba: unraveling the travels and metamorphosis of a popular Torres Strait Islander song', in F Magowan & K Neuenfeldt (eds), *Landscapes of Indigenous Performance: Music and dance from Torres Strait and Arnhem Land*, Aboriginal Studies Press, Canberra, pp. 12–28.

Neuenfeldt, K 2001, 'Cultural politics and a music recording project: producing *Strike 'em! Contemporary Voices from the Torres Strait*', *Journal of Intercultural Studies*, vol. 22, no. 2, pp. 133–45.

—— 2002, 'Examples of Torres Strait songs of longing and belonging', *Journal of Australian Studies*, no. 75, pp. 111–16.

—— 2004, 'Some historical and contemporary Asian elements in the music and performance culture of Torres Strait', in A Shnukal, G Ramsay & Y Nagata (eds), *Navigating Boundaries: The Asian diaspora in Torres Strait*, Pandanus Publishing, Canberra, pp. 265–75.

—— 2007, Notes on the Engagement of Indigenous Peoples with Recording Technology, *The World of Music*, vol. 49, no. 1, pp. 7–21.

—— 2008, '"Ailan style": an overview of the contemporary music of Torres Strait Islanders', in T Mitchell & S Homan (eds), *Sounds of Then, Sounds of Now: Australian popular music*, Australian Clearing House for Youth Studies, Hobart, pp. 167–80.

—— 2011a, 'Assembling a sacred soundscape: choosing repertoire for Torres Strait Islander community CDs/DVDs in Australia', in B Abels (ed.), *Austronesian Soundscapes: Performing arts in Oceania and South East Asia*, University of Amsterdam Press, Amsterdam, pp. 295–317.

—— 2011b, 'A case study of Indigenising the documentation of musical cultural practices', in G Seal & J Gall (eds), *Australian Folklore in the 21st Century*, Black Swan Press, Perth, pp. 73–91.

—— 2013 forthcoming, '"Sweet sounds of this place": an overview of contemporary recordings and socio-cultural uses of Mabuyag music', *Mabuyag Island*, Queensland Museum Memoirs Series, Cultural Heritage Series, Brisbane.

Neuenfeldt, K & Lawe-Davies, C 2004, 'Mainland Torres Strait Islanders and the "magical islands" of the Torres Strait: the music of Gaetano Bann as metaphor and remembering', in K. Dawes (ed.), *Island Musics*, Berg, Oxford, pp. 137–51.

Neuenfeldt, K & Mullins, S 2001, 'The "saving grace of social culture": early popular music and performance culture on Thursday Island, Torres Strait, Queensland', *Queensland Review*, vol. 8, no. 2, pp. 1–20.

Osborne, E 1997, *Torres Strait Islander Women and the Pacific War*, Aboriginal Studies Press, Canberra.

Paterson, A 1902, 'Thirsty island', *The Bulletin*, 5 April, pp. 74–6.

Pryor, C 2001, 'Northern delights', *The Australian*, 8 September.

Reid, M 2012, Personal correspondence, 30 November, Queensland Department of Aboriginal and Torres Strait Islander and Multicultural Affairs.

Ross, A 2007, *The Rest is Noise*, Farrar, Straus and Giroux, New York.

Seekee, V 2002, *Horn Island 1939–1945: Record of the defense of Horn Island during World War Two*, Vanessa and Arthur Liberty Seekee, PO Box 6, Horn Island, Queensland, 4875.

Sharp, N 1993, *Stars of Tagai: The Torres Strait Islanders*, Aboriginal Studies Press, Canberra.

—— 1996, *No Ordinary Judgment: The Murray Island land case*, Aboriginal Studies Press, Canberra.

Shnukal, A 1992, 'Pacific Islanders and Torres Strait 1860–1940', *Australian Aboriginal Studies*, no. 1, pp. 14–27.

—— 2011, 'Torres Strait Islanders', in M Brandle (ed.), *Multicultural Queensland 2001: 100 years, 100 communities, a century of contributions*, Department of Premier and Cabinet, Brisbane, pp. 21–35.

Shnukal, A, Ramsay, G & Nagata, Y (eds) 2004, *Navigating Boundaries: The Asian diaspora in Torres Strait*, Pandanus Publishing, Canberra.

Singe, J 1989, *The Torres Strait: People and history*, University of Queensland Press, Brisbane.

—— 2003, *My Island Home: A Torres Strait memoir*, University of Queensland Press, Brisbane.

Sterns, M & Sterns, J 1994, *Jazz Dance: The story of American vernacular dance*, Da Capo Press, Boston.

Thaker, L 2009, 'In our own words: The making of Malaytown stories', *Zenadth Kes: I, Torres Strait Islander*, Summer, pp. 50–2.

Titasey, C 2012, *Ina's Story: The memoir of a Torres Strait Islander woman*, private publication, Thursday Island.

Torres Strait Islands 2011, Queensland Art Gallery/Gallery of Modern Art/State Library of Queensland/Queensland Museum/Queensland Performing Arts Centre, Brisbane.

Watkin Lui, F 2012, 'My island home: re-presenting identities for Torres Strait Islanders living outside the Torres Strait', *Journal of Australian Studies*, vol. 36, no. 2, pp. 141–53.

Wilson, L 1988, *Thathilgaw Emeret Lu: A handbook of traditional Torres Strait Islands material culture*, Department of Education, Brisbane.

—— 1993, *Kerkar Lu: Contemporary artefacts of the Torres Strait Islanders*, Department of Education, Brisbane.

Wemyss, K 1999, From TI to Tasmania: Australian popular music in the curriculum, *Research Studies in Music Education*, no. 13, pp. 28–39.

York, F 1990, *Children's Songs of the Torres Strait*, Owen Martin, Bateman's Bay, NSW.

—— 2000, 'Torres Strait Islander Music', in S Kleinert & M Neale (eds), *Oxford Companion to Aboriginal Art and Culture*, Oxford University Press, London, pp. 340–4.

SELECT DISCOGRAPHY

Dan, Seaman 1999/2011, *Follow the Sun*, CD, Hot Records (1075), Sydney, produced by Nelson Conboy, Nigel Pegrum & Karl Neuenfeldt.

―― 2001, *Steady, Steady*, CD, Hot Records (1097), Sydney, produced by Nigel Pegrum & Karl Neuenfeldt.

―― 2004, *Perfect Pearl*, CD, Hot Records (1094), Sydney, produced by Nigel Pegrum & Karl Neuenfeldt.

―― 2006, *Island Way*, CD, Steady Steady Music (TI1001), Cairns, produced by Nigel Pegrum & Karl Neuenfeldt.

―― 2007a, *Somewhere There's an Island: A Collection*, CD, Steady Steady Music (TI1002), Cairns, produced by Nigel Pegrum & Karl Neuenfeldt.

―― 2007b, *Beautiful Land and Sea*, CD, Black Image Band and Seaman Dan: 'Singing the Blues', produced by Will Kepa, Nigel Pegrum & Karl Neuenfeldt.

―― 2009, *Sailing Home*, CD, Steady Steady Music (TI1004), Cairns, produced by Nigel Pegrum & Karl Neuenfeldt.

―― 2011, *Follow the Sun*, re-release with additional song, 'Sayonara Nakamura', CD, Steady Steady Music (TI1006), Cairns, produced by Nelson Conboy, Nigel Pegrum & Karl Neuenfeldt.

―― 2012, *Sunnyside*, CD, Steady Steady Music (TI1007), Cairns, produced by Nigel Pegrum & Karl Neuenfeldt.

―― 2013, *Still on Deck: Personal Favourites*, CD, Steady Steady Music (TI1008), Cairns, produced by Nigel Pegrum, Karl Neuenfeldt & Nelson Conboy.

Home: A Collection of Songs From Queensland Aboriginal and Torres Strait Islander Artists 2009, CD, Queensland Government/Q Music, Brisbane. Seaman Dan, 'Mango Rain', produced by Nigel Pegrum & Karl Neuenfeldt.

Mills, A. 2010, *Waltjim Bat Matilda*, CD, Skinnyfish Music, Darwin, produced by Michael Hohnen.

Mills, R. c.1998, *Blue Mountain*, CD, Zuna Entertainment, Cairns.

―― 2001, *Mata Nice*, CD, Zuna Entertainment, Cairns, produced by Nigel Pegrum.

Mills Sisters c.1992, *Frangipani Land*, CD, New Market Music (NEW10222), Melbourne.

―― 2002, *Those Beautiful TI Girls*, CD, Zuna Entertainment, Cairns.

Paipa/Windward Torres Strait Islander Exhibition 2003, National Museum of Australia, Canberra.

RAN: Remote Area Nurse 2005, Original Soundtrack Recording for the Special Broadcasting Service (SBS) Television Series, CD, music composed and produced by David Bridie, Blunt Label/Sound Vault Records (SV0501), Melbourne, Seaman Dan, 'Somewhere There's an Island', produced by Nigel Pegrum & Karl Neuenfeldt.

Rough Guide to Australian Aboriginal Music 2008, CD, 'World Music Network' (RGNET1207), London, Seaman Dan, 'Old Men and the Sea', produced by Nigel Pegrum & Karl Neuenfeldt.

Sailing the Southeast Wind: Maritime Music from Torres Strait 2003, CD, Central Queensland University, Rockhampton, Seaman Dan, Raymond Wymarra & Karl Neuenfeldt, 'Sailing the Southeast Wind', performed by Seaman Dan, produced by Nigel Pegrum & Karl Neuenfeldt; Seaman Dan & Karl Neuenfeldt, 'House Party Hula', performed by Rubina Kimiia, produced by Nigel Pegrum & Karl Neuenfeldt.

Saltwater Songs: Indigenous Maritime Music from Tropical Australia 2004, CD, Seaman Dan, 'The *Floria* Sails Again', produced by Nigel Pegrum & Karl Neuenfeldt.

Speaking Out: Celebrating 20 Years on Air — The Best of Indigenous Music 1990–2010 2010, CD, ABC Music (2748770), Sydney, Seaman Dan, 'TI Taxi Driver', produced by Nigel Pegrum & Karl Neuenfeldt.

The Straits 2012, CD, original soundtrack recording for ABC TV series, music composed and produced by David Bridie, Wantok Musik (W0008), Melbourne, Seaman Dan, 'Mena Menali', 'Ailan Kwiktaim' & 'Kapa Roa'ia Se Laloga', produced by Nigel Pegrum & Karl Neuenfeldt.

Strike 'em! Contemporary Voices from the Torres Strait 2000, CD, Torres Strait Cultural Festival Committee, Thursday Island, Seaman Dan, 'Mena Menali', produced by Nigel Pegrum & Karl Neuenfeldt.

Verandah Music 2003, CD to accompany G Seal & R Willis (eds), *Verandah Music: Roots of Australian tradition*, Curtin University Books/Fremantle Arts Centre Press, Fremantle, Seaman Dan, 'Forty Fathoms', produced by Nigel Pegrum & Karl Neuenfeldt, book and two CDs.

SELECT FILMOGRAPHY

Blue Horizon 2004, Produced and directed by Jack McCoy & Seaman Dan, 'Somewhere There's an Island', produced by Nigel Pegrum & Karl Neuenfeldt.

The Clouds Have Stories: The art of the Torres Strait Islands 2011, Seaman Dan interview, directed by Daniel Marsden, Queensland Cultural Centre and Whistling Wolf, Brisbane.

Cracks in the Mask 1997, DVD, featuring Ephraim Bani, produced and directed by Frances Calvert, Ronin Films, Canberra.

Frangipani Land Forever 2008, featuring the 80th birthday celebrations of the Mills Sisters, Cessa Nakata & Ina Titasey, *Message Stick*, ABC TV, Sydney, produced by Douglas Watkin, broadcast 24 February.

Girl in the Cafe 2005, directed by David Yates, BBC, London, Seaman Dan, 'Somewhere There's an Island', produced by Nigel Pegrum & Karl Neuenfeldt.

Hula Time: The Seaman Dan Story 2005, *Message Stick*, ABC TV, Sydney, produced and directed by Nancia Guivarra.

Jack Satin 2011, directed by Christopher Olness, Seaman Dan, 'Somewhere There's an Island', produced by Nigel Pegrum & Karl Neuenfeldt.

Malaytown Stories: First Wave of Torres Strait Islanders to the Mainland 2006, DVD, produced by Lenora Thaker, Double Wire Productions, Cairns.

Ray Mears Goes Walkabout (Torres Strait) 2008, Seaman Dan: interview, BBC 2, Bristol.

Seaman Dan 2002, Interview, 487915 Tape 1, National Film and Sound Archive, Canberra.

Seaman Dan and Friends: Welcome to the Torres Strait 2005, F-Reel, Melbourne, produced and directed by Fiona Cochrane.

Uncle Seaman Dan 2009, *Living Black*, SBS, Sydney, broadcast 13 April, produced and directed by Stefan Armbruster.

AWARDS

Australian Recording Industry Association (ARIA) Award Winner Best World Music CD (*Sailing Home*) 2009

Jimmy Little Lifetime Achievement Award, the National Aboriginal and Torres Strait Islander Music, Sport, Entertainment and Community Awards 2009

Australia Council for the Arts Red Ochre Award 2005

Australian Recording Industry Association (ARIA) Award Nominee Best World Music CD (*Island Way*) 2005

Torres Shire (Qld) Citizen of the Year Award 2005

Australian Recording Industry Association (ARIA) Award Winner Best World Music CD (*Perfect Pearl*) 2004

National Folk Recording Award 2001

INDEX

Aboriginal and Torres Strait Islander Arts Board, 118
Adams, Raymond, 46
Adams, Tidja, 16
African-American music, influence of, 30, 73, 141
Ah Boo, Manji, 14
Ah Mat, Budden, 32, 40, 124
Ah Mat, Jaffa, 14, 29, 79
Ah Mat, Sarina, 31, 90
Ahwang, Ernest, 132
ailan kastom, 3
'Ailan Kwiktaim', 88–9; use in *The Straits* TV series, 89
'Ailan Man', 122–3
Akee, Fred, 80
Aniba, Alfred, 146
Aniba, Wilfred, 147
Anno, Ketchell, 14, 33, 126
Anu, Christine, 151
'The Arafura Sea', 82
'Are You from TI?', 97–8
ARIA Awards, 64, 117, 118, 133, 148
Artback NT, 104
Arts Queensland, 104
'As the *Goodwill* Sailed Away', 29
Asai, Iona, 48
Australia Council for the Arts, 100, 104, 118
awards, 64

'Baba Waiar', 145–6; re-recorded for *Still on Deck* album
Bagiri, Norah, 118, 130
Bani, Danny, 151
Bani, Dimple, 68, 150
Bani, Ephraim, 70–1, 75, 96
Bani, Gabriel, 68, 85, 102, 117, 150
Barba, Marian, 63
Barkus, Russell, 130
'Barron Delta Blue', 93
Baudet, Andree, 101, 133
Beattie, Heather, 121–2
Beattie, Peter, 121
Beckett, Jeremy 3–4
Bell, Alistair 'Azo', 93–4, 106–7
Beloff, Jim, 123–4, 125–6
bends, the, 45–6, 54–5
Benjamin, Danny, 133
Benjamin, Yunup, 68
Big Talk, One Fire event (Cairns), 149

Bin Awel, Hassan, 134
Bin Awel, Karim, 134
Bin Dol, Jenap, 16, 17
Bin Gapore, Baddah, 14
Bin Garape, Doseena, 17
Bin Hoosen, Dahlia, 17
Bin Juda, Betty, 31
Bingarape, Desiree, 152
Bingarape-Minniecon, Sade, 152
Binjuda, Frances, 95
Binjuda, Leilani, 95
'Black Swana', 75–6
Bligh, Anna, 122
'Blues on a Ukulele', 123–4
Bolton, Helen, 74, 75
Bolton, Roger, 74, 75
Bon, Father Dalton, 116
Bonham, Emily, 114
Bowie, Mary, 31
Bran Nue Day, 102
Brandy, Peter, 103
Bridie, David, 120
Brockenshire, Libby, 85, 133

Cairns Gondwana Indigenous Children's Choir, 80, 151
Cairns; Alligator Creek, 29–30; cultural life during Second World War, 29–32; homegrown entertainment 30–1; Malay Town, 29–30, 141; periods living in, 60
Cam, Dave, 80
Carr, Bob, 122
Cedar, Olive, 31, 32
Cedar, Pensio, 3, 321
Charles, Brett, 133
Christian, George 'Toofie', 127–8
cinema on Thursday Island, *see* Thursday Island cinema
Clarke, Jenni, 68, 85
Cobb, George, 97
Cole, Malcolm, 133
Cole, Nat King, 43, 58, 95, 149–50; songs recorded for *Sunnyside* album, 150
Collins, Andy 'Sugarcane', 93
Collinson, Div, 42–3, 102
Collis, Winnie, 31, 32
Conboy, Nelson, 68
Consolidated Mining Industries, 56
Cook, Louise, 118
Cooper, Mike, 85

Cordona, Peter, 42, 102
Crabbe, Des, 80
Cropper, Steve, 140
Crowdy, Denis, 68, 85, 95, 101, 110–12, 115, 150
Cruz, Russell, 42
CSIRO, 44
Cubillo, Delfin, 42, 43
Cunha, Rick, 18
Cunningham, Josh, 136
Cyclone Mahina, 143

Dan, Bill, 52
Dan, Catherine Jaira (adoptive mother) [Granny Dan] 7, 9, 11, 18, 29, 34
Dan, Connie, 52
Dan, Darkie, *see* Dan, Henry Maynard
Dan, Elvianna, 52
Dan, Henry Gibson 'Seaman'; ancestors, 7; awards, 64, 84, 117; baptism, 9; birth, 7; contracting pneumonia, 149–50; diving accident, 52; early years on TI, 8–11; education, 9, 19–20; first job, 10; first performance with other musicians, 41–2; getting the bends, 54–5; Koolpinyah Cool Stores, 41–1; learning music, 26; learning to dive, 34–8, 81–2; learning to ride 23; iving on Hammond Island, 58–9; marriage and children, 52; meeting Karl Neuenfeldt, 66–7; mineral exploration in PNG, 56, 57; move to Cape York (Coen), 17, 18–19; multicultural heritage 7; mustering, 23–5; nickname, 7, 35; quitting diving, 55; recordings, 64; return to TI after war, 34; taxi driving on TI, 58–60; time on *Paxie*, 44–50; transporting fishing boat to Tweed Heads, 60–2; war years in Cairns, 27, 28–33; years in Coen, 18–26; years in Northern Territory, 39–44
Dan, Henry Jnr, 52
Dan, Henry Maynard (adoptive father) [Darkie Dan], 7, 8, 11, 13
Dan, Simon, 52
Daniel, Norman, 53
Daniel, Stephen, 53
'Danville', 74–5
Darnley Deeps, 46, 51, 52–5, 81, 116, 143
Darnley Island, 81
Darwin Festival, 104
Darwin; athletic life, 41–2; social life, 41–2; *see also* Parap Camp; Sunshine Club
David, Fred, 151
David, Michael, 53

De Torres, Luis Váez, 2
Deane-Freeman, Jesse, 68
death at sea, 144–4
Delacruz, Dorrie, 33
Delacruz, Nocky, 33
Dewis, George, 46, 70, 129, 134
Dewis, Margie, 63
Diefenbach, Dale, 118
diving suits, 44–5
'Dock of the Bay', 140–1
Doll, Nikki, 150
Doolah, Jeffrey, 14
Dorante, Bert, 60–2
Dorante, Clare, 52
Dorante, James, 52–3, 82, 138
Dorante, Owen, 60–2
Dorante, Vincent, 52–3, 82, 138
Dorante-Lyons, Jenetta, 152
Dow, Dave, 151
Dowling, Clive, 42, 43
Drummond, Ali, 123
Drummond, Cindy, 90, 118, 130, 150
Dubbins, Billy, 13
Dubbins, Eddie (Dubbo), 74, 75
Dubbins, Jumila, 17
Dun, Ken, 131
Dun, Loftus, 131
Dunbar, Bob, 134
Durante, Brianna, 152

Edwards, Webley, 90
Egan, Ted, 41, 68, 83–4, 104, 151, 153
Elarde, George, 35, 81–2
Ella, Peter, 150
Entrance Island, 77
Erub, *see* Darnley Island
Eyken, Thomas 12

'Farewell to the Torres Strait', 82–3
Farquhar, Sarah, 76
Fatiaki, Rev. Iveni, 119
Fell-Tyrell, Rita [Rita Mills], 16–17, 63, 73, 98–100, 151
Fernandes, Bernard, 122–3
Filewood, Alan, 108
Fitzgerald, Ella, 95
'The *Floria* Sails Again', 55, 138–40
Floria, 53, 82, 138–40; restoration project, 139
Follow the Sun album, 68–84; awards, 84
'Follow the Sun', 70, 92
'Forty Fathoms', 51, 55, 81–2; re-recorded for *Still on Deck* album, 151

Foster, Betty, 63, 130
Foster, Steve, 129, 130
Foster, Thomas, 76
Fox, Jason, 101, 118
Foyster, Clive, 56
Fram, 39–40, 56
'Frangipani', 106–7
'Friday Night Blues', 62–3, 80–1
'Full Fathom Five', 143–5

Gab Titui Cultural Centre, 133–5
Gaffney, Ellie, 63
Galton, 53, 138
Garcia, Joe, 40
George, Murray, 53
Ghee, Tony, 102, 117
Gibuma, Tim, 151
Gilbert, Steve, 68, 71, 85, 101, 103, 109, 150
'Going Back Home', 102–3
Goodwill, 29
Grafton, 53, 82, 138
Gray, Vicky, 114
groper, 49–50
'Gubaw Paruka', 96–7
Guivarra, Francis, 33
Guivarra, Ivy, 33
Guivarra, Joan, 33
Guivarra, Nancia, 75
Guivarra, Pedro, 39–40
Guivarra, Thomas, 33

Haddon Anthropological Expedition, 3
Hakalitz, Ben, 101, 150
Hakaora, College, 136
Hakaora, Taki, 136
Hakaora, Terina, 136
Hall, Dinah, 115
Hammond Island 58–9
Hancock and Gore Ply Mill, 32
Harold, 97
Harris, Russell, 85, 150
Harrison, Mat, 68, 85
Harry, Elda, 53
Hau'ofa, Epeli, 119
Hawaii, visit to, 125–7; *see also* Society for Ethnomusicology conference (Hawaii)
'The Hawaiian Turnaround', 125–6
Hawaiian War Chant, 63
Hazelbane, Dave, 42
Hazelbane, Ken, 42, 43
Hillier, Tony, 84
Hippie, Dorrie, 31, 32
Ho'opi'i, Richard, 126–7

Ho'opi'i, Sol, 126
Hodges, Harry, 30
Hodges, Noel, 73
Hodges, Patty, 17
Homberger, Ruedi, 85, 150
Hondo, Gladys, 17
Horn Island, 77, 95; *see also* Wongai Hotel
Hot Records 68, 85, 101, 117
hotels on TI, 80–1; Federal Hotel, 62, 63, 81; Grand Hotel, 62, 80, 81; Royal Hotel, 9, 11, 62, 80; Thursday Island Hotel, 153; Torres Hotel, 62, 80
house parties, 13–14
'House Party Hula', 32
House Party Hula event (Cairns), 90
Howard, Shane, 142
hula dancing 16, 31, 98–100, 127–8

Idalia, 35
'Island Lady', 78–9
Island Way album 118–32
'Island Way', 131–2
'Islander Drums/Warraber' 116–17
'Isles of the Torres Strait', 76–7
Ives, Donna, 105

Jackson, Christine, 133
Jacob, Ben, 30
Jacobs, Cecilia, 31, 32
Janke, Terri, 118–19, 131; *Butterfly Song*, 118–19, 131
Janke, Toni, 151
Jia, Kathleen, 16
Jia, Seri, 16
Jib, Robbi, 101
Jimmy Little Lifetime Achievement Award, 64, 91; *see also* Little, Jimmy
Johnno's Blues Bar, 136
Jones, Nadene, 133, 150
Jose, Becky, 31, 32
Jose, George, 31, 32
Joseph, Victor, 108
Joye, Col, 90
'Jymeekah', 128–9

Kailag, 97
Kala Kawaw Ya language 146–7
Kala Lagaw Ya language, 4, 62, 75–6, 88, 96, 133, 145–6, 148
Kalemo, Sopa, *see* Pitt, Sopa

'Kapa Roa'ia Se Lalonga', 119–20; reprise, 131–2
Kazamias, Charlie, 81
Keawe-Aiko, Genoa Leilani Adolpho, 126, 127
Kennedy, Florence, 126
Kepa, Will, 68, 103, 133, 144, 150
Ketchell, Franceen, 114
Ketchell, Stacee, 114
Ketchell, Thomas, 114
Kim and Jeff, 74
Kimiia, Rubina, 85, 150
Kismet, 97
Kiwat, Fred, 151
Kiwat, Richard, 151
Knight, Alan, 57–8
Kole Kabem Wed, 4
Koolpinyah Cool Stores, 40–1, 104
kores, 4, 62, 145, 151
Ku-Olga, Klare, 68

Laifoo, Ron, 108, 109
languages, traditional, *see* traditional languages
Lawe-Davies, Chris, 115
Lee, Reggie, 40
'Let's Get to Where We Ain't', 120
Levi, Miseron, 145–6, 151
Levi, Patrick, 151
Lewin, Jerry, 32, 59, 63, 90, 129, 134
Lewin, Sammy, 32
'Lighthouse', 135–6
'Little Pony', 18, 21, 67, 77–8
Little, Jimmy, 85, 85, 90–1
Lloyds, Chris, 68, 85, 150
Loesser, Frank, 115
luggers, *see* pearling luggers
Lui, Geoffrey, 118

Mabo, Bua, 71, 75, 83, 117, 134, 146–7
MacDonald, Tom, 18, 19
MacFarlane, Mrs, 97
MacFarlane, Rev. WH, 12, 97
'Magic Carpet of Pearls', 113–14
'Magic Island Moon', 131
Maher, Joe, 53
'Mak Taim', 146–7
'Makin' Whoopee', 43, 58
'Mango Rain', 136–8
Mannock, Mark, 68, 85
Mansfield, Ted, 19
maritime industry, 11; decline in 51–2; *see also* pearling luggers

Massey, Stella, 101
Matha Loose Choir, 85
Matters, Enid, 63
Mau Power, *see* Mau, Patrick
Mau, Patrick, 118, 122–3, 151
Mau, Royce, 114
Mauar (Rennel Island), 8
Maugham, Somerset, 5
McDowall, Jim, 19–20
McGinlay, Peter, 74
McGinlay, Tracy, 74
McGinness, Val, 26, 27
Mcgrath, Clare, 31
McGrath, Vic, 68, 130, 133, 134, 150
McIntosh, Wayne, 68, 85, 150
McKenzie, Kerry, 85
McMenamin, Simon, 150
'Mena Menali', 87–8; use in *RAN (Remote Area Nurse)* TV series, 88; use in *The Straits* TV series, 88
Meredith, Hazel, 33
Meriam Mir language, 4, 62, 87–8, 117, 133, 146–7
Messa, Salu, 152
Middleton, Cliff, 44
Mills Sisters (Darwin-based) 26
Mills Sisters (TI-based) 16–17, 62, 63, 73, 81, 98–100, 151; *Frangipani Land* album, 73
Mills, Ali, 26
Mills, Cessa, *see* Nakata, Cessa
Mills, Ina, *see* Titasey, Ina
Mills, June, 26
Mills, Kath, 26
Mills, Rita, *see* Fell-Tyrell, Rita
Milroy, Billy, 106
'Minna Murra Moon', 114–15
Moa Island, 145
Mohamad, Edna, 17
Montgomery, Ric, 101
Moyden, Jessie, 17
Mua, Makereta, 119
multiculturalism, 3
music on Thursday Island, 12–17; *see also* house parties; hula dancing; Torres Strait Islander music
Mye, George, 87–8

Nakasone, Seisha 'Harry', 126
Nakata, Cessa [Cessa Mills], 16–17, 63, 73, 98–100, 102, 109, 130
Nakata, Tommy, 124
National Folk Festival (Canberra), 98; Red Shirt Day, 108

National Folk Recording Award, 64
National Museum of Australia, 132
Neuenfeldt, Karl, 68, 134; meeting Seaman Dan 66–7; as producer 68, 85, 95, 101, 109, 118, 119, 122–3, 133; as songwriter, 85, 89, 92, 94, 95, 103, 109, 110, 111, 112, 114, 115, 119, 120, 125, 128, 130, 135, 137, 144, 146; as musician 68, 85, 103
Neuenfeldt Pearson, Kyana-Lili, 125
Newman, Neville, 134
Nicol, John, 85, 90, 150
Nicols, Lala, 31
Noah, Aven, 151
Noble, George, 33
Norfolk Island, 127–8
Northern Xposure, 151
Nunan, Carmen, 63

Odo, Richie, 85
Ohta, Herb Snr, 123–4, 125–6
'Old Men and the Sea', 124–5
Old Spice Boys, 106
'Old TI', 2, 29, 43, 67, 79–80; re-recording with Cairns Gondwana Indigenous Children's Choir, 80, 151
Oui, Tibau 103

Pacific Island Forum Leaders' meeting (Cairns), 72, 73–4
Paipa/Windward Torres Strait Islander exhibition, 132
Papua New Guinea; mineral exploration expedition 56, 57–8; recording 'Veiga, Veiga', 110–12
Parap Camp, 41–3
Passi, Charles, 102, 109, 117
Paterson, AB 'Banjo', 5
Paterson, Bill, 33
Pau, Raymond, 108
Paxie, 44–50, 51
pearling luggers, 35–6; food, 37–8; life onboard 36–8; need for cooperation, 38, 52; season, 83
'Pearly Shells', 89–91; duet with Jimmy Little, 91
Pegasus Studios, 118, 133
Pegrum, Amelia, 118
Pegrum, Carmel, 118
Pegrum, Laura, 102
Pegrum, Nigel, 66, 68, 69, 85, 89, 101, 107, 109, 114, 118, 119, 133
Perez Ray 'Rusty', 42, 43

Perfect Pearl album, 101–17; ARIA Award, 117
'Perfect Pearl', 104–6
Pigram Brothers, 102–3, 147–8
Pilot, Jacob, 133
Pilot, Kay, 133
Pitt, Agnes, 33
Pitt, Arthur, 33
Pitt, Douglas Senior, 7, 123
Pitt, Dulcie, 33
Pitt, Heather, 33
Pitt, Lucy Gaiba, 33
Pitt, Maisie, 33
Pitt, Maryann, *see* Savage, Maryann
Pitt, Sopa, 7, 123
Pitt, Sophie, 33
Plasto, Courtney, 114
Port family, 21
Port, Alfie, 21
Powers, Mary, 43
Prideaux, Ann, 19–20
Prince of Wales Island, 74
Prober, Leon, 90

Quinn, Jim, 56, 57–8

race-based laws; Queensland 10–11, 30; living under the Act, 11, 113, 147; Northern Territory, 43
Ramblers, The, 134
RAN (Remote Area Nurse) TV series, 87, 88, 89
Rattenbury, Wendy, 115
Raymond, Kasim, 30, 46, 47
Raymond, 'Slicky' Lawrence, 30
Red Ochre Award, 64
'Red Shirt Day', 107–8
Redding, Otis, 140
Rehder, Ken, 47, 57–8
Repu, Cygnet, 85, 133, 151
'Return to Me', 94–5
'Rhythm of the Hula', 127–8
Rich, Charlie 95
Rich, Tristan, 85, 101
Rivers, Harry, 118
Ross, Alex, 153
Rostoka, Crystal, 74
Rostoka, Dragan, 74
Rostoka, Jessie, 74
Rostoka, Mina, 74
Rotuman Churchward Chapel Choir of Suva and the Oceania Centre for the Arts and Culture at the University of éthe Pacific, 119

Ruby C, 52
Rudd, Kevin, 72, 122
'Running Aground', 93–4
Rupa, Gere, 102, 111
Rupa, Gima, 102, 111

Saibai Island, 146
Sailing Home album, 133–48; ARIA Award, 148
'Sailing the Southeast Wind', 133–5
Sailor, Fred, 30
Sailor, Louisa, 30
'Saltwater Cowboy', 147–8
Savage, Ellen, 31, 32
Savage, Kaffa, 31, 32
Savage, Kitty (birth mother), 7, 8
Savage, Lilly, 31, 32
Savage, Maryann (grandmother), 7, 8, 30
Savage, Sam (grandfather), 7, 8, 16, 31, 32, 72, 123
Savage, Sam, 85
Savage, Thomas (uncle), 34
Savage, Willy, 31, 32
Saveka-Levi, Gertie, 63
'Sayonara Nakamura', 41, 83–4, 151
Schenk, Kathryn, 85
Schuurbiers, Susan, 85
Scott-Halliday, David, 121–2
Seafoy 2, 56
Seaman Dan 'sound', 101, 150
Second World War; end, 34; outbreak, 22, 26; TI during, 28–9
Seden, Dahlia, 17
Seekee, Wayne, 68, 130
Seepoy, Tom, 101, 150
Segur Kaba Wed, 4
Select Sound, 68, 85, 101
Seranealis, Eddie, 13
Seranealis, Hubby, 13
Shadbolt, Norm, 80
Shakimra, 102
sharks, 48–9
Shibasaki, Hismile (Izzie), 63, 89, 129, 130, 134
Shibasaki, Lily, 63
'Shimmering Blue', 141–2
Shinjo, Nonya, 63
ships visiting TI, 5, 114–15; MV *Marella*, 115; MV *Merkur*, 115; SS *Airlie*, 5; SS *Changte* 5; SS *Chingtu*, 5
Silver Plains Station 22–5, 77–8
Sinatra, Frank, 95
Smith, Barbara B, 126
Smith, Bessie, 73

Smith, Giles, 68, 85, 150
Smoke, Jack, 29
Snake Gully, 136
Society for Ethnomusicology conference (Hawaii), 125–7
Solomon, Dulla, 13, 16, 17
Solomon, Henry, 40
Solomon, Lexine, 151
'Somewhere There's an Island', 86–7; use in *Girl in a Café*, 87; use in *Jack Satin*, 87; use in *Blue Horizon*, 87; use in *RAN (Remote Area Nurse)*, 87; use in *The Straits*, 87
'A Song for Leilani', 95
Sprinter, Natasha, 114
Steady, Steady Backroads Tour, 103–4, 121
Steady, Steady Music, 118, 133, 150
Steady, Steady album, 85–100; release in United Kingdom, 87
'Steady, Steady', 92
Steel, Kirk, 68, 85, 150
Stephens, Kuru, 151
Still on Deck: Personal Favourites album, 151–2
Subam, Tony, 101, 112
Sunnyside album, 149–50
'Sunset Blues', 67, 72
Sunshine Club, 43, 104

Taafe, Danny, 74
Taibobo, 4
Tardent, Tony, 116
Tate, Dick, 40
Tatipata, Johannes, 14
Taukave, Samuela, 119
taxi driving on TI, 58–60
Taylor, Kathleen, 17
Ten Days on the Island (Tasmania), 121
Thaiday, Kenny, 31, 32
'Thank You for Saying Hello', 95–6
The Straits TV series, 87, 88, 89, 120
'Thirsty Work', 129–30
Thompson, Amelia, 18, 21
Thompson, Herbert, 18, 21, 22, 77–8
Thompson, Jane, 17
Thompson, Romeo, 22, 25
Three Amigos, 130
Thursday Island (TI), 4–6; during Second World War, 28–9
Thursday Island cinema 10–11, 13; racial segregation 10–11
'TI Blues' 66, 67, 70, 72–4
re-recorded for *Still on Deck*, 151
'TI Taxi Driver', 51, 60, 108–9
Tindley, Sarah, 93

Titasey, Ina [Ina Mills], 16–17, 63, 73, 98–100, 102, 109
Toa, Tehega Afugia, *see* Savage, Sam
Torres Strait; annexation by Queensland, 2; population, 2; *see also* Thursday Island; Torres Strait Islanders; Torres Strait Island music
Torres Strait Creole, 62, 88–9
'The Torres Strait Hula', 98–100; as tribute to Mills Sisters, 98–9; ukulele version for *Still on Deck* album, 151
Torres Strait Island music, 3, 12–17; community role, 62; contemporary influences, 4; sacred music, 4; traditional styles, 4; *see also kores*
Torres Strait Islanders, 3–4
Torres Strait Islands: A Celebration, The, 113
Torres Strait Light Infantry, 28
Torres Strait Regional Authority, 104; community music projects, 151
Toulasik, Solomon, 14, 16
Tracking Kultja festival, 91
trade networks; after colonisation, 2–3; pre-European colonisation, 2
traditional languages 4, 62, 87–8, 133; *see also* Kala Kawaw Ya language; Kala Lagaw Ya language; Meriam Mir language; Torres Strait Creole
Tropical Troubadours, 33
Troutman, Jason, 71, 103

'The Ukulele Waltz', 11, 112–13
Umi Arts (Cairns), 149

'Veiga, Veiga', 101, 110–12; recording in PNG, 110–11
Victoria Memorial Institute Hall, TI, 14–16, 59, 62

Viti, Ron, 108
Vizzone, Giuseppe, 68, 85

Waifs, The, 136
'Waiting for the Ice Man', 26, 39, 103–4
Wallace [Wallis], Pedro, 40
Wallace [Wallis], Robert, 40
Wallach, 135
Walters, Amy, 33
Walters, Fred Jnr, 33
Walters, Fred Snr, 33
Ware, Freddie, 31, 32
Ware, Jack, 73
Ware, Kitty, *see* Savage, Kitty
Warraber Island, 116
Warusam, Moses, 133
'Watching the Weather', 34, 55, 109–10
'Water', 142–3
Watson, Mrs, 10
'Welcome to the Torres Strait', 70–1
Whittington, Stephen, 68, 85
Williams, Cal, 104
Williams, Megan, 85
Williams, Roy, 16
Willis, Margaret, 68, 85
Winship, Brandon, 114
Wongai Hotel, 130
Woods, Wally Snr, 13
World Expo 2005 (Aichi, Japan), 121–2
Wymarra, Nicholas, 134
Wymarra, Raymond, 64, 66, 68, 134
Wymarra, Ted, 134

Yeller, Jack, 97
Yothu Yindi, 104

Zani, 68